Project Focus:
A Forecast
Study of
Community
Colleges

Project Focus: A Forecast Study of Community Colleges

Edmund J. Gleazer, Jr.

President
American Association of Community and Junior Colleges

McGraw-Hill Book Company

New York	*Kuala Lumpur*	*Panama*
St. Louis	*London*	*Rio de Janeiro*
San Francisco	*Mexico*	*Singapore*
Düsseldorf	*Montreal*	*Sydney*
Johannesburg	*New Delhi*	*Toronto*

Library of Congress Cataloging in Publication Data

Gleazer, Edmund J.
   Project Focus.

   1. Municipal junior colleges—United States.
I. Title.
LB2328.G54   378.1'543'0973   72-10558
ISBN 0-07-023435-3

Project Focus: A Forecast Study of
                Community Colleges

1 2 3 4 5 6 7 8 9 0 E B E B 7 9 8 7 6 5 4 3

*The editors for this book were Paul Walker
and Patti Scott, the designer was Marsha Cohen,
and its production was supervised by James E.
Lee. It was set in Century by Port City Press.
It was printed and bound by
Edwards Brothers Incorporated.*

Contents

Foreword

The year 1970 marked the fiftieth anniversary of the American Association of Community and Junior Colleges. It was also the end of a decade of unprecedented growth in community colleges. Approximately five hundred new institutions were established during that period. To the leadership of the AACJC it seemed an appropriate time to examine trends in the community and junior college field and consequent implications for the objectives, functions, organization, and administration of the AACJC. W. K. Kellogg Foundation, long interested in community education and the community college, provided a $250,000 grant toward the support of the eighteen-month study.

The project team consisted of Edmund J. Gleazer, Jr., executive director of the AACJC since 1958; David S. Bushnell, former director of comprehensive and vocational education research for the U.S. Office of Education; and Francis Pray, chairman of Frantzreb and Pray Associates, Inc., a management consulting firm specializing in college and university advancement.

A random sample of nearly one hundred community and junior colleges was studied. Thirty of these were visited by team members. I personally spent several days in each of twenty-five institutions in twenty states. I also interviewed members of the legislature and other state officials in those twenty states. My interviews in the colleges included faculty members, students, administrators, and board members. Additional community personnel were interviewed in order to include attitudes from a cross section of citizens.

The research was described as a "forecast study." No attempt was made to evaluate or examine institutions. In order to obtain views of what was likely to happen and what ought to happen, interviewees were questioned about five major elements of change, which are discussed in Parts 1 to 5:

Part 1   Changes in the student population to be served

Part 2   Changes in how they are served—through programs, supportive services, types of instruction, people, etc.

Part 3   Change in organization and governance—who calls the shots, what are the shifts in locus of power

Part 4   Shifts in financial support—who pays and who should pay

Part 5   Trends in community relations

In addition to the interviews, an institutional self-study instrument was administered to all the sample institutions.

A report with recommendations for change in the AACJC was submitted to that organization in late 1971. This book deals with the context in which the AACJC does its work—the institutions it seeks to serve.

This book is not a treatise on all aspects of community college operations. A great deal is being published now in areas of finance, staff development, curricula, and governance. Many studies are underway in higher education, and a number of these deal with aspects of community college services. This book reports the impressions of one person who has been immersed in community college developments at the national level during several years of their greatest growth, one who left administrative responsibilities for a while to listen to people in the field talk about the future of their institutions. Their feelings, quite naturally, I related to my own experiences and views.

The tone of the book may strike some people as too critical. I have no apologies for that. The research approach itself was oriented to change. If you ask how the institution should change, you imply that the present state of affairs should not continue; and so a critical element is implicit. Moreover, community college accomplishments are evident enough not to require a promotional piece from me at this time. Their achievements are largely a basic assumption. I was impressed by the large number of board members, students, faculty, and administrators who were secure enough in their perceptions of the work of their institutions to be self-critical. That is a notable quality in a time when educators are frequently charged with having a great affection for the status quo.

More than anything else, I would like to feel that I have done an accurate job in reporting the perceptions of a great number of people who took time to talk with me. It was an impressive and encouraging cross section. This book, I hope, speaks for them.

Acknowledgment

Many persons had a part in the writing of this book. It was the suggestion by the W. K. Kellogg Foundation that led to my personal involvement in a learning experience both rich and meaningful. And it was through financial resources provided by the Foundation that I was able to travel those many miles and to have associated with me in the leadership team of Project Focus two respected and competent associates, David Bushnell and Francis Pray.

I am greatly indebted to a "field staff" who arranged appointments, made hotel reservations, and saw to it that my time was utilized efficiently. These include the presidents of institutions I visited, their assistants, and personnel in state community college offices. And, of course, the interview approach would have been impossible if people, hundreds of them, had not listened to my questions and responded. An illustration of their interest and assistance is found in the willingness of a seventy-year-old board member to drive 30 miles over ice-covered highways to talk with me for a few hours one evening.

My colleagues and critics on the staff of the American Association of Community and Junior Colleges gave their characteristically able assistance. Roger Yarrington, William Harper, and Richard Wilson were of particular value in helping me get my thoughts organized and articulated. William Shannon, as acting executive director of the AACJC during my absence, saw to it that the work of the AACJC went on without interruption, and Jack Gernhart did my worrying for me, as an accomplished assistant should.

Special congratulations must go to Edith Liebske for transcribing more than 1,500 pages of interview notes and typing the manuscript.

The list of acknowledgments would be incomplete without thanks to the AACJC and the board of directors for the privilege of fifteen years of engrossing involvement in one of the big stories in American education.

The colleges are going to have to come down to earth, get rid of the hierarchy that sits up there and feels superior rather than seeing education as a tool to work with. Education is not something to separate and divide. It should be seen as an everyday tool. There should be ways to integrate the tools of education into the community . . . . The college should be here, with the poor in the rural and migrant community.

Project Focus:
A Forecast
Study of
Community
Colleges

Part I. Changes in the Student Population to Be Served

The student brings a hell of a lot of things with him. He is black or Italian or something else. He brings with him a lot of notions, things that are in his mind. He might be anti-this or anti-that. It needs to be recognized by the people here that he does come as he is.

A Student

Chapter 1.
He Comes as He Is

It is impossible to determine what a college is, or what it ought to be, without looking at who goes there. Who are the men and women who use the institution? Or, more appropriately put, who benefits from it? Too often chroniclers and critics of colleges look at only what the college has to give instead of looking at what the student may have to offer, what his attitudes may be, and what he expects of the institution or of himself.

The student brings a hell of a lot of things with him. He is black or Italian or brown. He brings with him a lot of notions, things that are in his mind. He might be anti-this or anti-that. It does need to be recognized by the people here that he does come as he is.

That's the way T. C. saw it. He had started in a community college, later transferring to Stanford University. When he talked with me, he was a graduate student at a state college, working toward a master's degree.

His story begins earlier. He graduated from high school nine years ago, worked for four years, and became interested in criminal justice systems while serving in the Oakland Police Department reserves. He married, and his wife wanted to help him get his degree. He was sure of one thing: he didn't want to go back to his former job in an automobile plant. But something else stood in T. C.'s way. He described it:

> Where do you go with academic handicaps? I didn't have background for a university, so I came to the community college. I took all academic courses. My teacher worked with me very closely. I had a great deal of help. The teachers in English and political science took their time to help me through tutoring. I was in a hurry. I should not have been in English A, but my teacher helped tutor me. Other teachers gave me tips. I started out in a real shaky fashion. But I had inspiration. I wanted to do it. I looked back over my shoulder at the automobile plant.

The first semester was rough, but he developed confidence. The second semester was better. His instructors continued to help, and his grades were excellent in the second year. T. C. used athletics to get into what he described as a top-notch college. Offers came from Harvard, California, and Stanford. He said:

> I feel that 87 percent of this I got on my own, but the rest of it was help from counselors. I don't mean the regular counselors, but faculty who helped me. I had no contact with regular counselors here; I didn't want to be programmed. They would have told me to take remedial courses. I knew what the score was on my examinations, but that wasn't really me. I knew what I wanted, but they would have told me that I was not college material.

WHO ARE THE STUDENTS?

T. C.'s story provides one of many examples of who goes to community colleges, why, and what he brings to the experience. Obviously, he had that elusive quality called "college material." But what is that quality? Who does make up the "material" of a community college? Who comes? Why? How do they feel about it? What changes are coming about? Who should come? The usual reasons are well known: close to home; low cost. But those terms are almost as impersonal as "college material." Beneath the generalizations are people like the following.

Shelley is in her second year at the community college. She is majoring in sociology and plans to transfer to a state college. She is here because the cost is low and she was not sure what she wanted to do.

Peg is in education. She wants to go into dramatics if she transfers to another college. She came here from a missionary college in New York. She didn't want to go back to the missionary college and decided to stay in her home area. Also, money (or lack of it) was a factor.

Bob is in his first year. Education is his field too. He is not sure of his educational or vocational objectives. The college was close to his home, and he was accepted. So why go through the hassle of trying to get in somewhere else? He is not sure what he wants. He hopes to get straightened out here and then to transfer.

Veterans Are a Major Group

Joe is a second-year student. He is in business and data processing. He was discharged from military service and has been out of school for a while. He felt that he could carry the financial load here. He did not want to rely on his parents for financial assistance.

Russ is president of the Veterans' Association. He is in his first year and is interested in business. He would like to go to Lehigh University, but he needed some courses to fill out his program in order to be accepted there. Also, he didn't have enough money. He wants to transfer there if he can get financial assistance.

Bob is in his fourth semester and is in engineering. He came to the community college because of the low tuition and because it is a small school (5,000 students) compared to a university. He had been told by some of his friends that the four-year institutions are pretty severe, and he was just getting out of the military, so he was uncertain about how he could perform academically.

Rob had about the same story. He, too, is a veteran. He said it was pretty scary thinking about coming back to college. He didn't care much about grades in high school. He graduated almost ten years ago. People told him the university was very rough, especially in the first two years. So he decided to try it here.

Tom was somewhat older than the others. He is in his second semester in data processing. The low tuition attracted him. He said that he got out of high school in 1959, and his wife has been prodding him to go ahead with some college work. He felt that he probably couldn't "hack it" anywhere else. He said that it's "a hell of an adjustment" coming back to school. He really didn't know what he wanted, but now he thinks it's data processing. And since the university has just set up a bachelor's degree in computer science, he is going to transfer there.

Transfer Is a Common Goal

Elizabeth is a journalism major and plans to transfer to a four-year college. She was recently widowed. Some financial assistance was available. She had worked previously to put her daughter and husband through college. Now she is preparing for a better way to support her two sons, who are eleven and fifteen. She came because of the proximity of the college and its low cost.

Eugene is a veteran who spent eight years in the military forces. He is majoring in sociology and psychology and planning to transfer to the state university. He enrolled because of financial factors and because he wanted to come back to his home community. Out of school for ten years, he wanted to get into a situation where he could talk with people and have some sense of support by being in his home area. He said that a lot of people describe the university as being the "big house." The way they picture it, "You can feel like a cheese rolling down the hall with the big rats following you to eat you up."

In almost awed but approving tones the chairman of a board of trustees summed it up this way.

We are getting the darndest dukes mixtures of people: some coming here because of limited family pocket-book; some because they might be better off living at home for a while; others because they need opportunity for employment in this metropolitan area; and a lot of kids who don't really know what they want to do; more people in the evening division than in the daytime are married; people who are employed. The community college idea is so flexible that in effect you can wave your hand and say, "everybody."

So there's lots of "material" of all kinds. It's the opportunity as well as the challenge of the community college to mold and meld the the material into productive, interested, excited citizens. To do it the colleges must look at these people as people, anticipate or quickly identify what they bring, and measure up to their expectations.

ENROLLMENT IS INCREASING

There is an orthodoxy that community colleges are for those who cannot get into other institutions for various reasons: (1) they can't afford it; (2) they are not capable or ready; or (3) the other institutions do not offer what they really need or want. As someone put it, "In the beginning the community colleges in this state were really developed for the hardship cases. They served the disadvantaged. If you couldn't go to the university, you could go to the community college." That same spokesman then pointed to a development which has opened up a new set of problems as well as opportunities for these institutions. "There has been a marked change in this now. The community colleges now cater to every-one. . . . They are no longer looked upon as second choice."

They Should Have Gone Somewhere Else

Now the lines begin to form at the community college tables when college and university representatives are invited to the high schools. And in those lines are increasing numbers of valedictorians and others of more-than-mediocre academic achievement. At first glance this would appear to be cause for cheers by an institution which has looked long and hard for recognition and respect. But concerns like these are being voiced.

A lot of my friends really could have gone somewhere else, but the people in South Bethlehem are not coming and the institution ought really to be for them.

A community college is more attractive. There is real danger in this. Some students may not be served because of the influx of better students. Students today can go two years to community college and then they can transfer to their "father's college" and save a great deal of money in doing this.

They expressed the hope that perhaps there will be more good, close, cheap colleges developed. It would be good for the mission of their institution.

If he has a clear-cut goal, he should be encouraged to go elsewhere.

She is not sure that they ought to be attracting students who can afford to go elsewhere.

There are some students coming here who should be going directly to the university.

Let the rich ones, ones whose parents can send them somewhere else, let them do that, keep them out. Needs should be basic. Take the students who cannot get into other institutions because of money or academic problems. Priority on need, financial first.

What is happening to produce these questions and observations by students, faculty, and administrative personnel? Do they have an almost heretical sound? Is the community college faith under question by its adherents? If so, planners perhaps should stop short, for the outlook is for many more community colleges and heavier enrollments.

Although enrollments tripled during the 1960s, there is no leveling off in sight, assuming that the financial resources are available. Pressures will force acceleration of enrollments. Fueling this demand are factors that range from the persuasion of attractive new campuses and enrollment ceilings on state universities to stepped-up efforts to recruit students not previously served.

COMMUNITY COLLEGES LOOK BETTER

Those 500 community colleges established during the 1960s very often began operations in temporary facilities. Obviously they were not fully accredited since such recognition cannot be earned until a college has been underway for a few years. There was not much in the way of glamour and excitement to attract potential students. The appeals were low cost and proximity to home. Some offered programs not available elsewhere. (Remarkably enough, most of these institutions opened with more students than had been forecast.) However, during the subsequent years accreditation was obtained, campuses were built, and high school counselors more frequently pointed to the community college as a desirable educational option. The effect has been that in an area like Dade County, Florida, over a period of three years following high school graduation, Miami-Dade Junior College sees some 70 percent of the high school graduates.

LIMITATIONS ON STATE COLLEGES AND UNIVERSITIES

What happens to state colleges and universities will substantially influence community college enrollments. Limitations are often placed on the size of the four-year institution as a matter of state policy involving budgetary restrictions. As a result, large numbers of high school graduates who once would have gone directly to state universities and colleges are already entering community colleges first.

In a number of states (among them Illinois, Ohio, Maryland, and California) there are moves to put an upper limit on enrollments in the public universities. In fact, Phase III of the Master Plan for Higher Education in Illinois calls for a university enrollment freeze at the 1970 levels. Two upper-level universities have been established in that state. These have no freshman or sophomore students, and they follow the pattern established in Florida, where there are four upper-level universities. In Ohio it has been proposed that the open-admission universities become more selective and that two-year institutions be relied on for assuring access to all high school graduates. Whether the concern is for the size of the universities or for the costs involved, there is movement in many states to encourage students to begin their work in community colleges or similar institutions.

The University Is Too Large and Impersonal

Another factor, which may be transitory, discourages students from moving directly from the high school to the university. The university is perceived as too large and impersonal. When community college students were asked where they got the ideas that produced this negative image, they referred to reports from their friends or, in a growing number of instances, they had been there themselves and had transferred back to the community college. In a number of states, among them Washington and North Carolina, the number of students transferring from universities to community colleges has reached substantial proportions. In North Carolina 15 percent of in-state transfer was from senior to two-year colleges in 1970. In Washington it was 23 percent.

Other illustrations of the proportionate expected increase in students to be served by the community colleges are found in Maryland and Iowa. In 1971 in Iowa 19 percent of the full-time-equivalent students were in state community colleges. By 1985 this figure is projected to be 40 percent.

In Maryland there are now 17,000 full-time students in the state colleges, 30,000 in the university, and 21,000 in the community colleges. The forecast calls for 27,000 in the state colleges, 40,000 in the university, and 60,000 in the community colleges by 1980.

MORE OLDER STUDENTS WILL ENROLL

Most of the additional 40,000 students expected in Maryland community colleges will represent a different kind of population than those now enrolled. The projections assume an increase in older people returning to college, including a rising proportion of women and persons of low income. The trend toward increasing numbers of older students is already so apparent nationally that it is not at all accurate to refer to community college students as "kids."

One-fifth of the enrollment in one large community college is women over age twenty-five. The percentage of entering freshmen of age eighteen to twenty has dropped from 91 percent in 1967 to 74 percent in 1971. Those twenty-one years and older have increased from 7 percent in 1967 to 26 percent in 1971. This contrasts with 2 percent in the four-year institutions who are twenty-one years and older. Undoubtedly the large number of enrolling veterans has swelled the percentage of older students. Another factor has been the effect of the tightening economy in various parts of the country producing unemployment. In the aerospace industry, for example, people have looked for retraining opportunities such as those provided in occupational programs at community colleges.

OTHER GROWTH FACTORS

Adding to the community college load in some places has been the retrenchment by high schools in the face of tax failures in elections. Some high schools have been forced to cut back their programs to the essentials. As a result, community colleges are serving more high school students since looking for course enrichment is tending to lead them to the community college which can offer more advanced-placement programs.

This is not a new development, but until economic factors caused a limitation in high school courses, there were not many takers. Calculus for high school students, for example, is offered by a California community college at 7 A.M. By the time the student leaves high school and enters the community college or goes to a state university, he will already have earned credit for three semesters of college calculus. Similarly, community colleges are offering programs in vocational-technical education that are not available at the high school level because of limitation of resources.

These factors contribute markedly to the increasing numbers of persons of all ages served by these institutions. While the operation of factors external to the institution has augmented the enrollment, there is clearly a disposition among those identified with the college, from board members to students, to recruit persons from groups not served previously. These people may be in a low-income group or of a particular ethnic background or have physical handicaps such as deafness or blindness. Faculty speak of women who are separated from husbands, divorced, or widowed; of younger women receiving aid for dependent children; of those who left high school to get married. Some people return to forge a new identity; some are out of touch with the world of work and do not have the skills for handling institutional procedures; others have dropped out and now need to develop the skills to cope with society.

There is an idealism among many of the faculty, students, and administrative personnel of America's community colleges which, when fully expressed, would result in an educational assignment beyond comparison, not just in terms of numbers to be served, but in the spread of interests and needs to be met.

DIVERSITY IS THE DIRECTION

More students and greater variety, these are the prospects. It is likely that the impressive, sometimes confusing mixtures of persons now served by community colleges will diversify even more. No educational institution will confront a broader range of human talent, not even the comprehensive high school. For what adds another dimension of variety is that the community college cuts across many high school districts and reaches an older population.

COMMUNITY COLLEGES GET THE CREAM OF THE CROP TOO

As the hawkers used to say at football games, You can't tell a player without a program. The diversity of students in community colleges demands "program profiles" of who goes there that are better understood and defined. Despite criticism of schools, precollege training is improving. Through mass media the availability of intelligence from sources outside the schools is contributing to better-informed people at all ages. Aspirations are higher, rewards greater. The forecast is for more students who are at home in the academic world.

"In the beginning we did not get the cream of the crop. Now we are beginning to get some of the best. There are quality students coming," said the president of a young community college.

Test data support his impressions. Test scores are higher for many students. Faculty report a trend toward "better" high school graduates. They look for more who are "academically able" and "baccalaureate-bound." "In fact," reported a dean, "we have emphasized programs for the less able in our planning, but now we see that we will need honors programs as well."

Students, too, have views of what the institution ought to become if it wants to be able to match their interests. There is a call by some for the community colleges of the future to provide "intellectual atmosphere," including such accoutrements as residence halls. They declare that college education is more than the classroom, and some say that in time vocational-technical programs will be crowded out.

"I don't see this campus really as a college," a student said. "It doesn't have a college environment."

At this point I suggested that perhaps it was a different kind of institution and that the disadvantages he saw of a commuting population (students living at home and working part- or full-time) might be exploited to bring about educational benefits. But he did not warm up to that idea.

We are still a very young institution. It is going to take some time. Maybe some day we will have dormitories. We are going to have new facilities. You have to have something you can take pride in. At the present time our facilities are army barracks. But on the other hand it is a great thing here. We have small classes. We have good instructors. They are liberal. Some of them are superintelligent. They are great.

More Students from the Top Half of the High School Class

There are now community colleges drawing a large proportion of this kind of student. More of their students come from the top half than from the lower half of their high school classes. A state director reported that the students going to one of the largest community colleges in his state were not much different from those who were in their first two years at the state university.

"I guess our problem is that a lot of us want the same kinds of things that a four-year college can provide," mused one student.

In the same state, the chairman of the legislature's committee on education maintained that these colleges ought to "take most any high school graduate and should not have the intention of becoming a scholarly-type institution."

The apparent tension between expectations of student and legislator is highlighted by these two differing views of the president and dean of the *same institution*.

"I believe we are moving to what looks like a college now, and the new facilities and campus have had something to do with this. With the university raising admission requirements I feel that we will be getting better-prepared students academically." Such was the dean's picture.

As for the president: "I feel that the community college offers services to the student who is uncertain, who is not clear as to his goal. If he has a clear-cut goal, perhaps I would encourage him to go elsewhere. It is the role of this institution to provide opportunity for exploration and possibly for failure without so many bruises."

Each man was picturing what he saw as the most significant change in direction of the institution. Some would hold that these views are mutually exclusive, that the college must be one thing or the other. And herein lie a crucial point and a dilemma. The crucial point is that the tension generated from the conflict of direction is not likely to diminish but rather to intensify. The dilemma lies in the fact that indications are that the institution will be required to be both things.

MORE "UNCONVENTIONAL" STUDENTS

Just as churches tend to welcome to their fellowship those who live the good life, so colleges look with favor on the motivated, literate, and articulate. Therefore it may come as somewhat of a shock to find a large number of the community college family stating that a big part of the college mission is service to those academically less qualified. They see the institution as representing a new approach to education that can pick up the products of failure. They acknowledge that it is easier to teach motivated students, but their job, they say, is to teach those whose motivations are weak. Not all faculty concur in this. There are those who declare that too much time and money are wasted on students who are not ready.

The challenge of low educational attainment is illustrated in a Midwestern city. Of the students who attend this big-city community college, 80 percent are from elementary and secondary schools that ranked lowest in performance on citywide aptitude and achievement tests. Scores show that students performed three grade-level equivalences lower than their actual grade placement in reading and numerical ability. On each factor measured, the high school students averaged 40 percentiles lower than the national norms. These are the students sought by this college. Others are those who dropped out of the high school at age sixteen or seventeen.

Another population to be served has been suggested in many colleges: beginning adult learners. Often these come from the model cities area. They have been out of school for many years.

"I admire them," said a teacher. "But do they have the background? They will need help in reading. They need learning skills. They are insecure—insecure but highly motivated. Some of them carry very heavy loads trying to get training for a decent living and at the same time trying to keep their families together."

Community colleges in North Carolina can furnish at least a partial answer to that teacher's question. Out of the 293,000 different people who took one or more courses in the community colleges and technical institutes of that state in 1970, 47.5 percent enrolled to complete studies of elementary or secondary education level or to otherwise improve their general education.

Call them what you will (and the approved glossary terms seem to change daily)—educationally handicapped, disadvantaged, unconventional, the new students—community college people see a future with many more of them. A state commissioner of education believes it is appropriate to have in community colleges a concentration of students disadvantaged by poor secondary school experience, not because the community college is a second-class institution, but because it is closer to the high school and in his state the county superintendent sits on the college board. His seat on the board puts the community college people in the position to ask him "What the hell are you doing about the needs of these students who are coming to us not prepared for college work?"

DIVERSITY OR DISJUNCTION?

"As different as night from day" is a helpful euphemism in looking at characteristics of community college students. Most older students are in evening programs; however, a growing number are in day classes, and the trend is expected to increase. But whether enrolled in night or day classes, the older students are different from the younger ones. In fact, it is the older students who have had more than just academic experience against whom younger, apparently more indecisive colleagues are measured. To some teachers the evening and day students make up in effect two colleges. Evening students seem more dedicated than able, they say. The day students appear to be younger, striving for individualism and asking troublesome questions like Why do you require this? On the other hand, according to faculty, "The night people are middle-class, churchgoing older people, people who know what they want to do, people who have found out that they cannot advance without additional training."

Among the older students problems of motivation are minimal. By the time a woman gets a babysitter and travels to the college she is earnest about her studies. There is some question about rapport with younger students whose needs are somewhat different. Competition with the more mature is sometimes rough for the young person interested in getting grades.

Evening programs now represent more than half of the headcount in many community colleges. In general among students and faculty there is a high morale, a lively interest, flexibility in approach, and an informality and timeliness that prompt one to wonder whether the "night people" are harbingers of the community college to come.

Students voice concern at the assortment of enrollees and especially at the absence of a cohesive quality.

> Many are commuting students. They have an hour or two and then they are on their way. Or they are transient students. They are here for a semester and then somewhere else. Voc-tech people are engaged in welding or diesel mechanics or auto mechanics. I don't know any of those people. There is nothing that really keeps us together. There is no common bond for people from all walks of life.

In the face of a counselor's warning, the poignancy of this expression is disturbing, for the biggest problem, he said, in working with those students from homes experiencing college opportunity for the first time is a psychological one: the students' self-concepts. This involves a sense of identity and place in the group.

Large numbers of students say they don't know why they are at the college. Many would welcome an alternative.

> In the high school they ought to strike at that matter of the prestige of college-going. There should be some way of bringing to the high school student opportunities in the building trades or in technical fields because if that is the way you go, you are considered a dumbbell, and the counselor prods you into college. Your parents probably have the biggest influence. They say, "We didn't have a chance, so you go whether you like it or not."

Large numbers of new enrollees are not there six or eight weeks later. The reasons for leaving are not well known. Finance often appears to be a factor. Many recent high school graduates are in these institutions because they don't know what else to do. The community college may be viewed by these students as an opportunity to defer decision making at low cost—cost in terms of dollars and ego shock.

WHAT KINDS OF STUDENTS?

What does the future seem to hold for community colleges? A much broader spectrum of student differences, with striations of many kinds: motivations, age, culture, interests, academic achievement, objectives, race, socioeconomics, aptitudes, and intelligence. How can these differences be dealt with in productive ways? How can diversity become of value? Is there potential here for what might be considered a principal role of the community college—to advance the democratization of education?

Obviously some way needs to be developed to view diversity. There is a sorting out and labeling process which takes place now. But often the categories are misleading or false, not in harmony with the goals of the institution. For example, when faculty members or administrators were asked to identify the *kinds of students* who ought to be served by the college, repeatedly the response was in terms of *kinds of programs*, with transfer or occupational most often named. Similar traps of classification were evident in the linkage of "good" students with the academic or transfer programs and "poor" students with the vocational-technical courses. Was it just an unfortunate slip of the tongue when a president said, "We are getting a better grade of student now, as well as more vocational-technical people"?

Labels for the Ordering of Students

Other labels are used in an attempt to establish some ordering of the students served. These include regular and part-time, day and night, transfer and terminal, academic and occupational, older and younger, and occasionally A students and D students. Unfortunately there is a tendency to assign along with the label a slate of characteristics. If he is a transfer student, it is implied that in several ways he is different from an occupational student. Not the least of the limitations to this kind of inaccurate generalization is that no one really knows who the transfer student is until after the fact.

However, if a college is to work effectively with such a breadth of characteristics, there is need for an organizing approach to heterogeneity. The present misleading oversimplifications are not helpful; they are dangerous. They perpetuate classifications alien to the mission of the community college.

A helpful approach to study of community college students and their classification along lines of motivational interests has been suggested to me by Pierre Grimes of Golden West College in California. Dr. Grimes has had an interest for many years in the field of motivation dynamics as utilized in industry. He left industry to teach in the Orange Coast district and has applied his former techniques to studies of student motivation.

Four Categories of Students

Four categories of students emerge from this study of motivation: (1) The high schooler—he is close to the teacher and enjoys that association. He looks upon community college as a continuation of high school. It's fun, fun, fun. He goes to football games and plays cards in the student union. (2) The vocationalist—he has a clear idea where he is going. He is interested in preparing for a job, and that is pretty much what college is. (3) The future careerist—he has accepted the general idea of our culture. He has the feeling that the degree assures a white-collar job and that his future is guaranteed as a result of his educational program. (4) The "selfer"—he is looking for meaning. He is asking the big questions, What is life? Who am I?

If questions about certain aspects of college life are put to these different categories of students, the responses differ clearly. It is then possible to predict response to a particular situation, based upon this system of categorization. For example, it is probable that the high schooler will respond to questions about curriculum and student activities in different ways from the selfer.

Golden West College has large rooms called forums that seat up to 300 people and are equipped for multimedia use. The high schoolers and future careerists adjust to the forums. The vocationalists resent them; they can't ask questions nor prove themselves as to vocational choices. The selfers pointedly avoid the forums.

Grimes's method suggests predictable reactions to program learning, teacher characteristics, textbooks, etc. Withdrawal patterns can also be predicted. The high schoolers and selfers had some tendency to drop out—the high schooler when he found out that college was different from high school and wasn't all fun, the selfer when he found out that the college program was much more like the program the high schooler would want. The selfer found few people looking for meaning and asking the big questions.

Selfers Lose Out in Wrong Courses

Grimes had not realized how many selfers were lost (that is, eventually dropped out) because they enrolled in the wrong courses. He maintains that courses taught by different people are not the same courses. In utilizing his techniques a counselor could match up the student and the teacher (faculty may similarly be classified), and this kind of matching would make much more sense and be more effective than matching up courses and students.

Grimes estimates that 50 to 60 percent of the students at his institution are high schoolers at the beginning, and there is a heavy percentage of "leavers" from this group. The future careerists make up about 15 percent, and they tend to be the most constant. If a college is to be viable, it must be interested in the extent of movement from one type to another. It has to be both set up to facilitate this change and able to keep the selfers.

Grimes's classifications are less important than the fact that they result from a research approach. It is research into the nature and characteristics of student diversity which is called for here, as contrasted with operating methods guided by clichés and conjecture.

SUMMARY

Who goes to community college? Everybody. The mix of students is one of the challenges of community college work. There are students from educationally disadvantaged backgrounds, students who need honors programs, high school students in advanced-placement programs, and students well beyond the traditional college age group. They are enrolled in a variety of programs for many different reasons.

Enrollments will grow and the diversity will increase. The frustrations of faculties and administrators trying to learn how to cope effectively with such diversity will also probably increase. But this stress must be a creative one, for the students at the extreme edges of this diversity are simply the advance guard of the community college students of tomorrow. That is the way it should be if community colleges are to help democratize higher education.

One central problem comes of trying to deal with a diverse student population without appropriate descriptors. The traditional labels don't fit. With a nontraditional student population some nontraditional procedures and nomenclatures are required. Finding working definitions that adequately serve the information needs of the community college field may well be the most important task facing educational researchers today.

REPRISE

Hey man, take a look at me! I don't come from his side of town. I don't dress the way he does or the way you do, but I am here too. I come here because you've got to have an education. I just want to know that you've seen me, that you know I am here, and that there is something here for me. Don't tell me what I ought to be. How do you know that? Take me for what I am. If we can't do it that way, how can I become anything else?

Chapter 2.
Toward Equal
Opportunity for
Minority Groups

Mounting numbers of minority group students are enrolling in community colleges, many more than are entering four-year colleges. In 1971 of the full-time enrollees 30 percent were other than Caucasian in race.[1] A steep increase has occurred during the past two years.

There are a number of reasons for those accelerating enrollments. There was substantial development of community colleges in many big cities during the sixties, thereby putting postsecondary educational opportunities within reach of inner-city populations for the first time. The colleges were not only accessible geographically, but generally cost students less. Most had policies of open admissions which provided opportunity for many students whose previous academic experiences had been deficient. And recruitment efforts had been stepped up because of the view that a significant responsibility of the community colleges is response to the pressing needs of the black, Spanish-speaking, and Indian populations. One other factor is most important. In some places, students who had previously viewed community colleges as second-class institutions and as foreign territory had begun to see them as "their" colleges.

These figures are encouraging. They may ease the consciences of those concerned with equality of education by conveying a sense of substantial progress. But there remains a real question as to whether

[1] Data reported are taken from a questionnaire administered to full-time students and faculty at 90 institutions participating in Project Focus survey. For further information on student and faculty characteristics see David S. Bushnell, *Organizing for Change: New Priorities for Community Colleges*, Chap. 2.

change is taking place as rapidly as circumstances require. Out of many hours of listening to thoughtful, serious, and sometimes angry minority personnel—students, faculty, administrators, board members, people in various communities—I am convinced that improvement of opportunities for minority persons must become a matter of first priority in America's community colleges. In relation to the past and in relation to other institutions, community colleges appear to be doing well. But, compared with the need and in light of their opportunities, these institutions must do more and do it quickly.

I sensed unrest and frustration, impatience with changes that were perceived to be more facade than substance, and a belief that involvement at decision-making levels is long overdue. These feelings and their causes varied throughout the country and were not common to all minority groups. In some cities the days of violent protest, of militancy, were being superseded by work "within the system." Changes had already taken place to assure participation in educational decisions and program. On the other hand it was clear that in some areas the "roof could blow off" at any time. In some places gaining access to educational opportunities was a pressing problem. In others, access had been gained, and the crucial matters were the holding power of the institution—retention of students, the provisions of supportive services so that the student could complete his program.

To generalize about minority group students (or minority groups, for that matter) is just as rash an exercise as generalizing about students or Americans or parents. It is not the purpose of this book to attempt an anthropological analysis of racial and cultural differences, but there are differences to be considered just as there are rural and urban and regional differences that can be noted among the people of this country.

THE LARGER ENVIRONMENT

The community college exists in a social environment, and in general it represents a socioeconomic cross section of that environment. Matters of race, cultural differences, and class differences in the larger setting are brought with the student to the college. For example, he comes with a set of attitudes toward education and other social institutions which have formed and stuck through childhood and youth experiences. The community college is often viewed as a possible extension of unhappy public school tribulations.

The examples are numerous of the school perceived as an alien environment. I asked a Spanish-speaking student whether there had been a bilingual approach to learning in the public schools. He replied that when he was a kid, the teacher would hit him across the knuckles with a stick when he used Spanish words.

A young black student, being recommended for a Ford Foundation scholarship, looked back on his high school days. He was threatened with expulsion because he smiled in class. The students in his school wanted to commemorate the death of Martin Luther King. This was denied, and so they wore black hats and black gloves on that day and were sent home. "We feel like there is nothing we can do to change it," he said.

Problems Differ from Place to Place

Obviously, in other places the problems might be quite different. For example, in Tucson, Arizona, 56 percent of the Mexican-American youth have already flunked out after three-quarters of their first year in high school. And in Stockton, California, according to staff of the College Readiness Center, many of the minority students come to the college with fourth-grade reading ability.

In some of the cities, the losers outnumber the gainers, and their prospects are troubling. Black administrators and faculty say that in the future the larger number of minority students will be coming from inner-city schools that are already overcrowded and with services cut back because of financial stringencies. They fear that students will be even less well prepared for academic programs. A faculty member in an inner-city community college who has a son in high school described these institutions as "detention homes. There is high faculty turnover. There are many young teachers who are not well prepared, and a radical ideology is being promoted." He expects new tensions and increased frustration at the college level.

Another element in the larger society affects the community college in its work with minority personnel. Interviewees told me that people need to have some visual proof of what their opportunities can be. Black and brown students look for members of their races to identify with in the professions or in positions of responsibility in the community. But they find few of these in board membership, in the top-level administrative ranks, or in the professional life of the community. Look at how the minorities see it:

There is not one Mexican-American principal in the county. Why go to school to become administrators when the opportunities are not there? You look around. You don't see any brown faces. This cuts the motivation in half. Maybe some day you can wind up at an institution like Phoenix Union High School. So the brown personnel don't have visibility, and there is no credibility to the claims made by administrators that they are trying to employ Mexican-American personnel. It is not just the community college. It is the whole state.

It would be good for you to know that out of the 22,000 people who live in our community (predominantly black), we don't have one doctor or one lawyer. We need to educate enough people to build a community that people feel good about living in. Our sons and daughters have to see a doctor or lawyer to know that it is possible for them to become doctors and lawyers also.

They see no Spanish-speaking mayor or councilmen or Spanish-speaking people in the chambers of commerce, no dentists. So the young fellow asks, "Can I really be president?"

I never had a Chicano or black teacher until I got to Berkeley. So there are no models. I thought that Mexicans and blacks didn't have enough brains to teach. But if I can see somebody of my color there, I can recognize him. He is out there. Maybe I can be there too.

I walked down the main street of a Southwestern city with a leader in the Mexican-American community. He pointed to the buildings we were passing, the banks, the city hall, and noted:

One change definitely needs to take place. There must be recognition of people of caliber in the minorities and opportunity for expression of their abilities in the whole structure. The higher you go up in those buildings, the whiter the complexion of the people working there. The farther down you go below the first floor level, the darker the complexion. We want to be on the upper floors. We want to see some minority faces there.

They Want to Be on the Upper Floors

The drive to be on the upper floors, to be involved in decision making and policy determination, to be in on the planning and not be "programmed," this insistence upon self-determination is another factor to be recognized in consideration of ways by which the community college can move toward equal opportunity for minority groups.

One of the founders of Nairobi College in East Palo Alto, California, the president of Mothers for Equal Education, wrote:

I am forty-three years old, and for me this is the first time I have ever been involved in building or helping to build a school. We always saw people building the schools, and we never knew how it happened or what took place. As a result, those schools didn't mean much to us. The process of organizing the college and getting it off the ground, the process of involving the faculty, the students and people from within the community has given many of us hope. We have never had this kind of opportunity before. We are going to have to build our communities from within; we need institutions that will get large numbers of black people into college and out.

This same individual described another problem of contemporary society which affects the accessibility of community colleges. She reported that in a county already served by three campus-type institutions, the closest facilities were 30 miles away. There is no bus transportation, and many families do not have cars. Her criticism could be multiplied a hundred times. Public transportation in general is either not available or inadequate. When this factor is coupled with the tendency for community college facilities to be built where large blocs of land are available, the effect is reduction of accessibility to people who are most in need of college services.

Phoenix, Arizona, Monmouth County, New Jersey, Northampton County, Pennsylvania, and Prince Georges County, Maryland, are just a few among the majority of areas served by community colleges in which public transportation is poor. This is not a shortcoming which can be laid solely at the doorstep of the community college. Responsibility is broader than that. A society which is largely affluent has assumed apparently that its citizens all have the means to secure essential civic services by means of the automobile.

Sites chosen by many recently established community colleges are not far from people who find it easy to go to college but may be many miles from those who find this problem of distance just one more difficulty. The problem is not easily resolved. In densely urban areas land has often not been available. And removing structures from property tax rolls in areas where tax revenues have already declined has been resisted. Problems of building have appeared to be fewer by going to the periphery of the city. Land may cost less. Negotiations may involve fewer interested parties. But regardless of the reasons for moving to suburban areas, the fact remains that large numbers of minority persons do not find the college within easy reach. Long-range solutions will involve measures to improve public transportation, dispersal of college services as discussed in Chapter 5, and a scale of community values which (in determining where facilities are to be located) accentuates the needs of people who have not had educational opportunity.

MIXED PERCEPTIONS OF THE COMMUNITY COLLEGE

A growing number of minority students are coming with attitudes toward education which are shaped by previous experiences. They are looking for models of their own race with which to identify. And they want to be free to determine their own future. What happens when students and the college come together?

Views toward the college are mixed. Not all minority students enter these institutions singing psalms of joy for the privilege. Sometimes the community college is viewed as a "cop-out" on behalf of the white population. It is seen as another way in which society works out its cultural policy. The community college takes the pressure off the universities. In effect, it keeps the minorities in their places, they say. These same students feel pressures from the white institution to push them in the direction of bricklaying and similar trade occupations.

I got the impression in interviewing minority students in some urban areas that they would much rather be at a university than at the community college, but were prevented because of inadequate funds or academic preparation. Accenting this feeling was the supposition that the "good" minority student goes to the university where he gets more financial aid and a better program, and those who need compensating educational experiences for academic deficiencies go to the community college. Salt is further rubbed into the wounds when "remedial" courses are required for which no academic credit is given but for which he must pay tuition. And the student questions the justice of it all. Why should he pay in terms of time and money, he asks, for courses which convey no credit? Why should he be penalized because of inadequacies that can be traced to ineffective elementary and secondary schools? In this student there may be a smoldering anger and a resistant attitude because he didn't want to be there in the first place, but he felt that there were no good options.

New Attitudes Emerging

On the other hand, there are dramatic contrasts to these views and attitudes that represent substantial and recent changes in student and institutional spirit. These new attitudes are profoundly significant as a forecast of what the future can be. In some institutions student morale is high, and the community college is first choice. Minority leadership, substantial numbers of minority students, programs directly related to interests and backgrounds, and new attractive facilities such as those at Malcolm X College in Chicago and Merritt College in Oakland, California, appear to contribute to this recent and dynamic reshaping of the image of the community college for some minority personnel. Other factors of significance would include staffing, financial aid, supportive educational services, educational programs, and relations with other institutions.

STAFFING: A MAJOR CONSIDERATION

Although 30 percent of the full-time students in community colleges are from minority groups, only 5 percent of the faculty are black or brown. Obviously, minority students who seek to identify with persons of their own race in the professional ranks do not have an easy task. The problem of identification is made even more difficult by the fact that minority group faculty tend to be from middle-class backgrounds. Yet, the majority of students may be from different socioeconomic strata. If teaching-learning styles are crucial, if opportunities to develop social, psychological, and political links are important, what are the implications for the staffing in relation to the characteristics of minority group students, particularly those in the urban areas?

Almost without exception there is a call for more black, Spanish-speaking, and Indian faculty and administrative personnel. However, students, faculty, and presidents are not inclined, as judged in their responses to institutional goals, to rank among the top institutional goals that of attracting a representative number of minority faculty members. Faculty and students, though, assign more importance to this purpose than do presidents. This would suggest that the concern expressed over the growing participation of faculty in appointments, as it might affect a president's specification of more minority faculty, is not necessarily justified.

There is an advantage in employing bicultural people, according to Mexican-American interviewees, which is that such individuals can relate to both kinds of students, to the Anglo- and the Mexican-American. But often it appears that the Ph.D. degree or university credits count for more than life in the community and knowledge of the community. Those who appear to be most successful in working with minorities are those who know the culture of the students and know the community. Students hold not only that such knowledge is important, but also that there should be recognition of their previous environment and acknowledgment of their life-styles. One black instructor who was very popular with the minority students had a Phi Beta Kappa key, had worked as a longshoreman, and had held a broad variety of jobs. This was the kind of man they could understand and who could relate to them. They wanted more faculty with this kind of breadth of experience in the workaday world.

Faculty Should Be Involved

A black president insists that faculty personnel become involved in the community. In some way they need to become acquainted with the various parts that make the community tick. They need to know what people are thinking, what they do, where they live.

Several minority students proposed that just as all high school graduates are presumed to have some English, it should be assumed that all faculty members have some kind of preparation or training to deal with other people, particularly people who are culturally different, some kind of educational experience by which they can take a look at themselves as well as others. They further proposed that these concepts be expressed in policies of employment.

However, the need for faculty and counselors to be oriented to different cultures has been given little attention in preservice professional training. A dean of students at a leading university in the Southwest declared, "The university did not teach a damn thing about minorities in the counselor education program."

In-service training has value at this point. There is usually sufficient motivation present because (1) what is learned has an immediate and direct relationship to the teacher's task and (2) the results or feedback necessary in effective learning is not long in developing.

Talent Being Identified

More institutions are identifying and finding ways to tap talent in the community, despite the fact that talented people may lack the conventional credentials. One leading urban community college selected its key staff from the community and provided suitable training. Efforts of this kind need to be stepped up, for large numbers of faculty at this time are frank enough to say that they fail to understand and lack sensitivity to different learning styles and psychological needs. Peace Corps volunteers are given intensive training before moving into different cultural settings. The need in community colleges would appear to be no less essential.

The Carnegie Commission on Higher Education, in recognition of underrepresentation of minority groups in the academic community, advised:[1]

> Until we can produce a more representative ethnic distribution of persons with advanced degrees, the Commission urges that interim alternatives for hiring faculty be sought by educational institutions. All those with the desire to teach classes for which they are qualified by talent and experience should be allowed to do so. The conventional standards of competence are not always relevant.

The problem of racial or social distance between faculty and students may be particularly acute in the vocational-technical fields. Here the problem is compounded because of what seems to be an aversion of minority personnel in general toward vocational-technical education. Some studies show the vocational-technical faculty to be conservative in values and outlook and inclined to expect minority groups to conform to those values. Resistance to vocational programs may be reinforced by difficulties in identifying with faculty in these fields. As is well known, the negative attitude toward vocational programs is not unique to minority youth in the United States, but up to this time they seem to be particularly resistant. Pressures to place them in vocational-technical programs start in high school years, as they see it.

"If you have a Spanish surname," said a student, "you are automatically put in the vocational-technical programs, and when you get to community college, you lack the basic skills which are required if you want to move into the transfer program."

Other students and faculty point out that blacks and browns have not had a chance to see the successful personnel of their races in action in the vocational-technical fields: "You don't see the black and brown faces there. These young people don't know the kinds of job opportunities opening up. So college is just a generalized good thing to them that conveys status."

If the fruits of completing a vocational-technical program were evident, that is, if graduates got jobs, if training led to meaningful employment, and if the route were open-ended, many more students would be interested.

Job Attainment Is Difficult

It is reported that another deterrent in some fields, such as building trades, is the difficulty minority personnel experience in getting jobs

[1] *A Chance to Learn: An Action Agenda for Equal Opportunity in Higher Education,* Carnegie Commission on Higher Education, Berkeley, Calif., Mar. 2, 1970.

and thereby entering apprentice programs. A closer relation of the college with business, industry, and labor unions is called for in order that the training cycle be complete. Recruitment, training, and job placement could give visibility to new kinds of job opportunities and enhance the attractiveness of occupational programs.

There is another faculty consideration crucial to the success of the community college in opening new opportunities for education. It transcends matters of race and culture but is related. Will there be warmth, the sense of personal relationship which so many students seek, in relationships with faculty and among students, faculty, and administrative personnel? As will be discussed in Chapter 3, there are tendencies toward impersonalization and a formalization of relationships which would press most heavily against those to whom the ways of the academic world are not well known and institutionalized and regulated behavior is suspicious. How flexible will be the professional roles? How quickly can needed change come about? What mechanism can be established for decision making to assure that needs and interests of students are high among the considerations?

MONEY PROBLEMS

Among minority students the primary reason for leaving the college before goals are attained is lack of money. A recent study at Malcolm X College supports this assertion, which was made in a number of community colleges. The dean of arts and sciences reported that 80 to 90 percent of the "dropouts" stem from financial reasons. No tuition is charged students in the Chicago city colleges. In other parts of the country, in Maryland, for example, where $300 is the tuition charge, a financial aids officer says that people are often surprised at what it costs to go to a low-tuition, publicly supported community college. In addition to $300 for tuition and $30 for fees, there is $150 for books and supplies. Transportation cost is estimated at $320, which covers only gasoline for a car. Meals and clothing and personal costs come on top of that. She talks with people in terms of a minimum budget of about $1,700 per year without any contribution toward buying groceries for the home or taking into account the earnings sacrificed because the student is attending college.

Financial aid plans frequently do not take into account the particular problems of low-income minority group students. For example, students plead for something to be done about the parents' confidential statement for financial aid. Frequently the mother or father, they report, can't read or understand the thing. The three- or four-page document "turns them off."

A Mexican-American counselor said that students he was contacting were uneasy about coming to the college. The procedures of getting in were unknown to them. They didn't know how to secure financial assistance, or whether financial assistance was available. They were hesitant to come in and apply. Personal contact must be made with them.

A problem referred to repeatedly is that those students who are at home in the academic institutions take initiative in procuring information about financial aid; they observe the requirements for submitting applications, turn in the materials on time, and often follow up with personal contact. On the other hand, minority students who are uncertain about attending the institution and who finally decide to try it often contact the college just before the term begins and indicate their need for financial assistance. Nine times out of ten the funds have been committed months before.

Pressure on the Student to Help Support His Family

There are other problems which are not often taken into account. I was told that the Chicano who is not contributing to his household after age 18 "feels like a fifth wheel." He is surrounded by poverty and finally he can no longer stand the pressures of feeling that he ought to be contributing toward support of the home, and so he drops out of school.

There were many good words said about work-study programs, although college personnel still have to find the jobs for the students. But there were very few good words about the guaranteed-loan program. According to students, if you don't have an account in the bank for six months, then the banker won't look at you. And it was emphasized again that you have to look at life-styles. Counselors in working with high schools find that the students tend to pick the work-study programs. They avoid anything like a loan. They are told that you can borrow up to $5,000 over a four-year period for college work. Their reaction:

> Suppose the family makes $3,000 per year. Somewhere in that person's gut is the feeling that he can't possibly pay back that much money. So most people don't apply. In fact most people don't even know how to fill out the financial aid application.

Work-study program difficulties also were recognized:

Many of these students are trying to make up for deficiencies in past education. If you add a heavy load of employment, then it becomes an impossible task. Should they be in the reading laboratory working at reading skills or out on the campus picking up paper for income?

The greatest blow of all, though, occurs when funds are presumed to be available, tentative commitments are made, expectations stimulated, and then federal or state funds are cut back or delayed. Veterans have financial assistance under federal legislation, but there is need for a similar program for others who are financially disadvantaged and who have no benefits. Helpful though the work-study programs have been, there has not been enough of this money to meet the needs. Clearly, if the community college is to serve financially handicapped minority group students, there must be a new and more realistic understanding of what are the actual costs of attending the college. If the states and the nation are committed to extending educational opportunity to all, regardless of income, then the financial consequences must be recognized in terms of programs that fit the needs of this segment of our population.

SUPPORTIVE SERVICES

Closely related to the financial problem is the need for supportive services, At a college in California, I saw small children accompanying young mothers and fathers to the classroom because care was not available for the children. Child-care services are among the most needed forms of aid. In one institution it was considered so important that the major part of a state grant for disadvantaged students was spent to provide day-care services. However, the state is now asking whether that is really an educational service. A number of black administrators told me that it was a most crucial need, second only to financial aid.

Some might question whether ethnic studies are appropriately referred to as a "supportive service." For minority students they often are. Interests and motivations are generated that spur the student to improve reading, writing, and mathematical skills. Fear of writing is reduced when the student is encouraged to write about those things *he* wants to write about, and matters of race and culture, especially his own race and culture, are very much on his mind. This same recognition of the special interests and needs of the student is reflected in other services of the college. The word *remedial* has fallen into disrepute. Students who required remedial courses often perceived themselves as "losers" and as stupid. Negative attitudes toward themselves and the college often inhibited their learning. Instructional remediation implies a value judgment that anyone below the "norm" is inferior because he doesn't measure up to the verbal skill level (as determined by achievement tests) of the middle-class white.

Who is to say what is the appropriate norm for someone who has been reared in an urban ghetto, who has learned to cope with the demands of such an environment, and who speaks his own language derived from his subculture? "The learning skills center attempts to deal with the student where he is 'at' with reference to his particular level of development," says a director of a Learning and Instructional Resources Center in an urban college. The concept that all students have the ability to learn is gaining acceptance, and some institutions are being structured to accommodate students' strengths. Skill centers, laboratories for reading, writing, and mathematics, and tutors—often other students—as well as peer counselors, are available to help the student move at his own pace. These services assume variable rates. If the student apparently is never going to be a fast reader, he is taught how to survive as a slow reader. In terms of past provisions, tremendous support systems are required to move in the direction indicated, and there are consequent financial costs. However, what are the alternatives? Merely to admit the student to the college is far from assurance of educational opportunity.

California Recognizes a Need for Greater Resources

The state of California (SB 164) has recognized the need for additional resources in setting up the Extended Opportunity Program:

> ... that the California community colleges recognize the need and accept the responsibility for extending the opportunities for community college education to all who may profit; ... regardless of economic, social, and educational status. It is the intent and purpose of the legislature to encourage local community colleges to establish and develop programs directed to: ... those students affected by language, social and economic handicaps, to establish and develop services, techniques and activities directed to the recruitment ... and their retention in community colleges and to the stimulation of their interest in intellectual education and vocational attainment.

Of forty-six projects originally funded, forty were for general support in counseling, tutorial services, and individual grants.

Reference to ethnic studies has so far been in relation to motivation of the minority student in improvement of reading, writing, and mathematical skills. Obviously, much broader interest exists. Substantial developments are under way, particularly in the urban community colleges. The national picture reveals a number of differences in approach. In some areas, black and Chicano studies are offered, as well as similar courses for other minority groups. Or there may be a broader approach such as cultural history of the Southwest as taught by a Mexican-American in Kansas City (who also edits a bilingual magazine, *Entrelineas*). Emphasis appears to be on what such studies can contribute toward the total learning process rather than on these studies as ends in themselves.

"I will not hire a student because he got A's in black studies," said a black publisher. "I want that, but in addition I need to know, can he write, can he type, can he contribute to my business?"

And an attorney stated: "You should slip in the basics such as mathematics and those programs dealing with the reasoning process."

Chicano or black studies, or their equivalent for other minority groups, are not just "academically oriented programs" but serve to establish the self-identity and historical links which are so important in the growth and development of any student.

California's ninety-three community colleges have been directed to offer ethnic studies courses by 1975. The order, from the board of governors of the community college system, allows each college to decide how many courses to offer and what courses should be defined as ethnic studies. Of the ninety-three colleges, seventy-seven already offered such courses when the mandate was issued.

Ethnic Studies for All

There has been some push toward a requirement that all students take ethnic courses. But many minority students shy away from this approach as much as they do from other required courses such as physical education. However, it is clear that there is general agreement that a college needs to make available those ethnic programs that are of particular interest because of the composition of the student body and the community.

There are other difficulties experienced by minority students. A faculty member reported that two black students came in at the last twenty seconds of registration. To his colleagues he said,

You know what is left by that time. Sure they can take Typing I, Shorthand II, and Spanish III. You might say they should have come earlier, but they didn't, and there is nothing left for them. High school counselors will often say to the minority students: You are not college material, go somewhere else. They are not accustomed to how you go about getting into a college or when you report for registration.

In addition to the frequent handicap of not knowing the procedures and timetable for gaining admission, students emphasize the need for an orientation program which will assist in getting acquainted with the place and where they go for various things. "Otherwise you come in, you get lost, you go out, and you are another black statistic, and this just confirms the notion that you can't make it anyway."

Perhaps these problems could be eased through early recruiting efforts by the college and improved relations with the high schools. A Mexican-American teacher who was contacting future students said:

I find that the college is here and the students are there, but they are not getting together. We need to do away with the alien pictures that the student has of this institution. Personal contact must be made with them. Their attitudes do not prepare them to be aggressive and take initiative in his regard. The Chicano attitude is different from the Anglo. There may be a negative attitude in the home and a negative attitude among his friends. The community college needs to work more closely with the high schools. The big problem is retention. The institution needs to change so students feel that this is their institution too, so they are comfortable here. There are so few of them and so many others.

Better contact with the public schools was emphasized many times. Why not coordinate the junior high school and the high school and the community college in tackling the problem of learning to read? The teacher went on:

There is need to make a commitment to the student while he is still in the eighth grade through contacts by professionals and counselor aides. The eighth grade is crucial because if he can't pass the tests and if he can't take algebra then, he is cracked out. He needs to be told the things he is going to need, not four years later, but at that time.

Ethnic Specialists Suggested

It was suggested that "ethnic specialists," perhaps paraprofessionals, be prepared to work with elementary school and junior high school children, so that problems of attitude that would affect later learning experiences could be recognized and dealt with much earlier in the individual's schoolwork.

There is another set of relationships which is important. As has been reported in this chapter, many more minority students are entering community colleges, and there is reason to believe that they will be staying longer. Changes are occurring in institutional programs, structures, and student attitudes which are causing more students to complete programs in the community colleges. Larger numbers then will be looking for access to four-year colleges and universities. And at the present there are signals in the environment, many of these financial, that suggest a lack of space or a suitable program for the minority student who wants to move on. This problem is just now beginning to make its presence known and will require prompt and serious examination on the part of educational planners, the state legislatures, and the taxpayers.

In other words, my impressions cause me to be optimistic about the community college's capacity to attract and serve minority group students. If this is the case, if in effect the community college broadens the base in higher education, it helps put in motion a wave of events which will move toward other colleges and universities with surging force. There needs to be a place for those students who want to continue. Otherwise, the buildup of aspirations is lost, perhaps never should have been encouraged in the first place.

There is another cause for concern. In a large Midwestern city I heard a president describe a "growing backlash from lower- and middle-income groups toward 'disadvantaged' blacks." He attributed the first millage defeat of the college to that factor. In effect, he said, the sentiment appeared to be, "We are no longer going to give you money to educate people who are uneducable." And one of the outstanding programs for the academically disadvantaged in the entire nation was terminated because no more money was available. I had never seen that president so disturbed. What the community college can do is directly related to understanding and support from the many communities it serves.

It is true that other segments of the population, that is, other than black and Spanish-speaking and Indian, have educational needs to which the college must be sensitive and responsive. The events of the past decade have focused American attention on the racial minorities, especially their lives in the big cities, and have forced an awareness which required constructive action. However, the many changes coming about show benefits much broader than only those accrued by minorities. For example, it is essential that community colleges acknowledge and relate to community groups and interests. Uncomfortable though it was in many places, that process was greatly stepped up during the past five years. It was time to question teaching styles, faculty qualifications, and administrative ways. Many good questions had been long deferred that dealt with grading and evaluation, tests and their validity, curriculum content and organization, and learning styles. A much closer look at individual differences and how college structures and program ought to relate to these was in order. Has there been any other five-year period in the history of education which has been so full of questions and searching and criticism?

A good share of the unrest, the dissent, and the constructive change which is coming about can be attributed to response by educational institutions to segments of the population who insisted upon being heard. I have reported that a major theme of the people I listened to was agreement upon the mission of the community college to provide educational opportunity to those who had not had it before. Large numbers of people of racial minorities fall into that category. Manifestly, there are others, too, to be served. The college's response to the needs of the minorities, as I see it, strengthens the institution in serving all its constituents.

SUMMARY

High on the priority lists of community colleges must be improved services for the increasing number of minority group students. Students from the ethnic minorities represent an increasing percentage of the community college student body. They come with unique needs and, in many cases, built-in frustrations with the educational system. Unless the college is prepared to offer services to meet their needs, their frustrations will be multiplied rather than reduced.

For community colleges to serve such students well there must be ethnic minority representation on the faculty, in the administration, and on the board. Faculty members must be sensitive to the special needs of minority students and committed to the philosophy that all are to be served and that all are capable of learning. Financial aid and other supportive services must be structured to meet actual needs. A complete service, from preenrollment counseling to job placement, must be offered as a complement to classroom and other learning experiences.

The system—whether it be the registration system, the learning system, or whatever—must be organized to help persons who may not be accustomed to dealing with academic systems.

All this can be done if persons within the colleges and within the communities that support them realize that the extension of such services is not only a legitimate activity for community colleges but central to their reason for existence. Such services are the means for giving life to the philosophy of extending higher education opportunity to all.

Part 2. Changes in How They Are Served

If you're more interested in what you're teaching than in what they are learning, don't come to this community college. A Requirement for New Faculty

Chapter 3.
The Structures
Don't Fit

What the community college promises to do can contribute toward a social revolution in this country. It would be a revolution characterized not by disruption and disorganization, but by greater individual freedom, competence in vocations of worth, and responsible citizenship. But a promise will not do. There are evidences of growth; a significant increase in student numbers is projected. But what is actually happening to these students? That is the question of consequence. Are their needs being met? What kind of an institutional environment is there for the student who "comes as he is"?

QUESTIONS ABOUT ORGANIZATION

Personnel in the community college field are uneasy about institutional structures. They express strong feelings that the conventional academic patterns and processes are not appropriate to the stated missions, that "the structures don't fit." "Our structures have let us down, and yet the present structures are determining our goals," says a community college leader. "We are living in times of almost uncontrollable change, and we don't know how to deal with it," adds another. Many students, as reported before, seek self-actualization and a supportive environment. They need flexible arrangements to accommodate diversity as well as an integrative influence to establish relationships with many personalities and goals. But, in the face of this, symptoms of impersonalism, rigidity, and absence of cohesive influences are appearing. Moreover, flexibility appears to be greatly restricted; in fact, the colleges are unreasonably dominated by the universities to which some students may transfer.

Apparently the community college has been evolving a new consciousness of educational mission, but change in organizational frameworks and administrative concepts lags noticeably. It is an eclectic institution which counts both secondary schools and colleges among its antecedents. During the past fifteen years it has taken on new tasks. Some of these have been "thrust" on it by state-level agencies, as will be discussed in some detail later. From its progenitors and from its many tasks have come forms and structures which seem to resist assimilation to this new setting, leading to a situation which is most ironic: the community college now needs urgently to establish within itself a condition of community. More attention has probably been given to examination of college functions and purposes in order to plan buildings than to constructing suitable forms of organization and administration. Insistent, probing, and sometimes aggravating questions from architects seeking to design buildings which facilitate their particular functions have forced educational planners to think about what the college is to do. "Functions precede structures" is a well-worn cliché, but it has not so often been applied to matters of educational organization.

And so in arrangements of students and professional personnel for learning experiences in the community college, the old structures tend to persist. If we assume that educational opportunities are needed that contribute to such goals as self-direction, self-help, personal development, occupational training, and development, are commonly found organizational forms and structures suitable? The response must be that in general they are not. Rather they represent a past which was different in its expectations and demands.

Lack of Cohesive Influences in the College

Mrs. Smith, a highly rated teacher of political science at a leading community college, had some interesting thoughts on this vital matter arising from her own education and experience.

She came into teaching when she was older than most. She described herself as very idealistic. Her graduate program was taken at a state college, and she thought that a community college would be the place for her. She wonders now if her assumption that administrators and faculty would be working together for the student was naive. She had hoped that a new school would provide a creative challenge.

"I found it was another political group," she said. "You have to develop your own power group in order to get things done. I tried things, but finally this year I have given up."

Take the public-speaking area at Mrs. Smith's college. In order for students to use it, they have to fill out innumerable forms. She once led a war moratorium group when a faculty advisor was needed, apparently because nobody else was willing to do it. She was called into the president's office repeatedly because he feared violence during the speeches and wanted assurance there would be none. The dean of students conferred with her because he had heard that the flags were going to be torn down. The president insisted that there also be a pro-war group and a pro-war speaker so that both sides of the argument could be heard.

Mrs. Smith declared that the students she was advising were against war and that those in favor of war should organize their own group. But the president won out. Both sides were heard from.

Mrs. Smith says that now the "free-speech" area isn't free and nobody uses it.

Rigidity in the Classroom

Mrs. Smith reported on still another experience, this one being connected with Jerry Farber's article, "The Student as Nigger." She had intended to use this controversial piece, as well as one by Sidney Hook representing a different point of view, as a basis for discussion in her political science class. The dean's office, notified of the plan, indicated that Farber's article could create dissension in the community. And so the issue committee was called into session.

This committee of administrators and faculty considers possibly controversial matters and how the college should deal with them. The use of the articles was approved by the committee, but its action was vetoed by the dean. The president had already decided, Mrs. Smith had heard, that regardless of the committee's action, he would not permit the article to be used. The issue went all the way to the chancellor, probably creating far more dissension than the article really merited.

This incident simply points to a need for change in attitudes and policies regarding teaching, learning, and thinking today. Such change must seem long overdue if the community college is to truly embrace the notion of community, a dimension of which it seems so proud. Mrs. Smith observed:

> The basic change required is that of placing more confidence in the abilities of faculty and students to make responsible judgments and to act wisely. The college has a responsibility to the community, but the question is, do you look toward more openness and the stimulation of new thoughts and ideas on the campus and in the community, or do you respond to present mores of the community? There is the concern about property taxes. But the community should not be telling us what to teach. There is concern about rocking the boat. However this might be a function of age. This is a new institution. People want to do things right. Perhaps in time they might become more relaxed.

I asked Mrs. Smith for her reaction to the systems approach to learning, that is, technological aids such as the TV and computers. She reported some students complaints, particularly about the computer. "The students feel that they really have nobody to talk to." "Another thing is that they still don't have people who know how to run the things."

Mrs. Smith teaches a large class of 115 and then holds seminar sessions with 25 to 35 students in each. This method doesn't work in her estimation. When the institution first opened, her classes were small. She could take the students into the community to visit the jails and government offices to give them firsthand knowledge of social and political situations.

She has helped get jobs and VA checks. She counsels and advises them. They came to her because she knew them from class, and they hoped she could help with some of their other problems. That personal interaction has changed as classes have gotten bigger, the system more complex. She doesn't get to know the students, and they can't know her from use of TV tapes or the computer.

Teacher/Student Rapport Is Difficult

Ahead of her she sees large classes and students being processed with little personal relationship. "In the use of the computer you tend to just get at the facts. I realize that what I put on the computer is of minimal value." Her lectures are put on videotape for students who miss the forum. "Some teachers are described by their students as fine and having a sense of humor, but these same teachers seem to lose their humanness on tape, and their humor is taken out," Mrs. Smith complains.

"Let me speak honestly. The Social Science Department here

started out fresh and with new ideas. These have gradually been squashed. Now I feel that I will come to teach my classes and then go home." When I asked why she felt that her efforts had been squashed, Mrs. Smith cited a number of things which could all be wrapped up in such terms as red tape, bureaucratic regulations, indifference. Initiative must be approved by committees. All kinds of forms must be filled out. Spontaneity is ruled out by the need to plan far in advance for any creative learning experience.

Mrs. Smith related another example:

> When a student is placed on probation, he has the right of appeal to the College Affairs Council. However, the council, after having made a decision with regard to a student who was placed on probation for using an obscene word in the free-speech area, was overridden by the administration. There are faculty and students on that council. Students feel the administration is not for us. They ask, What's the use?

Some radicalism is needed, in Mrs. Smith's view, to change things, that is, the system which the students feel doesn't work. She doesn't feel that the faculty is organized to exert their influence, but the possibility of a union may change matters.

I asked whether the program called "Explorations in Communications" was helping some with regard to communication on campus. Students report to her, she said, that people are often one way in those sessions and their old selves again after it's over.

What would you do, I asked her, if you had administrative responsibility? She took some time to reply:

> I would really get down there and find out what they are looking for, I mean those Mexican-American students and others. I would help them organize politically.
>
> So few students really go on and there are many students that are just wasting their time. If the college were to help them really work in society and find ways of dealing with the critical issues of these days, students would get excited. They would have something to work for.
>
> The faculty meetings are really boring. We rarely talk about important issues. We don't even know each other anymore. However, when I talk with George Jones, our dean of academic affairs, it's great, but we just don't seem to find the time.

She reported that a new forum has been planned and will be operational soon and that faculty are being asked what they would like in it. But she would like things to develop much more spontaneously and quickly, rather than see people waiting to be asked.

For example, there was some interest in Russian conversation, and there are people on the faculty who can teach that kind of course. There are other things that we would like to do to respond to community interests. Why can't we just start out and do these things? You have to go through so many administrative levels and such masses of red tape in order to get anything started.

Mrs. Smith, in short, is overwhelmed by "the system."

If there are substantial numbers of other faculty in the community college field who share Mrs. Smith's outlook, there is cause for alarm because of the characteristics of the young people and adults seeking to be served by this kind of educational institution. Large numbers have not been initiated previously into the mysteries of post-secondary education. They are in process of formulating views about themselves and their potentials. There are decisions to be made concerning vocational, educational, and personal objectives. Some want to find the quickest way to "get some bread on the table." Others are uncertain in a society where the options are clouded. To those people who want to be recognized as individuals, who they are and the quality of their relationships are vitally important and will have a great deal to do with a sense of inclusion or alienation. Repeated reliance by administrators on regulations and citations from the law leaves these students cold.

In the Shadow of the University

Students and faculty play their roles within the community college system. The college, in turn, is part of a state system of post-secondary education. At the state level there is evidence of inappropriate organizational relations between the community colleges and universities. Despite all its growth, the community college still stands in the shadow of the university. The weight of the university on community college programs and processes is far out of proportion to the one community college student out of three who enters the university. Remarkably, this influence has persisted beyond the time that there was any justification for it. Fifty years ago there were universities that performed an approval or accrediting function for junior colleges. Twenty-five years ago a substantial number of community colleges were not regionally accredited. Fifteen years ago only one out of five students began his college work in community colleges. Now conditions are markedly different. Almost one college freshman in two is in a community college, in California four out of five. Now most community colleges are accredited by the regional agencies that accredit four-year colleges and universities. More importantly, research data are readily available on great numbers of community college students who have begun upper-division work in other institutions.

Enough is known about community college students who transfer to suggest that university paternalism, no matter how benevolent, is no longer in order. The community college mission to its variegated enrollments has no greater obstacle than its own long dominance by four-year institutions. Whether this control is actually expressed or simply exists tacitly makes little difference; its effect still restricts inventiveness and initiative shown by the community colleges.

For example, a dean describes a growing willingness in his institution to recognize accomplishment without consideration of the time involved in the program. "But," said the president of that college, "the university hovers over us like a cloud of radioactive dust, inhibiting to some extent what we can try. They still want us to have F grades which follow the student along for the rest of his academic experience. Everything needs to be put on the transcript." It was his impression that in some ways his institution had progressed farther than the university in the search for more effective learning processes, but it was boxed in by university entrance requirements. As he saw it, the problem was not with the president or deans, but with the department chairmen.

Blocked by Transfer

And in yet another case, a dean observed, "We are blocked by the transfer function. We would like to have our own program, but we can't quite make it. Upper-division people so often have in mind that people taking science are going to be looking toward the science field as a career." He wants freedom to build programs upon current interests and in present surroundings, to give people the opportunity to learn *how* to study science. He feels forcibly limited to the "know what" rather than the "know why and how."

A swelling concern about the multiple commitments of their institutions is aggravating in many teachers a long-repressed frustration with university requirements and the consequent need for "course matching."

"We are steeped in the transfer tradition along with other junior colleges. Anything innovative can be shot down by irritated or capricious registrars at the university."

The result of the community college's need to comply with university entrance requirements has been a wrongly placed focus of interest. Eyes of faculty and counselors have been on the university's set of requirements, its course patterns, and order of sequence rather than on their own students and appropriate responses to their needs. To be sure, the desire that the transfer students not lose credit is among the impelling motivations for this obsequiousness. But one must ask honestly whether this objective deserves first place in an educator's catalogue of concerns.

Community colleges not closely tied to university requirements and patterns can serve their students better and with more flexibility. And yet, at this time, as discussions are under way within universities to change programs and achieve greater flexibility, community colleges seem to be waiting to see what the university will do.

What will be the effect of a three-year bachelor's degree program? General education patterns are bound to change. What are the implications for our programs? How will the external-degree and open-university concept affect us? These questions reveal a feeling among community college planners that they cannot initiate change; rather they must wait and respond to change initiated by other institutions.

PEOPLE IN THE SYSTEMS

There are conflicting pressures within the colleges, and differences appear almost irreconcilable. Administration has one view about how to get the educational job done, faculty another. Students fault much of the system. Some want to change it completely. The community wants to be involved in the action. Once again, the community college comes down to people.

"Unless there is a tremendous increase in income," states a president, "we must find a method or system that permits the institution to considerably increase the number of students who will work with the teacher without harmful effects."

But it is apprehension about that system that concerns many students: "You get the feeling that you are a computer being programmed by a computer. Learning is stimulated by love, by one personality touching another. There is no substitute for the teacher who will look you in the eyes or grab you by the shoulder and say, 'Hey, look, here's what I am talking about.' "

The system, the organization, is seen as antithetical to spontaneity and freedom. Some of these feelings are expressed in reaction to physical facilities, buildings, and their relationships. The symmetrical placement of trees on the campus, the master plan, the techniques and format of the classes—all these appear to stem from the concept of a pattern human beings must fit. There is opposition to the architect who continues to influence the school by prescribing wall colors and insisting that changes correspond with his notion of what is suitable.

I wonder how much time he has actually spent in reflecting upon his effect on people's lives. For example, our classrooms really don't have windows. They have little slits through which some light comes, but you can't look through them. But the administration building is nothing but glass. And the buildings are built like a Tinkertoy arrangement so that they can be added to easily. This gives you a sense of being temporary and transient.

Presidents, Too, Fear Restraints

These feelings about restraints on spontaneity and individual expression which are voiced by students and teachers are echoed by community college presidents. Sit for a few hours in a session of chief administrators when they share their own concern with each other, and the same impressions will come through. Innumerable regulations and rulings seem to hedge them in. One state, California, has been described as a "code" state, meaning that only those things specified in the educational code may be done. Community college regulations are a part of the voluminous educational code for elementary and secondary schools.

An observer gets the impression that the state legislature sits as a school board for the state. A multitude of educational matters ranging from the major to the minuscule are prescribed through legislation. Bills become acts and part of the school code. Under these circumstances it is not clear how much initiative and creativity can be exercised by community college leadership in relating to new societal requirements.

Others are also concerned about the "systems." Community college board members say that their institutions are affected by what Congress does as well as by the state of the economy, availability of the tax dollar, and actions of the state legislature. They have a sense of being acted upon, of being shaped by forces without opportunity to influence those forces. In many respects they say much the same thing as the faculty members. The board members declare that it may be necessary to "exercise their clout" in order to get the money they need, even if it means taking away some from the state colleges.

Within the college, faculty personnel are concerned about the forums and the red tape, about being overruled by administrators. They perceive decisions as being made without their participation. Spontaneity, creativity, and self-determination, they believe, are stifled. And the view develops that to work at the problem is to organize power blocs. And so it is reported that the American Federation of Teachers is growing out of a sense of need to organize. People both on campus and on the board have the notion that the larger system is dealt with through the organization of more systems and interest groups.

Quandary of Self-actualization

This leads to the quandary of self-actualization. Comments are heard about large classes, the necessity of work orders in order to get a picture hung in a teacher's office, color surveillance by architects, orders to students not to paste posters on the columns, alleged role-playing by the president and other administrators. There are the procedures, the committees, the systems approach, the computer on the one hand; on the other, the strong desire of faculty and students to be involved in decisions affecting them. Are these symptoms of rigidity and impersonalization a function to some extent of rapid growth and size? Lack of time seems to be a factor.

"He is a great guy, but we don't have opportunity to talk anymore." You get the feeling that people are asking, Is anybody listening? "You can't fight the system," they are saying. And there is the possibility of the "cop-out," with faculty saying, "I'm not going to try that anymore. I will teach the forum and let it go at that." Or the student declares, "I am here to prepare for a job; let somebody else worry about the college."

Increasingly, cries are heard for a leadership with the capacity to listen, to understand, and to respond.

The Demarcation at USOE

An additional example of questionable organization is provided in the demarcation between academic and vocational education which persists from the U.S. Office of Education through the state administrative levels into almost every institution. On the campus students observe, "There is very little comingling of students on this campus. The autoshop kids are down there in the corner working eight hours a day. The law enforcement people are away over there."

In several state capitols, the separation of the vocational and academic streams is yet to be bridged. A commissioner of education reports that a major problem is how to relate the technical institutes and area vocational schools to community colleges. "There still seems to be the same kind of orientation and drive as in those days when vocational agriculture was the big thing." I observed that since all these institutions are under his board, cooperation would be facilitated. "Are you kidding?" was his reply. "These people have a very strong political organization, and moves toward the comprehensive institution seem almost anathema to them." Landmark action in his state was about to bring together the vocational-technical institutes and the community colleges. This was to be done with the support of the governor.

A FRESH APPROACH TO ORGANIZATION IS NEEDED

It needs to be pointed out that in several states housing vocational-technical and academic programs in the same institution, the community college, is still relatively new, at least in its implementation. And the search is on for effective arrangements. Also the vested interests on both sides now give some evidence of joining forces. But the point is that if we must look to the student and the learning process as referents, then a fresh approach is needed in organization of resources and personnel. Unfortunately approaches that blend, mix, and stimulate interaction of the college people have seldom existed. Rather, the ways of lower-division colleges and those of the vocational and technical schools seem to have been transferred to this new institution; they are now under one roof. There is little evidence of a curriculum design that gets at common interests and concerns, cuts across subject matter, and seeks to utilize diversity for enrichment, motivation, and excitement.

CONCERN FOR STUDENTS IS THE FOCUS

Solutions to the organizational problems described by community college staff and students have their beginning in focusing on the students to be served. They must be the continuing reference point. Three young staff members of a college-readiness center declared:

Concern for students is what the community college needs to be all about. Many of these students have been crippled in schools. They need someone to lean on. You have to take a person where he is . . . . For many students, this college is all they have. The only way they can get jobs is to have the kind of preparation they can get here. Many of these students, minority group students, are at the fourth-grade reading level, and in effect the open door becomes a revolving door because they are able to last only two semesters and then they are out. But what is happening is that they are fighting eighteen years of neglect.

Counseling in the Tutoring Program

These staff members often find themselves counseling in the tutoring program. They feel it is much more than just teaching people to read, that they deal with all kinds of problems that the student has, with the teaching of reading only a part of this broader context.

"Some of the students come into this reading laboratory as to a womb where they are looking for security," the staff members said. "They are comfortable. They feel at home here. They don't seek out the counselors in the college. They talk to us about their problems of drug abuse and mental health."

They repeated that students come for all kinds of help—information about money and insurance and advice about day-care services for their children.

Young married students who have children are actually taking them to class, or they take turns watching the youngsters. The institution itself does not make provision for this particular situation, according to these informants, other than going through some questionable motions.

An attempt was made by students and staff members to set up a day-care center. They tried a church which had a large nursery. But community response was negative: "We have private day-care centers, and this new effort would compete with them. There would be duplication of services." The question of morality was raised. Some of these children had been born out of wedlock.

College Leadership Is Vital

As these young men see it, leadership in the community college is important. They have the impression that the leadership tends to perpetuate the status quo. Although the college is responsible for community education, it seems to be merely reacting to what the community wants rather than seeking out what should be done.

There ought to be an atmosphere in the college that encourages people to try, but instead there seems to be an atmosphere of fear that you might do something to make somebody unhappy, like the dean of instruction. We bring ideas and they say, "That's not the way to do it" or "We don't have the money." The channels of communication are not open. Information is not there for us; we have to dig for it. Instead of bringing us into the fold, in effect you feel that you are a bastard child.

COLLEGE RESPONDS WITH COMMUNICATIONS PROGRAM

Response has been initiated at one college through a program called "Explorations in Communications" which is open to students, faculty, and administrators. Board members have also participated. Several hundred people are now involved on a voluntary basis. This invitation to share describes the needs which gave rise to the program:

In the new college community the individual will not feel alienated nor anonymous but will "belong." Organizational "distance" between faculty, administration, and student will be overcome. Communication will be effected through human-to-human, not role-to-role, interaction. All will be involved in the decision-making process. Education will concern itself with the "now," relevant issues. Meaningful human interaction will counterbalance the depersonalization of bigness and automated education. You can join a successful struggle for personal and group identity. Faculty and administrators will become people and not positions. How? Small communication groups of faculty, administration, students. Limited to fifteen. Group determines its own agenda. Six weekly meetings of two hours at various times during the day. Co-led by a student and a faculty member. No roles; just people who have the freedom to risk interpersonal interaction will focus on issues relevant to the group's own members.

The fact that more than 600 people would take part in the program signals interest, especially since no academic credit is given and leaders contribute their time. Still, it is meeting the needs of relatively few faculty and students. And the trained facilitators essential to work with each group apparently will continue to be difficult to recruit because under present circumstances these are additional responsibilities built onto a regular faculty load.

Two students said they felt it was great, but wasn't it the kind of thing that ought to take place in regular, small classes?

Clearly new ways must be sought to conserve the values of the person in an institutional structure that tends to be more complex and ponderous as its tasks multiply.

LEARNING CENTERS

A new community college which describes itself as learning-centered appears to be moving in these directions. It does not have the conventional academic departments or divisions. Instead programs and personnel are grouped into four institutes, each with three or four learning centers that are described as kinds of minicolleges with projected enrollments of 1,500 each. The learning centers are places more than subject areas. There is an attempt to decentralize counseling into the learning centers as well as to provide learning resources and other activities there that give a specific identity to each center.

Institute of Applied Humanities
    Humanities Program
    Communications Media Program
Institute of Business and Management
    Accounting Program
    Business Program
    Business Administration Program
    Marketing Program
    Secretarial Science Program
Institute of Human Affairs
    Community Mental Health Assistant Program
    Education Program
    Education Aide Program
    Law Enforcement Program
    Social Science Program
Institute of Natural and Applied Sciences
    Automotive Technology Program
    Computer Science Program
    Drafting and Design Technology Program
    Electronics Technology Program
    Engineering Program
    Inhalation Therapy Program
    Medical Laboratory Technician Program
    Nursing Education Program
    Science/Mathematics Program

This warning is found on the cover of the brochure prepared to interest new faculty personnel: "If you're more interested in what you're teaching than in what they are learning, don't come to Brookdale Community College."

The college has found many teachers eager to work in an institution with that philosophy.

STOP DEAD-END PLANNING

What are other ways that the college can organize to reflect the worth of its various activities and relate them to each other in order to achieve the educational goals of the greatest number of enrollees?

Students have some views about this. They call for a stop to "dead-end curriculum planning." They ask that occupational programs be integrated with enough of the academic that the student could move to the university if things change for him. They see the duplication in present vocational education as a dead-end track which "very often turns out to be a tunnel in which you have to go back up to get out and to change your course." They object to finding in the community college the two- or three-track programs that they experienced in high school.

Younger students choosing their goals want assistance which would include orientation to college, self-awareness, social awareness, and communication skills, a program involving counselors. One of the problems, they say, is that when you come to the college, you get a list of courses that looks like a computer chart. You are confused. You are told, "Fill this out." You are asked which program you want to elect, and you're not sure. But an attempt is made to push you into a curriculum, and you don't know anything about it.

Students question the traditional sequence of courses. Why must American history be taken before a course in government? And as far as that is concerned, why does the state require students to follow the programs? Why is it necessary to take Introduction to Psychology before Principles of Psychology? Why is physical education required? Through their state organization students in the California community colleges were successful in getting introduced into the state legislature a bill which would abolish that requirement. The proposition came within one vote of carrying.

THEY BRING RESTRICTIONS ON THEMSELVES

Without doubt, community college personnel have literally asked for some of the restrictions they experience. In effect they have asked the universities what they should teach. In discussions of curricular change, questions arise about what the universities are doing or what textbooks they are using. One university president asserts that this is a mistake. He thinks that it is more a matter of what community college people think and particularly what seems best for the student. He maintains that people in the university ought to work with community college personnel as colleagues in attacking problems of common interest.

Need for a Common Language

Many faculty personnel are aware of the need to change this situation. They feel they should face up to the conflict between what they believe and what four-year institutions think community colleges ought to do. I asked some of these young teachers why they were concerned about the attitude of the four-year institutions. In answering, they revealed a justifiable perplexity about how to translate an educational philosophy into academic bookkeeping. Their college has a philosophy of "nonfailure." An appropriate means for evaluation has been developed. Now they are concerned that college programs, not just students, be understood and accepted. However, they are under the impression that the community college is viewed as a babysitting institution when the university looks at the evaluation and grading programs.

Suppose a college holds that almost anybody can learn if given time. Then how can the student's acquired knowledge be recorded so that it can be validly understood and interpreted by institutions to which the individual might transfer? Many community colleges have changed grading systems to eliminate letter grades. They have established a system of evaluation based upon performance levels, only to find that the university requires them to retranslate these evaluative terms into ABCD. But the ABCD performance represents an analysis of how the student compares to somebody else rather than to the course's desired performance level. The college is required to speak in the university's language rather than its own. Clearly there is a dilemma in trying to dovetail two different kinds of institutions, each with its own appropriate forms.

While these comments have centered on the preoccupation of university and community college faculties and administrations with the transfer function, there is another factor affecting the initiative of community colleges as well. It is the marketplace. Ultimately the consumer determines the value of a product by his interest in and use of it. In this case, the consumer is the student. More often than not, his first question about a course is, Will it transfer? This is not surprising, though, because in high school (through parental advice) or even in the community college itself, the prospect of transfer has been stressed while other values were overlooked or neglected.

MANDATES AND COMPACTS

Opportunities may be greater in the future for community colleges to develop learning experiences appropriate to their students without paralleling universities. The state board of higher education in Illinois views the community colleges as part of an integrated system of higher education. Consequently it has said, in effect, to the universities: Thou shalt accept credits from associate-degree transfer students. In Ohio, the Master Plan for Public Policy in Higher Education (published by the Board of Regents, March, 1971) makes the following recommendation:

> An Ohio resident who graduates with an associate degree from a publicly sponsored two-year institution of higher education shall be admitted without further qualification to a baccalaureate program of a publicly sponsored university, but only such course credit hours may be transferred to a particular baccalaureate program as are applicable to the requirements of that program.

A Need for Cooperation

Other states have made it clear: important as the public now considers college work and expensive as it has become for state and local jurisdictions, unnecessary duplication of effort by the student will not be condoned. An implicit mandate exists for the higher education community to work out its own voluntary relationships lest state agencies or the legislatures intervene.

A compact arrangement between community colleges and the state universities was pioneered by the state of Florida in 1959. In effect, the articulation agreement provided that after a public institution of higher learning in Florida had developed and published its program of general education, the integrity of the program would be recognized by the other public institutions in the state. Once a student had been certified as having satisfactorily completed a prescribed general education program, no other public institution of higher learning in Florida could require any further lower-division general education courses.

A new articulation agreement formulated in 1971 restated the provisions of the earlier compact and further specified that students receiving the associate of arts degree would be admitted to junior standing within the university system. These measures acknowledged a changing mix in the upper divisions of the universities. The authors recognized that in the near future more than half of the students will have a community college origin. This, it seems to me, represents realistic, sensible planning.

SUMMARY

Time and circumstances have put the community college in a position enabling it to act as a leader in a new view of education that looks first to the needs of students (rather than to tradition) in determining forms for buildings, curricula, administration, teaching, and learning.

Community college people seem to recognize an opportunity to make some significant breakthroughs in serving learners: the institutions are new and developing. Many options are still open. But traditions die hard, even in the 1970s.

In general, evidence shows that frequently "what they are learning" is not the basic value forming concepts and structures of organization within the community college. The influence of educational antecedents persists despite the fact that this generation has different educational needs. The rapid growth of these institutions leads us to ask, Are formal relationships and representation by interest groups an inevitable concomitant of large size? Further, the tasks perceived in the future are more complex than the ones at hand. What must the community college do to pull itself together, to establish its own integrity, and to harmonize its diversity?

That the organization of the community college be purposely structured to achieve these ends is essential. The fears of anonymity and helplessness in the grip of the system and other anxieties reported by students, faculty, administrators, and board members are not indigenous to the community college. However, students coming to community colleges now, and increasing numbers in the future, are particularly vulnerable to those fears; they are sensitive to these anxieties because they grew up around them. They come to the college seeking something else. If they are able to achieve a sense of personal worth, if the institution can be flexible enough to accept and encourage them, and if it can establish a sense of community among those it serves, then the community college will be an agent of change in the democratic direction, that is, toward providing better education for more people.

What is needed for such change is strong leadership and the kind of forward momentum that will enable community colleges to break out of traditional systems and away from attitudes now tending to discourage creativity and drown fresh concepts. The need for these qualities is so great that institutions must do everything possible to ensure that individuals with ideas and ability receive encouragement and support in trying new ways of implementing learning. Community colleges must provide new organizational forms that put a premium on responsiveness and flexibility. Most important, the college's clientele must provide a motive power for change by supporting the concept of a college structured to serve people, not to fit some previous mold.

Chapter 4.
Managers
for Learning

Growth and change in community colleges have no participants more interested and concerned than the faculty and the presidents. In general, they welcome growth as evidence of the college's recognition and acceptance. However, the probable directions of change prompt mixed reactions. Community college faculty have little to do, as they see it, with the educational philosophy of their institutions. It seems that the signals are called elsewhere—sometimes in a legislative mandate, perhaps in a state master plan for education, or by some administrative directive; the result is that faculty implement the institutional task as defined by somebody else. Their sense of minimal involvement in forming institutional goals ripens into perplexity and frustration when the student population appears not to fit traditional collegiate patterns and presents new social and educational needs beyond the scope of their training.

WHO OUGHT TO BE SERVED

A low-key puzzlement was experienced by a faculty group in a relatively new institution. I asked who ought to be served by the college. The response was "those who are willing to learn but who have not had the opportunity so far." A teacher of Spanish and sociology who had been at the college only one year asked whether it was to be a sophisticated place. There is nothing academic about learning to type, he said, or preparing people for menial tasks of that kind. Perhaps the world needs them, he suggested, and maybe we ought to do it, but let's not call it academic. He said that the same thing was true about learning to draw. When you talk about the academic, you are talking about the development of the self.

Is Typing as Important as Physics?

Somebody disagreed forcefully with the assertion that typing was as important as physics: "We are a community college, and we are here to serve the community, whether it is physics or typing, and if a teacher can't adjust himself to that kind of philosophy, then he ought to look for another job." Another person confessed that he had to grow into that kind of attitude, that in the beginning he did not have that broad view of the work of the institution. Another man in his first year at the college declared. "We really don't know where we are going."

The group agreed that the college needed both transfer and terminal programs, and discussion ensued as to whether these ought to be two separate streams. It was proposed that some mechanism was needed which would permit the terminal student to transfer. I pushed the questioning at this point by asking about the possibility of setting up two separate institutions. They responded by building a case for a single comprehensive institution on the grounds of economy rather than educational values; that is, the same laboratories could be used in both programs.

Let's face it, someone said, the community college really is a continuation of the comprehensive high school. I asked how they felt about living with that concept. They thought they could, although one person said we could do it but probably we would fall back into the old two-stream concept now and again.

Repeatedly I was impressed by the intensity of the discussion my questions triggered among the faculty members. They tended to talk with each other rather than to me. Who are our students? Who should be served by the college? What is academic? What is college-level? Where are we going? How do we teach at the levels for which we have been trained? Shall we concentrate on the better students or on the poorer students? Many teachers wanted to ventilate issues and problems that these questions bring up. They had been concerned for a long time and welcomed the opportunity provided by my visit and my questions to talk with their colleagues. Whether it was due to a lack of time or a lack of occasion, there was little indication that those with teaching responsibilities were spending much time in a common, general examination of basic educational issues affecting both the institution and their work. But the concerns are there and they pour out.

Students Cope Inadequately with the Academic World

A bright young president of a faculty senate in a large, well-established community college recalled his student days in that institution. He was excited by the faculty, and he had decided to return to the college to teach. Throughout his college and university work he was an honor student. He came back to teach economics to what he thought would be students of "real professional quality." Now he is deeply troubled. Increasingly, he feels that students are coping inadequately with the academic world represented in his institution. They bring with them the problems of broken homes. There has been a tremendous increase in other kinds of student emotional problems. They are inadequately prepared academically. This factor, plus the rapid growth of the institution which resulted in employing faculty with inadequate preparation, has brought the college to a crisis situation. In his opinion, "Lots of people don't belong here. They don't have the aptitude or interest." He sees them as afflicted with drug problems, poverty, illiterate parents, exposed to all kinds of despair.

In the past these people were not passed along through the high school, but now they are, and they wind up in the community college. The mean scores on the A.C.T. are falling. We have remedial programs and basic studies programs. But to some extent these are frauds. The whole place needs restructuring. We need to face squarely what is our philosophy. It is not well defined. We have ambiguous goals.

Young faculty are coming here who are devoted to high standards, but they are confused in direction. Pressures are being put on probationary teachers with regard to grades, to lower the standards, to dilute their work, and some of these pressures are put on by the legislature.

He feels the failure rate is much too high, that kids who can't read are sitting in the classroom. "It has even been suggested that if they can't read they be given oral examinations," he said. "It is a mistake for the community college to try to make up for all of the ills that these people have suffered throughout their lives."

There was diversity in earlier years, when he was a student. But then the objectives were different, the pressures of a different nature.

The principal aim was to prepare students for transfer, with faculty making the assessments, often ruthlessly, as to the fate of the students. Furthermore, the financial support came primarily from the local level. But now, with the state providing 70 percent of the financial support, there is pressure to accommodate even greater numbers of students and abilities.

It was his view that the institution should either face the issues candidly or abdicate responsibility for comprehensiveness. Administrators and faculty need to sit down together, set goals, determine how to achieve them, and recognize that such goals may not be attainable within the present structure.

Teachers Uncertain about the Direction They Are to Take

Another experienced teacher completed a similar interview by saying, "That's the plight of the academic man, and I am trying to hold the line because that is the tradition that I have come up under." I asked him what would happen if he could develop a course that would respond to the various student needs and interests rather than concentrate on the matter of university transfer. His eyes brightened at this thought. That is exactly what he would like to do, he said. But, "Nobody has ever told me that I am to change and to do what you suggest."

To say that there is a high degree of frustration evident among faculty members in community colleges would not be an overstatement. Some of it stems from uncertainties or differences of opinion about the educational mission of the college in terms of the people it is to serve. A community college president was quoted by a big city newspaper saying that his institution was not a Harvard, nor was it trying to be one. Reportedly the comment provoked a great deal of wrath in the community and particularly among members of the faculty because he seemed to be downgrading the institution.

"But," said the director of the financial aid program at that college, "I thought it was a good, honest, and reasonable statement. However, the faculty like to consider themselves intellectuals, although they are not hired for research and publication. Many do not understand the purpose of the college, and their first goal is what they consider scholarship." Regardless of whether her assessment is accurate, it does reflect a commonly found difference in attitude between presidents and teachers.

Frustration is also evident among those who accept the great diversity of students as appropriate to the role of the college. Here the problem seems to be, How do we do it? How can this broad variety of humanity with such diversified needs be effectively served? In calling for a collective approach toward problems of this kind there is another factor with which to reckon. Community colleges are characteristically commuting institutions. Not only does this affect student relationships and student life within the institution, but it bears on how faculty relate to each other. In one large city, for example, the community college population comes and goes almost constantly from 8 in the morning until 10 at night. It is a highly diversified community of comparative strangers, representing the entire metropolitan area.

The faculty are a widely dispersed group of people coming together for a few intensive hours, then departing for homes or jobs elsewhere. Nearly one-half of them have worked together one year or less. In addition, there are 266 part-time faculty members who work or attend school elsewhere most of the time. A survey of full-time faculty home addresses showed that they were living in thirty-one different postal zones within the principal Zip code area and eighteen-Zip code areas further away. *Two* faculty members lived within walking distance of the campus. The college ombudsman reporting these facts to me said, "Obviously this is a setting in which lack of communication and understanding, oversight, and a general feeling of estrangement from one another can be expected to generate problems."

In this kind of setting corporate faculty life may be almost nonexistent. Under these circumstances, a sense of collegiality is difficult to achieve. It is not easy to develop mechanisms for common approaches to issues of institutional philosophy. However, the level of frustration is rising high enough to insist that, even in the face of extreme pressures, problems long existent but deferred be dealt with now. Teachers told me that there has always been a variety of students in community colleges and that the needs of many had not been met simply because the pressures to do so were not strong enough. Now, however, many conscientious faculty members appear to be wondering whether they can teach at all; as someone said, "They now have got to fix it." To "fix it" may well require a special kind of teacher, one who is different from the conventional college teacher in a senior college or university. My general impression of faculty members is that they are sincere, dedicated people. Most are uncomplaining about the kind of task shaping up for them, but they are deeply concerned that their skills do not match this changing, most complex, educational assignment.

What Does It Take to Teach?

What does it take? What qualities does community college teaching call for? A dean answered those questions by describing the task to be performed:

The community college with open-admissions policies has a large enrollment of educationally disadvantaged students with substandard academic skills and weak motivation for conventional academic learning. Conventional instruction with lectures, competitive testing-grading, and research papers may be an adequate approach for the typical teacher in a senior college or university, but in the community college instruction based on the "academic production assembly-line model" is detrimental to the student as evidenced by high failure and dropout rates. Community college students with undeveloped academic skills and nonacademic motivational styles need reinforcement of personal development before they can function effectively in a conventional academic setting. Traditional teaching with its tired lecture-listen-test approach toward pumping data into the student is clearly antiquated, if not Stone Age instruction, for many community college students who are academically disadvantaged.

As has been implied, the qualities looked for in a community college teacher and hence the kind of appropriate training directly relate to what the teaching function is going to be. It is at this point that severe tensions are developing between faculty and administrative personnel in a number of institutions. The expectations may differ. The duties of a teacher are defined by a president in the following way:

Contributing to the development of an academic environment on campus. Assisting in development of educational policies, innovative programs. Participating in plans and preparation for North Central Association review. Participating in the development of co-curricular activities. Participating in developing research proposals and related activities. Participating in seminars to upgrade or update professional skills. Preparing proposals to secure government and foundation funds. Encouraging student-faculty interaction under informal circumstances. Visiting other campuses and cultural centers and making other field trips with students. Serving as a professional authority in the community. Analyzing community needs, becoming involved and sensitized to the community's problems. Evaluating library offerings and preparing book acquisition lists. Attending programs of the college. Participating in the academic advisement of students. Planning the teaching environment.

Time to Redefine the Function of Faculty

The president thinks it is going to be necessary to redefine the function of a faculty member in these broader terms. On the other hand, the faculty union has negotiated a contract which calls for twelve student contact hours per week plus three additional hours on campus. The president asserts that "Under no circumstances can twelve to fifteen hours per week of service be considered full-time. Such a definition would be immoral, if not illegal, and probably both."

Obviously these perceptions of faculty responsibility differ substantially. Whose concept will prevail? That issue has not been decided. However, I heard many references to the importance of qualities like the following:

1 The ability to relate effectively to people from different cultural and socio-economic backgrounds and to be in touch with the community the college serves
2 Work experiences beyond the academic field
3 The facility to keep up in the teaching field
4 Competence in the "individualization" of the learning process

TO RELATE TO PEOPLE FROM OTHER BACKGROUNDS

Twin factors heighten the need for faculty who can identify with and understand the student in a social environment: the emerging concept of the community college as a community-oriented institution and the diversity of student needs which requires a diagnostic, individual response. The reference point becomes the student as part of the community rather than the academic divisions or departments. College resources of personnel and materials become a part of that environment whose purpose is to supply opportunity for stimulation of new patterns of learning. Learning *continues* at the college; it does not begin there. The level of effectiveness, as represented in changed attitudes and new skills and concepts, is linked to previous learning. A base of common experience can facilitate teacher-student communication. There is need to talk a common language. The teacher may know the student language as a result of his own early experiences, although he can forget and may need reminding. Or, if he has the capacity, he can learn to be bilingual and bicultural or multicultural. For people who would teach in community colleges today, I heard many say, these cross-cultural skills are equally important as competence in economics, political science, biology, or electronics.

FACULTY EXPERIENCE BEYOND THE ACADEMIC AN ASSET

"He stood up on that stack 300 feet up in the air and did the welding for himself. He has been there. He didn't learn welding from somebody at the state university who learned it from somebody else at the state university."

Thus the point was made for the advantage of work experience beyond the academic for community college teachers. If they have never known failure, if their experience has been limited to the academic world, can they deal with a diversity of talent? Will they have feeling for students? These questions were asked frequently by students and faculty. The career ladder for a teacher often consists of a series of academic experiences. He does well in high school and college and tends to enter graduate school for preparation as a teacher without interruption for other vocational activities. He knows the world of the classroom, laboratory, books, and tests. He has mastered the system—that system. What appreciation does he have for the large number of community college students who come from a different world, who have mastered other systems but initially are ill at ease and not "at home" in the college setting?

Community college students are calling for teachers who have had a variety of experiences, who know the world, who have experienced more than an academic life. To qualify for a teaching post in the technical colleges and institutes of Wisconsin, for example, requires work experience. This might be expected of those who are to teach vocational-technical courses. But the requirement applies also to those who teach in the general education fields. There is broad support for the idea that teachers are better in their jobs as a result. On the other hand, military service requirements and world travel are becoming more common for recent college graduates before they enter teaching responsibilities. And so a specific work experience requirement may not be a necessary credential. However, I would strongly suggest that experience beyond the academic field might prove valuable to the faculty member who wishes to relate to students who are practical, literal minded, and interested more in performance than in philosophy.

FACULTY NEED TO KEEP UP IN THE TEACHING FIELD

Community college faculty are confronted with an impressive set of demands:

Learn how to teach

Keep up in your field

Study subcultures

Change your attitudes toward students and the academic processes

Some of these are self-imposed and stem from an impression that their professional training had been deficient because it had not prepared them for what they are doing. Critical of graduate school programs that did not relate to the actual requirements of community college teaching, they were equally critical of their own institutions for providing little opportunity to rectify those deficiencies. They asked for specialists to be brought in to work with them.

"We know our own specializations," they said, "but we want systematically to be taught to teach. Industry has experts who come in to help solve problems. Why can't the college do this?"

A president supported that need. There were 3,500 applicants for sixty teaching positions at his institution. Faculty members are involved in the screening process, and so he thought chances were good that they would get people who are philosophically committed to their particular learning approach.

"But," he said, "they don't know how to do it. They have to move away from the dissemination role, to which they are accustomed, to that of 'manager.' " He is convinced that "More and better in-service training than ever before is essential."

Colleges Can't Close to Retool

And many faculty agree. They assert that it is necessary to get people who are ready mentally to bring about change, who are honestly committed, who see the needs, and who are ready to devote time and energy. But, one of the big problems is that the institution cannot close down to retool the way an automobile plant can. There is need, therefore, for an ongoing problems clinic where people who are presently involved in the learning process would find resources to help them solve professional problems. I detected in many places a strong feeling that a structured preservice program is not as valuable as in-service training for people in the middle of problems and highly motivated, therefore, to seek solutions.

Clusters of community colleges are stepping up in-service training under provisions of the Education Professions Development Act. For example, in Tennessee where the community colleges are newly established, six-member faculty teams are brought together from nine institutions to study the problems involved in teaching high-risk, low-achieving students. A consortium of five community colleges and the University of California are assisting faculty to qualify for broader assumption of new kinds of administrative responsibilities which are coming their way, for example, in evaluation and staff selection.

The Coast Community College District in California offers a Faculty Fellowship Program which encourages developmental work toward improving learning experiences. The district establishes a fund each year to finance instructional and research projects conducted by faculty, either individually or in groups. Funds may be used to provide supplies, minor equipment, and assistance to those with projects they want to work on. Further, funds may provide for time released from a faculty member's regular assignment, may involve overtime pay, or may provide for a summer job. An example is a project which is to result in a complete audio-tutorial, multimedia approach to teaching physical science. The completed course will provide students with a general survey of the physical world around them in a far more stimulating manner than is possible under present conditions.

Florida Leads in Staff Development

Notable national leadership has been demonstrated by the state of Florida in directing to staff development 5 percent of the amount of state money available for the minimum-foundation program. This means 5 percent of the instructional budget. This is an excellent arrangement and ought to be available in other states.

Roger H. Garrison, in his 1967 study of community college faculty members, found that the most frequently expressed need was that of "time for renewal, time for professional refreshment." I found that same desire. There was repeated reference to the "need to go back occasionally." Usually that meant back to the university. After probing that matter, however, this did not appear to be the most productive possibility; it usually was the simplest to arrange, and it provided the credits necessary for a step-up on the salary schedule. But many faculty thought other experiences could be more beneficial. National Science Foundation institutes were judged as helpful. However, opportunities for faculty to work with people in industries related to their teaching fields would be most welcome. A teacher of physics thought it would be great to work as a physicist in optics where he could learn so much more than just theory, or to have opportunity to work with the physics of the medical field. Teachers want to keep alive professionally, and many believe the best way to achieve this goal is through linkage with industries related to the various professional teaching fields.

Teachers Trained in Business

A teacher of business economics at Mesa College in Arizona participated in a program initiated by the Maricopa County Junior College District and Valley National Bank. The teacher spent the summer as a bonded employee of the bank, a modest salary was paid, and the teacher was granted the maximum allowable credit toward professional advancement by the college district. The program was built upon the expectation that actual business experience would improve classroom teaching. Numerous teachers have expressed deep interest in programs of this kind, and these may represent a way of professional development just as significant to the community college teacher as further graduate work.

A large proportion of community college teachers continue graduate programs beyond the master's degree level. Salary and tenure requirements may provide at least partial motivation for this interest. However, of those who are continuing, 60 percent are in doctorate programs, and the question must be raised of whether the conventional doctorate program is the most effective means by which the community college teacher enhances his competence. Some people never seem to get out of the educational field. They are always talking to educators. Would there be greater value in making it possible for the faculty member to change his environment for a year, to go to work in business and industrial fields or in the community life which the college seeks to serve in its various programs? Alternatives to formal graduate programs are needed— alternatives that relate to the nature of the community college teaching task. Regardless how it is done, in-service training and provisions for professional renewal are among the most critical needs in the community college field. A complex, dynamic, and emotionally wearing profession entails expenditures of the teacher's intellectual resources that must be acknowledged.

INDIVIDUALIZATION OF THE LEARNING PROCESS

An experienced teacher with a Ph.D. degree and several books to his credit alluded to something that was hinted at in several institutions.

He asserted that there have always been students who required a different kind of approach, but two things have changed: the institution, which is at least finding out that these people actually exist, and society, which has made a similar discovery.

It is going to be necessary to deal more and more with students on an individual basis, and to think in terms of that student's own academic achievement.

It does not demean me as a teacher to speak with people who have what might be considered inadequate backgrounds in the field. They come to me for learning, and it is not important whether they understand it immediately or take a little longer.

He considers the "output" much more important than the "input." By the time the student leaves the institution, particularly if he transfers to another college or university, he needs to reach a level of performance which would predict success at that other institution, even though with some students this will require more time than for others. Sophisticated, capable, and with credentials to gain access to teaching posts in almost any college or university, this teacher made the following closing comments:

It takes a great teacher to teach in a community college. The purposes have been determined by the founders. They are reasonable. Change takes time. Moreover people ought to take the objectives and purposes of the institution into consideration in determining their own professional interests.

A College President Calls for Liberators

A college president called for "liberators." "We need antiremedial innovators. We cannot talk about bringing people up to snuff. In many respects these people are already up to those levels or beyond."

Students second the motion for change:

The teachers dig authoritarian roles. They really like that business, standing up there in front of the class. And so may some of the students like that approach. They don't have to think things through themselves. You are called upon to recite. That word *recite* should have been long gone.

In some instances teachers recruited from elementary school backgrounds have apparently been successful in community college teaching. They are reported to exhibit flexibility as well as an awareness of subject matter which cuts across several disciplines. Because they have been trained to start with students "where they are," they tend to be less prejudiced on issues dealing with verbal skills and grade-level achievement. Elementary school teachers, it was suggested, unlike high school or college instructors, are very often forced to be aware of the wide-ranging needs of students, needs which go well beyond the boundaries of mathematics, social studies, or English.

High school teaching background is also given a high mark as preparation for the teaching task in the community college. Breadth of experience and the capacity to relate to students are associated with secondary school teaching. Something needs to be done, I was told repeatedly, to develop people who have this ability to relate to students and enough formal background to take care of the technical requirements.

PRESIDENTS AS MANAGERS OF LEARNING

Clearly, presidents are required to be managers of learning situations, just as faculty are. They may not spend many hours in the classroom, though some exposure might help. But to create learning experiences requires input from those who direct policy as well as those who come face-to-face with the learners on a day-to-day basis.

Faculty members see the president's role this way:

We would like to just sit down with the president occasionally and talk with him. Lots of people don't know who he is. He ought to come down to our world, to the cafeteria, rather than our coming to his world. We need to bridge the communication gap between the offices and the cafeteria.

If the president is going to be successful, he has to occupy a daily role with teachers and students which provides for this kind of interaction, face-to-face contact.

The view of the administration seems to be that this is *my* school, not *our* school, and you are not going to tell me how to run it. When the faculty begin to ask some rather pointed questions, the president can't seem to take it and has difficulty in keeping his composure. But this needs to be considered our school, for all of us.

If the administration continues to initiate programs that have an effect upon you without involving you in these decisions, then the American Federation of Teachers at this place will grow.

The biggest problem by far is the friction between faculty and administration. They need to work together; there needs to be full participation of all elements. The administration understands the mission of the community college, but it is in strategy that it breaks down.

The effective response of the community college as a learning environment and as an organization will depend upon harmony among the values and attitudes of participants as well as superior skills in interpersonal relations. A changing community college, participating in a changing society, cannot leave the role of president unaffected. Past circumstances often called for knowledge of buildings and finance, competence in means more than in ends, how more than why. The future demands a leadership which can facilitate the process of interaction from which purposes are identified and articulated, a leadership which can assemble resources for accomplishment of those purposes and assist in establishing a conducive environment.

Personality Is a Big Factor

Although many presidential skills may be learned, there is a growing body of opinion which suggests that those seeking presidents look for qualities of the personality.

They should have the capacity for listening. When faced with an unknown situation, they should not go in with a plan. They should evidence sincere interest and concern and indicate by the way they listen to people that the information they are receiving will be helpful.

Those comments of a board member were supported by another trustee:

He needs to be a political animal, to have the capacity to feel what other people are thinking without being told. He needs to be a pacifier and needs to have the capacity to explain things. It is very important that he be emotionally secure and able to argue and disagree as well as to accept and understand disagreements. He cannot go by the book and play it safe. I think it is really a matter of temperament rather than training.

The need for a sense of humor, the capacity not to give up, and a commitment to everybody's right to free public education were other elements considered important: "He needs to be flexible, have the capacity to change, and to share administrative prerogatives."

Students see the president as an organizer,

. . . somebody to make the structure functional and to make sure all elements are involved; to coordinate those elements, to make sure that all functions are carried out and that all of the segments make input. He should not dictate. College presidents should come from the community or from like communities. But they come with a different life style, and they seem to say, What can I do for you, my child?

Programs to prepare presidents require, as a strong and essential element, selection of the candidate upon the basis of personality characteristics. He needs to be able to live with mistakes and open enough to recognize diversity around him. A sense of commitment is frequently referred to: "It has been so long since I have heard somebody say, 'I believe this' and then go ahead and act upon it."

One of the problems to be confronted in selection is that we do not yet know how to predict reactions of people under stress or how well they can tolerate anxiety. Ways are needed by which the personal qualities and potential of prospective presidents can be assessed and resources made available to them by which they can develop abilities for this kind of job. Many have not had preparation to be politicians, to be articulate. Yet an excellent political sense and the ability to establish a role of community leadership are among the qualifications of successful community college presidents.

Various segments of the community have goals which they want the college to assume. Particularly in urban areas there has been accelerated participation in the political processes in order to achieve those goals. But power groups as well as critical issues come and go. Long-term planning based upon current status will often turn out to be faulty. For example, a few years ago in a West Coast city, the Congress of Racial Equality and the National Association for the Advancement of Colored People were two very influential organizations. They had substantial impact upon plans for the future. But their present political influence in that area is very small. Now other organizations possess political and social power. The first job of the president as administrator is to exercise his political sense in recognition of the political makeup of the college's environment. A director of community services, a former newspaperman, urged that every community college president read the history of Tammany Hall "and abide by the precepts they find there. When I develop a program," he said, "I am developing another ward in effect. I am developing patronage, if you like. We get votes from those areas that are served."

A new president arrived in an area where it was necessary for him to demonstrate community leadership before he could successfully exert college leadership. He spent his time visiting the bars and the churches, getting acquainted with the power alignments of the area, and winning their confidence. He identified with them—with their goals and their needs. He built his own role. He recognized organizations that could serve the ends of the college. And he was able to redirect hostilities and energies. In some cases student "vice lords" in the area put on a shirt and tie, enrolled in the college, went to work in banks, assumed a new set of responsibilities. Leadership of the college was impossible without a keen awareness of political realities in that community, as well as the capacity to identify with its predominant values, life-styles, and leadership so that community resources could be directed toward attainment of college purposes rather than in opposition.

Said the president: "I have taken a position which almost amounts to arrogance so that people in this community and in the higher education fields see me as an equal or better. It is necessary for the president of a community college to promote the prestige of his institution."

How Can the President Be Mr. Inside and Mr. Outside?

A leading businessman commented favorably on the leadership given a new community college by a president who was formerly a high school principal in the area: "He knew the area; he knew what buttons to push to get things done." The president expressed some discomfort at learning new administrative roles including the delegation of more responsibility and authority. It still bothers him that the Instructional Council meets without him. But he feels that one of his primary contributions to the success of the college is his knowledge of the area.

A dilemma confronting the president is not whether he can be "Mr. Outside" as well as "Mr. Inside," but how to be both. Demands for his presence are as insistent within the college as they are from the community, and his particular and unique role as institutional leader is necessary.

"We don't know what they are doing over there," say the faculty, seeing the administration as a group that justifies its own existence rather than one that serves the learning process.

> The administration has not taken time to explain things—for example, some of the financial problems of the district. Too often they do things and they don't tell us why. This embitters the faculty. There may be good reasons, but we are not told. Given the facts, we might make the same decision, but we need to know the facts, and that is what is missing.

Even the very setup of the buildings seems to create separation. The administrative offices are up on what is called the "bridge," and the faculty offices are "away down there."

Students say that the president is an important figure and that they would like to get acquainted with him. "He seems to have time enough to go to community meetings. How does he know that he is representing us unless somehow we can become acquainted?" A counselor suggested a need for the president to move out from behind his desk to meet and talk with faculty and students in their environments.

I like to think about the president and administrative personnel as not only evaluating me but really giving constructive support. Perhaps administrators ought to get paraprofessionals to assist them with their daily routine so the president can get out where the processes are going on. Perhaps we need to raise some questions about administration. What really is its role?

Maybe the President Should Give Up Speeches

It is obvious that the president faces hard decisions with regard to his time. Will he spend more with faculty and staff? Faculty say yes. People can learn to trust him, they say, and want to work with him, and this kind of spirit and influence can permeate through the college. "But he is going to have to eliminate some things. Maybe it ought to be talks to Rotary clubs. Perhaps other personnel in administration should give the speeches." The relatively gentle note of reproof in comments of this kind represents one end of a continuum of faculty alienation. At the other end is a formalized, rigid relationship which threatens the mission of the community college.

In several states community colleges found themselves, often to their surprise, covered by state collective bargaining laws. In the bitterness which ensued, there is evidence that neither administration nor faculty were prepared to deal with the new situation.

In Michigan, for example, college faculty members were brought under the Public Employment Relations Act in 1965. "Everybody was plunged into a new situation and a power struggle ensued." It occurred to me that in industry there did not seem to be the same degree of bitterness and alienation between management and labor. Apparently collective bargaining hit Michigan education very hard, and in the beginning it was warfare, the kind that probably has worn off in industry. Educators were not accustomed to this kind of world. A new fact of life has appeared to challenge to the versatility and competence of the president.

Unions—A New Fact of Life

Regardless of the extent to which management-labor patterns are adopted in community colleges, it is clear that relations between

faculty and president and other administrative personnel will be
different in the future than they have been. The president of an AFT
(American Federation of Teachers) unit in a large community college
told me that more faculty members are being driven into the union.
Two years ago, there were twelve, now there are fifty. But, he said,
good administration will destroy a union. There is no need for it. But
many people now are being alienated. They have the sense of not
being consulted or involved. They are all supposedly professionals,
but they are not treated as professionals, as they see it.

Presidents face difficult and complicated circumstances. People
call for change: "more participatory administration," "walk with
faculty and students in a different way," "build more trust between
administrators and faculty," "delegate more authority." And presidents, themselves, generally are aware that the old patterns and ways
of administration are not working well. They say, "We need to be
less authoritarian." "We will play a less conspicuous role." "Now
you identify mutual problems, and go to work on them."

Occasionally I had the impression that presidents were figuratively
being drawn and quartered by divergent forces. For in addition to
faculty and student insistence upon being heard, seen, and involved,
boards of directors show increased desire to exercise the "review-
and-evaluation" function of the board. How can their interests be
expressed, they ask, without the president feeling that they want to
take over the institutions? They, too, call for more trust, and they
ask for better, more evaluative information. And there is the state
legislature. An increasing number of decisions that bear upon the
college are made in the state capitol. These decisions often are
money matters. Presidents see contact with the legislature to be a
responsibility which must be observed. Through all these calls to
duty, the note is repeatedly sounded: "There needs to be leadership
at the top. I mean by the president. You have got to get people to
feel that they are on the same team. Only the president can do that."

Perhaps in that statement there are clues toward solution of what
appears an almost impossible situation—responding to this broad set
of demands.

What is it that only the president can do? Providing leadership for
those involved in the work of the institution so that common goals
are identified and accepted is a paramount responsibility. Goals of
the community college are seldom set entirely within the institution
or by the local participants alone. Major goals may be established by
the state legislature or by a state community college board, or a local
board may have legal responsibility. Few matters, however, are more

important than participants having a common understanding of what they are to do together. And it is for leadership of this kind that I heard the greatest desire expressed. (It seems somewhat short of the mark to say, "I tell them what our philosophy is," as a president said in an aside about the faculty).

A Plan of Activity Is Required

If goals are to be achieved, a plan of activity is required. With other interested parties, the president develops a program appropriate to the goals sought. A president, who acceded to the value of greater faculty involvement in program formulation, denied himself the benefits of such involvement, it seemed to me, with his view that "We are reaching the point where we will need to sell our programs to the faculty rather than impose them."

Implicit in that statement is the notion that ideas are formed in the minds of a few administrators, or perhaps the president himself and faculty, while other personnel, including students, serve as implementers. It seems unlikely that any one man can be wise enough or have the energy to fulfill the requirements of that kind of role. Community colleges are in many cases large and complex institutions in a rapidly changing society. "We cannot have one person calling the shots; this institution is no longer a mommy-daddy type of store," said someone in homespun recognition of the need to broaden responsible participation. And another president shared that view: "All I can do is to provide the environment for change to take place. If I try to guide it too closely, this will really destroy it."

Great differences exist among community colleges in the way the presidential role is perceived both by the president and by others. In some places the president is the "take-charge" type. He makes the decisions as he is expected to. On the other hand, and at the other end of the continuum, a growing number of institutions call for presidential leadership which is quite different. For example, one college states in the preamble to the provisional constitution of its representative legislature:

> The people, many and varied, representing a diversity of ideas, backgrounds, and experiences, who comprise the family of Brookdale Community College herein commit themselves to a basic assumption: Those who live and work together can and rightfully should assume responsibility for directing and controlling their joint endeavors so that maximum benefits may accrue to all. Recognizing the interdependence of each segment of the Brookdale community, we have set forth in this constitution a structure for governance predicated upon this assumption.

The college legislature includes representation from:

1   The nonacademic staff
2   The faculty
3   The administration
4   The student body

The college assembly participates in formulation and amendment of educational policies and standards; establishment and elimination of college credit courses; standards for evaluating student performance; maintenance and development of student life; criteria for appointment, reappointment, and assignment of academic rank; academic freedom; and criteria and techniques for the evaluation of personnel.

The Trend toward Involvement of Groups in Program Formulation

Obviously, the president in this situation plays a vastly different part, or he plays his part in a vastly different way, from his colleague in the more traditional structure. Which is the better way? The answer must be sought in the goals of the individual institution. What works best in terms of those goals? However, there is an unmistakable national trend toward broader involvement of component groups in formulating college programs. This fact will affect the job definition and style of the presidential office, and hence the criteria for selection of chief administrators, as well as in-service experiences considered appropriate for renewal and updating of skills.

A third major responsibility of presidential leadership is to assemble, in concert with others, the resources required by the program: people, buildings, equipment, land, and money. Presidents give the impression that they are at home in this work. They are knowledgeable about tax levies, building construction, and land acquisition. Many are active personally in recruitment of other administrators and key faculty personnel. Of all their principal duties this one appears to be conducted with most facility by executives who are inclined to be of pragmatic bent. Moreover, this is terrain somewhat more solid than matters of goals and program development. However, a look to the future provokes a question: Will the circumstances within which community colleges operate reduce the comparative importance of this aspect of the president's work?

I heard repeated references, for example, to the need for programs to take precedence over concerns about buildings. And with regard to finance, strong indications exist, as reported in Chapter 8, that the

state will provide a larger share of the educational dollar and will
exercise more control over that dollar. To be sure, staffing will
continue as a critical element in making the institution go. However,
the size of many community colleges precludes the president's
involvement in other then key appointments. These factors suggest
that activities that the president now feels most capable of dealing
with will diminish in importance relative to other major challenges
represented in tasks which he had previously avoided or approached
with diffidence.

Evaluation Is a Major Challenge

One of the major challenges to leadership is the process by which the
college evaluates the effectiveness of the resources and of the
program in achieving established goals. Evaluation and the corrective
measures which that process requires are conducted by participants
in the college program and are primarily for their benefit. Self-
correction is the most effective response and is a result of
participation in the process of evaluation. The increasing demands at
state and federal levels for accountability of educators leaves no
doubt—unless those engaged in the learning process develop the will
and means for continuous assessment of both the individual's
progress in learning and the institution's productivity in terms of
resources utilized, agencies outside the institution will do it with the
danger that yardsticks inappropriate to the goals of the institution
may be applied.

Local boards, state-level agencies, and the federal Congress show
dissatisfaction with the quality of data reported by institutions of
higher education. The colleges collect a great deal of information but
appear, to their critics, to store it rather than use it for managerial
purposes. It is seldom used to measure effectiveness. However, a kind
of economic determinism is bringing an end to any casual attitudes
about institutional evaluation and accountability that educators
might have. In effect, state legislatures are saying to the colleges, "We
want to know what this state is getting from our colleges and
universities in relation to the taxpayer's investment." Accordingly
the governor of Michigan has requested institutions of higher
education to develop an evaluation system of a program budget, a
budget related to goals, programs, program objectives, and outcomes.
Appropriately, the Western Interstate Council for Higher Education
has developed a Management Information Systems Program. Clearly,
state legislatures will be mandating program planning and budgeting

systems as a requisite for state appropriations to the colleges. Some community colleges have demonstrated sophisticated leadership in the development and application of management methods. For more to do so, leadership must be trained. Few community college presidents had "management by objectives" as a part of their graduate programs.

In goal setting, resource assembling, and evaluation, the major role of the president is to set free the potential of the participants in the enterprise and to cultivate an environment which encourages and supports. In acknowledgment that demands are made of him which are beyond satisfactory response by any single individual, and in recognition of the function of the college as a learning institution, the president plays his role most appropriately when he is a manager of learning. He joins with others in accomplishment of goals which represent mutual interests.

The teacher in the community college is also a manager of learning. In a world exploding with knowledge he cannot expect to serve as a conveyor of information. His role is to provide leadership to the participants in the learning experience as they shape up their objectives, and to assist in tailoring educational programs to achieve the objectives. He helps make available resources which will be useful to the student, information through computers or books or tapes, laboratory equipment, and perhaps work-study opportunities. He participates in the process by which evaluation is conducted on a continuing basis so that learners are able to correct errors and identify deficiencies. Both president and teacher, in fact, are managers of learning.

Recognizing common responsibilities and a large community of interest helps close the gap which too often exists today between faculty and administration. There is no logical reason for a dichotomy. The artificial divisions which now exist, if perpetuated, will handicap the college in attaining its goals. It is the span of responsibility rather than the substance of the task which differentiates the roles of chief administrator and faculty member (if they hold to the tenets of administration and learning process proposed here). But more is required than a profession of faith. New skills and understanding are needed. The community college has an obligation to provide opportunity for that kind of learning.

SUMMARY

A special kind of person with special skills and attitudes is going to be needed for community college work. This is already apparent, and the need will become even more apparent in the future because of pressures already at work.

Faculty face the challenging assignment of improving the learning process in an institution with an ever-increasing breadth of program and an ever-increasing diversity of students. They come to their task with good academic credentials but not necessarily good preparation for the actual work they will do.

Administrators, too, find themselves facing an assignment that is changing in its requirements for success, and not all find themselves well prepared for the way the job is shaping up. Traditional presidential skills, as perceived by some, will probably have to give way in importance to increased emphasis on working with broader constituencies to make the learning process work more efficiently.

At present, these factors are causing frustration among both faculty and administrators. The frustrations are likely to be intensified if the two roles are separated even more widely by the collective bargaining process. The transition from where we are to where we are going will be made easier if faculty and administrators see themselves as partners, not adversaries, in the management of learning. There is also a need for a broader view of appropriate in-service education experiences. The nature of the community college assignment indicates that involvement in the life of the community may serve as well (or better) in some instances as additional course work in the university.

The way to bring the picture into its best focus, when seeking solutions to such problems, is to look first at the student in the community and to try to see his needs. When that picture comes into focus, the rest of the scene is perceived more clearly.

Chapter 5.
Dealing with the Assignment

Who is responsible for the student's success or failure? The community college or the student? Obviously the answer must assume shared responsibility, but the point is that views are changing. There is a shift in educational philosophy which places more weight on the institution's role. A teacher of economics, reminding me that he was educated under the "old school," recalled a pyramid chart used by the U.S. Office of Education which showed that, of the number of students who begin school, a smaller number graduate from high school, and even smaller numbers go on to college. He commented:

The educational system was based pretty much on the process of elimination, and the weak and disinterested fell by the wayside. Those who survived were competent. But all of this has changed, and it seems to be the attitude now that we should bring all of these students along with us, even those who are incompetent or not interested. The philosophy of what we are trying to do has changed completely. Now, what I need to know is: What are we really trying to do?

A SHIFTING EDUCATIONAL PHILOSOPHY

The attitude which places the burden for learning almost entirely on students is based on two somewhat contradictory beliefs. One belief is that a student can learn if he really applies himself—works hard, studies, and pays close attention to the instructor. The other is that each person has limited capability, usually called intelligence or aptitude. Therefore, some people are college material, and others are unfit.

Normal Curves

One popular practice, the application of the normal curve to determine the distribution of grades, illustrates the second belief. It is one of the best examples of a self-fulfilling prophecy. Prospective teachers were taught to expect a normal curve distribution of grades, and once teachers, they applied the curve to achieve the expected distribution. In retrospect it is astonishing that this practice ever became acceptable. By using the normal curve to determine grades, instructors were in effect abdicating the responsibility for student learning, and colleges denied themselves the primary measure of effectiveness.

The application of the normal curve ignored how much or how little was learned by the students. The significant element was the relationship of one score to other scores. Students could learn everything or nothing about an assignment, and the same combination of grades would be awarded. The explanation for surprisingly high or low scores was the abilities of the students, not the behavior of the teacher. The use of the normal curve to grade students was supported logically by the widely held belief that mental ability, the ability to learn, was distributed in varying amounts among individuals and that the distribution followed the normal curve. This belief also absolved instructors of any appreciable responsibility. The bright would learn, and the less bright would barely survive or fail, regardless of what instructors did or did not do.

College Responsibility for Student Learning

There is a trend now toward greater institutional accountability for student learning. Admission into a community college implies college acceptance of considerable responsibility for student learning. In some cases leadership in this direction is provided by community college people. In their opinion the only valid measure of institutional performance is student performance. Some state it succinctly: "If no learning is evident, it can be inferred that no instruction occurred."

There is growing acceptance of the view that all are capable of learning as well as mounting concern about students who leave college with poor grade records, goals not achieved, and feelings of frustration and failure. Many people are convinced that steps must be taken to reduce the number of failures. Since many of these people are also advocates of open-door admissions, they recognize that community colleges must dramatically change to better serve their students. The old "revolving door" and "cooling out" concepts are unacceptable. In their view the admission of a student does obligate a community college to do more than just present information, periodically award grades, and maintain records of courses taken and grades, certificates, and degrees awarded.

Reasons for Change

There are three major reasons for this apparent change in attitude toward responsibility for student learning.

One of the values often stated in this nation has been "equality of opportunity." This value is closely related to and supported by a belief in egalitarianism. Even before the Revolutionary War people were arguing that all men were created equal and that every individual was entitled to an opportunity regardless of the circumstances of his birth. The belief in egalitarianism has never been embraced by all people in this country, and at times many were afraid it would destroy the government itself. But, despite the changing tides, there is evidence of renewed support for egalitarianism and the value of providing equal opportunities to all people; this is the first reason for changed attitudes about responsibility for learning. The civil rights struggle has reemphasized these feelings in recent years. The GI Bill that entitled veterans to educational opportunities demonstrated that people can learn, regardless of their backgrounds.

A second reason is the growing belief that most people can learn. This thesis is best explained and supported in a paper written by Benjamin Bloom, a professor of education at the University of Chicago, entitled "Learning for Mastery." This short paper expresses the view that 95 percent of the students can achieve a high degree of mastery of given materials if a variety of instructional methods and media is provided and if sufficient time is available. Furthermore, the paper asserts that aptitude is really a measure of time, not of capacity, and that a high aptitude simply means the individual can learn quickly. The person of lower aptitude can learn and comprehend if he will persevere and if the information is available in various forms. With the exception of a small proportion of the population, all people can learn. But some will take longer. Almost everyone can learn to run and type; it's the 4-minute mile or 150 words per minute that will elude most people.

A third reason is found in the increasing demand for accountability by people who see the evidence of higher costs—human and financial—but who see no commensurate evidence of accomplishment. After all, they say, a community college should conduct purposive activities. Community colleges draw resources from their broad communities and are given certain rights and authority. Therefore, community colleges are accountable to their broad communities for the achievement of certain goals.

THE COLLEGE MISSION

The concept of college responsibility and accountability requires a statement of mission by each institution. Whom is it to serve? How is it to serve them? What are its goals? A primary purpose has already been stated: the community college is to facilitate student learning. Essentially, the mission of the community college is to assist in the development of its community's human resources. There are many means to accomplish this mission. A community college should identify these means and assure that they are available, but not necessarily from the community college.

An examination of statements of goals reveals great diversity. Some institutions emphasize what could be labeled the custodial function. Their primary concern is evidently knowing where a student is at a certain time and keeping him out of trouble. Other institutions emphasize the "rite of passage" or "coming of age" attitude. Each student must satisfy certain requirements and pass traditional tests regardless of a student's needs and interests. Once the requirements are satisfied and the tests are passed, the student becomes a "mature person." Prior to that he is something less.

The mission I am proposing here assumes no rigid patterns and schedules to satisfy either the "custodial" or "rite of passage" function. It assumes that each individual has potential and should have opportunities to develop it.

The goal of providing successful learning experiences for every student is idealistic and probably unachievable; however, that is no reason to reject it. A goal provides direction and a basis for measuring performance, has implications for intermediate objectives, policies, and practices, and has especially profound implications for institutions that historically have "weeded out" people by failing and discouraging them. The mission is no longer to develop the select few, but to develop all.

There is another important and timely element to be considered in the declaration of mission. Community colleges are interested in developing human resources beyond relatively narrow career or occupational spheres. There is more to life than a career. This is true, despite the fact that American society places major emphasis on an individual's occupation.

People are devoting less time to their careers and becoming more interested in other aspects of life. Community colleges can assist this development by providing more learning opportunities in avocational, cultural, social, and political spheres. Courses and programs in these areas are just as appropriate and valuable as traditional courses, and they deserve the same support and recognition.

In the final analysis, the significance and value of a learning experience depend on the learner, not on tradition or the opinions of educators.

METHODS OF FULFILLING THE GOALS

Variety in Curriculum

A narrow curriculum will not do. A community college cannot ordinarily achieve its mission by limiting its offerings to a narrow band of career programs or general education courses. It must offer a wide variety of courses and programs.

Unfortunately, community colleges are saddled with a variety of public expectations based on tradition, experience, and prejudice. In many cases these expectations are reinforced by state laws and funding procedures that force a college to distinguish between college-credit and non-college-credit courses, between vocational and nonvocational courses.

It is all too common for states to help pay for traditional liberal arts courses but not community service courses, or to pay more for students enrolled in vocational courses than those in nonvocational courses. In one state a distinction is even made between health-related and other vocational courses. The results of these policies and practices that arbitrarily divide and subdivide curricula are confusion, frustration, and invidious comparisons.

A community college should avoid the questionable dichotomies commonly used to classify courses and programs. Unfortunately this will not be possible until many state laws and administrative practices are changed, but it is another major challenge to the institutions. Such differentiations serve purposes of dubious value and result in comparisons that negatively affect students, faculty, and institutions.

There is no consistency to a scheme that classifies medical laboratory technician, dental assistant, and legal aide as occupational programs and classifies premedicine, predentistry and prelaw as academic programs. An even more illogical differentiation is college level versus noncollege level. A few years ago college algebra was college-level mathematics, but selective admissions and better prepared students enabled some colleges to alter their requirements. Since the average student has already completed college algebra, it became a requirement for admission. College algebra was no longer college level. Examples of inconsistency are endless.

Community colleges should champion the view that what is "worth" learning need not and cannot be reliably classified and that the courses and programs offered should be dependent on the needs and interests of the people and institutions, not on tradition and so-called normal, college-level programs.

Personal Assistance to Students

The community college assignment calls for radical change in the usual concept of the work of the counselor. His role in institutions boasting of their counseling service has been uncertain. He has been described by presidents as "neither fish nor fowl," neither faculty nor administration. When the funds are cut, he is often the first to go. However, students and faculty are calling for services that suggest the need for a whole new approach to the "functions" commonly associated with the area of "counseling."

How do you get counselors out of their offices? What do you do about the negative image of counselors; i.e., is something wrong with the individual who goes to a counselor? On the other hand, what can counselors do if ten to fifteen students are waiting and the counselee load is 600 students?

We are involved in putting out brush fires. We place vast numbers of freshmen in classes, counsel with them for vocations, work on transfer requirements, and see to it that graduation requirements are met. There is no time to settle down and take on the role of counselor as described in the textbooks.

Perhaps it is appropriate that the textbook role cannot be played. Rather than support a small professional counseling "corps," a substantial part of the educational budget (5, 10, up to 20 percent) might be thought of as a concomitant effort to make the "educational program," classroom, laboratory, and independent study effective—through adequate counseling, guarantee to the individual the kinds of assistance which will orient him to effectiveness, motivate him to positive action, and assist him in the perceptions necessary to take advantage of the more formal aspects of education. Perhaps we really ought to begin to think in broader terms than "counseling." It might be called personal assistance to students.

If we could break out of the "professional counseling" syndrome, and if we could begin to develop by a substantial reallocation of educational resources the counseling potential inherent in involvement of students, faculty, and laymen from the community including business and professions, we might find it possible to add very substantially to the effectiveness and productivity of the educational program. In other words, instead of thinking of counseling as "remedial" or "corrective," if we thought of it as a way of increasing educational effectiveness and as a program to be related to each individual student (rather than just to those who trouble us with their problems or make themselves embarrassing with their failures), we might be able to make progress in reducing dropouts and improve utilization of educational programs in ways which would astound us.

This fundamental appraisal especially ought to be undertaken in the case of students with perceptions of education different from those of so many middle-class and upper-middle-class youths. Where perceptions of role, of career possibilities, of social change, of the possibility of class mobility are lacking, incomplete, or negative as in the case of so many minorities, then this whole concept, if applied, might represent a significant leap forward.

This concept presupposes that we break out of the proposition that student counseling can only or can best be done by professionally trained personnel. While this training may be desirable and possibly even essential for those aspects concerned with application of tests and measurements, or in those areas of psychological and psychiatric assistance, the big areas of counseling largely neglected include those providing the intangibles of encouragement: assistance in changing perceptions by example in areas of career choice and preparation; peer assistance in overcoming such personal problems as those created by drug use, sex hang-ups, feelings of social inadequacy, etc. These, while very real and severe to the individual, do not necessarily require professional attention.

Peer counseling in the area of personal problems may be very effective if the peer counselors are guided and aware of the limitations of their roles and shown how to identify cases where individuals should be referred to more expert help. I have seen instances where laymen from industry or business or the professions (educational laymen) provided insight about preparation tracks, occupational requirements, and satisfactions and motivations which could not have possibly been provided by "professional counselors."

Change has been inhibited by two factors. One is believing that "counseling" in education is mostly a professional activity which must be accomplished by and through "professional" counselors. The second factor is the belief that the whole counseling operation is an appendage made necessary by the aberrant or unsophisticated preparation (or lack of it) of a minority of students. As a result, counseling is perceived as a troublesome necessity rather than as a major opportunity to increase the effectiveness of the educational program.

College administrators and counseling professionals argue that much more could be accomplished "if only the budget for counseling could be increased." If the lack of counseling is indeed the single greatest factor in causing the underutilization of the educational program, then a *reallocation* of budget resources to strengthen this area, even at the cost of support for the formal education program, would result in a clear gain in the effectiveness of the latter.

Grading Systems

Several community colleges are experimenting with nonpunitive grading systems and procedures which eliminate failure in the traditional sense. Supporters of nonpunitive grading argue that it is important to know what a student has mastered—what skills he can perform, problems he can solve, and information he can apply—but that it is not necessary or advisable to record failures in addition to successes.

Nonpunitive grading is another manifestation of the growing concern about students. The future of this approach to evaluation will depend in large part on the reactions of universities and four-year colleges. Their acceptance or rejection of the idea, with its impact on the transfer problem, will have much to do with the spread of this approach.

Only a few colleges are trying nonpunitive grading, and initial reactions are mixed. It is an issue that arouses emotional reactions. It is logically compatible with "learning for mastery" and the development of all human resources. If those two ideas are accepted and put into practice, it seems reasonable to expect the adoption of nonpunitive grading by a growing number of community colleges.

Concepts of Time

The notion of higher education as an activity most appropriate to eighteen- to twenty-five-year-olds is being dispelled. Education as a lifelong activity appears to be gaining acceptance philosophically and practically. Education can no longer be limited to a few years. Educational closure is no longer a reasonable concept. Being educated is a very tentative and temporary state in this era of accelerating change.

Other time constraints are being questioned. Theoretically the idea that aptitude is a function of time—that people can learn if sufficient time is provided—calls into question academic calendars and grading policies that have been attached to them. Practical considerations of students, their work schedules, and personal idiosyncrasies have led to weekend colleges, fourteen-hour days, and greater flexibility in scheduling. Rigid restrictions associated with traditional registrars are being replaced by flexibility and concern for individual students. For years registrars have been stereotyped as bureaucratic and unfeeling, but now many of them are advocating flexible calendars and the granting of credit for nontraditional educational experiences.

New Locations, New Instructors

Campuses will continue to be appropriate to some people, but many of the "new" students will function more effectively in other environments. Off-campus centers in neighborhoods and industrial locations will be more convenient, inviting, and realistic.

Communities can be used as laboratories. There is no need to duplicate a community's resources on a community college campus. Educational opportunities can be taken to people where they live and work, using mobile facilities if necessary.

Both urban and rural colleges are experimenting with alternatives to traditional campuses. Urban colleges are placing centers in the neighborhoods to attract people who are afraid of traditional higher education or in some cases of leaving their neighborhoods. Rural colleges are experimenting with instructional delivery systems, such as television, self-instruction materials, and small educational centers, that will enable people in a sparsely populated area to continue their education at a reasonable cost.

The acceptance of greater responsibility and willingness to organize and implement different routines to achieve greater student learning calls for a new breed of college faculty. Instructors, like students, have their self-images and measures of worth. Until recently, many college instructors have measured their own worth by the judgments of other college professors.

The criteria most often used by professors to judge one another have little relationship to learning. Rather, they are generally measures of scholarship, such as work published and research endeavors, that may demonstrate what a person knows about his discipline. It has never been established that an instructor's scholarship increases the likelihood that his students will learn. But, common sense supports the contention that time spent on scholarly activities is time not available to students. This line of thought does not reject scholarship, publications, and research, *if* those activities increase the likelihood of student learning.

Research to identify the effectiveness of certain methods and media in certain subjects for students with certain characteristics is desperately needed. And the results of this kind of research must be shared so that many people will benefit. Only when faculty members are primarily concerned about the educational progress of all their students and when they accept considerable responsibility for their student's successes and failures will a dramatic change occur in community colleges. The preparation of faculty—both inexperienced and experienced—to accept this new and demanding assignment may be the most difficult challenge confronting community colleges.

Methods and Media

To satisfactorily meet their assignments, community colleges must utilize a variety of instructional approaches and media. There is no panacea, no one combination of methods and media that will facilitate learning in all subjects. The lecture method may work for some students in some subjects, but it is not effective for large numbers of students enrolled in many courses. There is a great deal of discussion about individualized instruction. Several colleges are experimenting and trying different techniques on a modest scale, but few colleges are making a massive effort to individualize instruction.

There is a trend toward utilizing different instructional approaches, and resistance to change and experimentation is diminishing. There are a few people who adamantly support a certain instructional technique to the exclusion of others, but a more frequent reaction is a mixture of curiosity, hope, and skepticism.

The "show me" attitude is demonstrated by the efforts of people to visit places where things are happening, to see with their own eyes whether a new idea really works. Some administrators asserted that the best investment for producing change was to send faculty members to other colleges where they could see different instructional techniques in practice.

Because of financial and other constraints, the feasibility of doing something different is getting more emphasis now. One question commonly asked is, On what basis should methods and media be selected? More people are concluding that the best evidence is not the "authoritative opinion" of an instructor or a faculty committee. The best test of a film's or book's efficacy is its effectiveness with learners. Media and methods should be tested with "typical" learners in realistic settings.

Improved Teaching

It seems apparent that community colleges will have to rely in large part on in-service education to change the attitudes and practices of current faculty. A community college cannot close for several months to permit faculty to return to universities to be reeducated. And even if it could, there is reason to believe that few universities would know how to prepare faculty members for these new roles. The new roles are still relatively undefined and vague. Only a few community colleges are seriously reexamining them. They talk about "managers of learning," "learning facilitators," and "differentiated staffing." But there is no agreement on faculty roles even among the more experimental community colleges. There is a general recognition of the limitations any instructor has.

Few people are good at everything, but most are proficient at some things. But how can the faculty be organized and prepared to better serve students? Team teaching that turns out to be rotating lectures is hardly a major improvement. Too much specialization can fragment the assignments and responsibilities to the point where it becomes impersonal and no one really feels responsible for student learning.

Perhaps a solution or a partial one will be found in some of the cluster experiments. Several community colleges are organized into clusters or small collegia. I was impressed by one college's organization into "institutes." The cluster concept has many interpretations. It is essentially a way of closely relating faculty and students. This arrangement is intended to lead to a greater acceptance of responsibility for student learning by all parties—faculty and students. The value of the cluster concept remains to be established, but the search for better ways for faculty to work with students, beyond the traditional departmental structures, is a heartening development.

Until the roles of community college instructors become more clearly defined, universities will have an insoluble problem of developing relevant preservice programs. Community colleges will have to devote considerable effort to preparing their own faculty and staff. One administrator of an urban, predominantly black institution stated that he preferred people recruited out of elementary schools. It was his observation that these people were much more concerned about students and how well they learned. They were not "hung up" on their own disciplines. They accepted students as they were instead of lamenting that they were assigned inferior students. These people were student-oriented, and in his judgment that was the primary qualification for effective teaching.

It does seem clear that universities will have to develop preservice programs that place much more emphasis on the facilitation of learning and less on learning more about a narrow discipline.

A growing dependence on in-service education and other methods outside of typical graduate programs will lead to a reexamination of criteria used to determine academic rank and salaries. In-service education could be much more supportive of a community college's mission than more graduate credits in a particular academic discipline. Current practices seldom recognize in-service education, but graduate work, even work unrelated to an instructor's role, is often a basis for higher pay. A few community colleges are giving credit for in-service work, but they are the exceptions.

ACCOUNTABILITY AND MEASUREMENT

Community colleges are confronted with increasing demands for evidence of accountability—accountability to students for appropriate learning experiences and accountability to taxpayers for productive results. Many educators urge cooperation with proponents of accountability. They argue that it is better to participate in identifying significant and measurable purposes than to continually criticize and thus run the risk of having questionable goals imposed upon the institutions.

There are many advantages to cooperating in the selection of the measures and many dangers to doing nothing while asserting that nothing can be done. If the value of an educational activity cannot be demonstrated, critics and others, such as legislators and taxpayers, can reasonably contend that nothing of value has been added and that there is no need to continue supporting the activity.

Measuring inanimate materials is relatively simple. Even the value added by fabricating or processing inanimate materials can be measured with relative accuracy and ease. But measuring the value added during the educational process is much more difficult. Some would claim it is impossible. Although it is unlikely that the consequences of a particular educational activity can be determined precisely, it is possible to test for certain intended results. Initially the measures may be gross, but refinements based on experience could lead to fairly accurate and valid measures. It does seem apparent that some measure of worth will be used by people responsible for appropriating funds.

Community colleges may have to use the deceivingly simple concept of value added where *value added* is what the student obtained of value as a consequence of his education. In some cases this may be the only valid measure. Perhaps it is the ultimate form of accountability because it makes a college dependent on the evaluation of its clients—its students and its community. If the students are dissatisfied and assert that they received nothing or little of value, and if other measures, oftentimes dependent on student responses, corroborate their claims, revolutionary changes in a community college could be achieved.

In the process of ascertaining costs as related to benefits, consideration is usually given to salaries, utilities, supplies, and buildings. In addition, however, there is the obvious human cost. Perhaps the greatest and least-recognized cost is the human cost that can result from failure. Failure can arouse feelings of bitterness, frustration, lowered self-image, and alienation. Failure can lead to the antithesis of developing all human resources. Assigning quantities to the human costs of failure is another complex, if not impossible, task. But it is a cost that deserves more recognition and concern.

What to Measure

Educators are quite familiar with measures of inputs, having used them for years as determinants of quality and bases for granting accreditation. Examples are the academic and experience qualifications of faculty, the amount of money spent per student, the amount of floor space available for each full-time–equivalent student, the number of books in the library, and the intellectual stature of the students admitted, oftentimes determined by percentile ranks on "intelligence" tests and rank in a high school graduating class. These are all measures of inputs, resources that are put into the college, resources that may or may not have any significant effect on how well a college performs.

In the minds of a growing number of people, the determination of how well a college performs depends on its accomplishments, on its output. These people will not accept input information as valid evidence of performance. They argue that the key question is: Given the inputs of certain students, faculty, and other resources, what were the results? Did the students accomplish what was expected of them? Is a community better off because of a community college's activities? Did the students in the career programs acquire the needed job skills and knowledge? Are they performing well in their jobs? How well are the students doing who transferred to other colleges and universities? Did the community services programs achieve their stated objectives? There are many ways to measure output and determine effectiveness. What is needed are clear statements of objectives and criteria that will be used to measure the output. Output is the beginning as well as the ending point because it provides the sign posts and standards that are needed in planning the processes, structuring the organizations, and determining the needed inputs. Output must be carefully and clearly specified in advance if it is to be achieved efficiently and effectively.

Even though the precise measurement of results is not fully possible, it is possible to measure most of the intended and important objectives. This requires the identification of fairly specific learning objectives in advance. Interest in identifying specific, measurable objectives is evident throughout the country. Dozens of colleges have faculty members who are basing their courses on objectives. This is quite a change from the old "lesson plans" that stated what material the teacher would cover, which was often different from what students learned.

Statements specifying the conditions and the level of proficiency required to achieve the objectives provide what has long been needed to evaluate educational activities: objective standards for measuring performance. The learner thus has clear targets and is not forced to "second-guess" instructors.

In some cases objectives may be affective, such as changes in attitudes and personal satisfaction. These are perfectly appropriate for many courses. Although the achievement of these objectives is more difficult to determine, achievement can be measured by using attitudinal scales or simply asking people for their evaluations of their experiences.

Asking students to evaluate their educational experiences is especially appropriate in community colleges. Many students know why they are in community colleges and what they expect to achieve. They can be excellent judges of the value and effectiveness of instructional programs.

Measures of Evaluation and State Control

Because of the institutional flexibility evidently needed for the community college to deal with its assignment, a discernible trend toward greater state control (as discussed in Chapter 7) may be ominous. It does not necessarily follow that more state control will result in inflexibility, but initial steps appear to move in that direction. State laws that restrict faculty assignments and state guidelines that rigidly prescribe the utilization of space limit what a college can do. Inflexibility will be present as long as states focus on input and process variables.

Now that the emphasis is shifting toward measures of output, educators find themselves with the albatross of past practices hanging about their necks. Some state legislators and staff are just as anxious, perhaps even more so, to change the focus to output variables. If educators want to retain flexibility and some control over their institutions, they need to assist in identifying valid measures. In the long run this may be the only way of avoiding complete state control of community colleges.

A COMPLEX ASSIGNMENT

It is evident that the assignment for community colleges is large and difficult. It is also apparent that many changes in views, practices, and standards are needed to effectively deal with the assignment.

There is a growing demand for validation, for evidence that a certain method or medium does work. Several people lamented that there is not enough concrete evidence of how well some of these new things are working.

There is also a need for better mechanisms to share findings, to learn from the efforts of others. One of the clichés is, We don't want to reinvent the wheel. But it does not take long to realize that many community colleges are experimenting while unaware of similar attempts at other colleges. The communications network appears to be improving, but it is an agonizingly gradual process.

My observations are that the signs are good, progress is uneven but evident, and the momentum appears to be building.

SUMMARY

"The concept of the open door and our concepts of college-level work are on collision courses at this college." That was the report I received at one institution, and I felt the same anxiety on other campuses. But, at the same time, I detected the beginnings of new attitudes of responsibility for learning and recognition of the diverse student population the community college is going to have.

The referent is changing. It has to change. The old method of looking at everything in terms of "Is it college-level?" is giving way in community colleges. The new referent is the learner. Is it useful to this particular individual and his needs? is the appropriate question.

This kind of change in thinking, this new view of the assignment, is a difficult thing to achieve. On many campuses I saw hostility developing between faculty members and between teachers and administrators because of their different views of the college assignment.

For community colleges to successfully deal with their assignments, there must be development of a clearer understanding of institutional mission in the ranks of trustees, administrators, faculties, counselors, and students.

The more I saw this need, the more I was bothered by the organization of instruction into departments. These kinds of divisions, and the split of terminal-transfer, occupational-academic, have got to be replaced by programs organized in ways that recognize many different educational goals, all of equal worth.

Community colleges are in the business of developing human resources for the good of the individual and society. They work at this task by helping persons strengthen their self-images and their skills through successful learning experiences.

A variety of new approaches is being recommended and tried. Some will work well and some will not. The search will continue, however, in those institutions that are committed to the mission of helping persons attain their potentials. Society's growing commitment to equality of opportunity, its growing belief that all persons can learn, and its growing demand for institutional accountability require this kind of response.

The problem ahead of us must be recognized. But the indicators are very encouraging. I think community colleges can handle their difficult assignment.

Chapter 6.
The Vocational Education Dilemma

No part of the community college assignment is beset by more confusing eddies about what is respectable and legitimate in college offerings than that of preparing people for employment vis-à-vis (as often perceived) transfer to the university and the bachelor's degree.

Count the votes forecasting trends in the next ten years in community colleges, and a majority favor more vocational-technical programs and a greater range of technical skills developed. Legislators want more students enrolled in these programs. They voted for legislation with the understanding that many young people and adults need job training opportunities and that the state needed a supply of "skilled manpower." Community colleges were sold to sometimes reluctant taxpayers on the basis of providing vocational education. Most administrators, many faculty, people in the communities, and boards of trustees express a strong desire that more attention be given to job preparation. Too large a proportion of the students, they say, are enrolled in programs designed for baccalaureate-aspiring candidates. There are some dissenting views, particularly among recent high school graduates.

DISCREPANCY BETWEEN EXPECTATIONS AND ACTUALITY

What accounts for the call to community colleges to prepare more people for jobs in nursing, law enforcement, electronics, public administration, diesel mechanics, business, and a hundred other fields? Many reasons are given. Legislators may say we can't afford a bachelor's degree for everybody. And educators may assert that not everybody wants or needs a bachelor's degree. Some will point out that technicians and craftsmen in many fields are getting jobs, that employment opportunities exist for people with specialized skills. In that same vein, the role of the institution in *re*training is highlighted by changes in technology, such as in the aerospace industry in Southern California and the Seattle area during the late 1960s or the transition from farming to industry in the state of Mississippi.

State master plans for postsecondary education assign greater responsibilities in vocational-technical education to the community colleges. Economy is often cited in encouraging further development of these programs within an institution that also offers academic options leading toward the bachelor's degree. People assume that the costs to the state are lower for the comprehensive institution compared to that of supporting separate, specialized institutions.

More Students Will Seek Employment

Expectations are high, generally, that the next ten years will see many more students intent upon entering employment after their training is completed in the community colleges. But administrators and other educational planners acknowledge a difficult and perplexing dilemma. Although there seem to be many good reasons why more students *ought* to be interested in occupational education, the fact is that present and possibly future enrollments will show a sizable discrepancy between what educators and legislators think ought to be and what the students will do. Students are often saying, "no thanks." Frequently they prefer to enroll for a year or two, or less, in a program described as academic and which may lead to transfer to the university. But a large proportion will not complete two years; they will not transfer. They leave the institution with destination and whereabouts unknown. The occupational program would have made sense, declares conventional wisdom, but they avoided it.

At least half of the students *should* be in such programs, it was stated frequently, but that percentage was seldom reached. The programs exist; for example, at one institution 60 percent of the facilities were designed for occupational education, but less than 25 percent of the students were enrolled in those programs.

What accounts for the obvious differences between what many responsible people feel *ought* to be and the actual number of students enrolling in vocational-technical programs?

The Prestige Factor

Vocational-technical education and the kinds of employment such programs lead to lack prestige for many people in American society. "Back to the cotton fields." That's the way it looks to some black students. And many of their colleagues of different color seem to share distrust in educational programs purportedly designed to prepare for early employment. One president said he had a "deuce of a time selling hotel-motel management and food processing programs." "They make sense," he said, "they are natural outlets for placement in the area." But the pressures for establishing the programs did not come from the students. They "made sense" to the president. As he saw it, the basic problem was that a poor job of "selling" had been done of the kinds of opportunities available in these industries.

Is "poor selling" the basic problem? Why the apparent distaste for vocational-technical education? A union representative in the building trades told me, "We've got to raise the prestige level of occupations of this kind. The trouble is, fathers will say to their sons, 'I want you to become a lawyer, or a doctor; I don't want you to follow in my footsteps.' " He thought the rapidly rising wages in his field would help some.

I heard other references to attitudes of union members. At the same time that union leadership in the state of Wisconsin was pushing for vocational-technical programs, the rank and file of the unions, according to one of their number, were saying to their own children, "The last thing I want you to be is a plumber." Their children were urged to take the academic programs and to seek the baccalaureate degree.

On the other hand, a college teacher with graduate degrees described her father as a "first generation Polack" who didn't go to school. Her mother went as far as the ninth grade. They told their children, "Go to school, get a college degree." The college teacher reflected, "But now, parents who have gone this route, like I have, think this is not the only way for the success of their children." In general, though, in the minds of many, "success" is associated with the college degree. Anything less is "second class." These perceptions may appear most frequently among those who have been shut off from the social and economic mobility ladders.

Blacks Associate Vocational Education with Menial Labor

Blacks frequently associate vocational education with menial labor. "So often," a black student told me, "you see a mechanic in dirty surroundings. You don't see him pictured in a comfortable home with an automobile and boat. On the other hand, you see doctors and other professionals in nice clean circumstances."

Age and responsibilities may have something to do with these perceptions. A director of evening programs said:

More than anything else motivation gets to be a matter of bread and beans to adults. When they get out of high school and find they are not able to get jobs without additional training, then we find them coming back with motivation greatly increased. The necessity for training is something we can't preach into them when they are younger.

Some fields, however, appear to be attractive. Seldom are there problems in recruiting all the students who can be accommodated in the associate degree program in nursing which prepares technical or "bedside" nurses. And institutions could concentrate upon the data processing field with the exclusion of everything else. These exceptions serve to point up the problem of prestige.

In the words of a community college dean,

Black students want and need jobs which give status and which are also lucrative. The status striving for a depressed group is often more important than economic returns. When the occupations are shown in their true roles with corresponding status and respect, more blacks will be eager to enter these fields.[1]

Critical of the treatment in the mass media of occupational education, she called for community colleges to join with industry in building a favorable image for the occupational fields, one that did not smack of "second class."

The prestige "problem" does not have its genesis within the community college. Clearly, its roots are found elsewhere, possibly in the home. The chairman of a state board of education, who was also a university president, expressed his perplexity about how attitudes

---

[1] "Occupations & Education in the 70's: Promises & Challenges," American Association of Junior Colleges, Washington, D.C., p. 15.

could be changed. He hoped that someone with the Madison Avenue know-how would give it some thought because it was a fundamental problem in making effective their state plans for educational opportunity.

Vocational Schools Perceived as Punitive

Vocational schools and anything that resembles them on a post-secondary level, the way many students and teachers see it, have an image most difficult to change.

"In former years," said one student, "if you dropped out of high school before age eighteen, and if there was a vocational school in your town, you were required to go there. So going to a vocational institution was interpreted as a punitive and custodial type of assignment."

The dean of community services in a large metropolitan community college said that the high schools that concentrate on the occupational or industrial arts programs have the reputation of getting the "dumb" students and students think that there will be more of the same when you talk with them about occupational programs in community colleges. Many comments were heard about high school counselors who, in effect, said to their counselees, "You are not college material; why don't you go to a vocational school?" At least that's the way the students see it. And so people perceive the vocational programs as being for people who can't make it and are kept in custody until they satisfy the age requirements for leaving school. And these attitudes are part of the "baggage" which accompanies the high school graduate as he moves to the community college.

Many Students Are Not Ready to Decide

Large numbers of young students may avoid the job preparation programs, not because they find those opportunities distasteful but because they are not ready to choose educational and vocational objectives. A reason frequently given for enrollment at the college is "I'm here to get my bearings." Students who are undecided find that the relatively low-cost close-to-home institution, approved by society as a legitimate place to spend a few years, offers a chance to postpone what are feared to be irrevocable decisions about what they are going to do. Many students are not ready to make the plunge. The world of vocations is confused and complicated. It is difficult to find out what the options are and what the future might be if a given route of development were followed. There is apprehension about making mistakes, getting into a "dead-end street," or investing some years of effort and then finding out that they prefer some other vocational field.

If a student enters a curriculum in automotive technology or nursing or law enforcement, specialization begins early in the game. He has to declare his commitment to a program. However, in the usual lower-division transfer curriculum he can engage in academic exploration, and the pressures for decision making are not as early or insistent. There are large numbers of undecided students in the transfer programs. Many of them will not transfer, at least not at the end of two years. But this fact is not inconsistent with the notion that the community college curriculum should provide reasonable opportunity to students to sample various areas of human experience and, with the help of good counseling, to establish goals.

Thus a good deal of uncertainty is expected. However, the task of effectively preparing students for employment after two years or less of education calls for earlier decisions. It is in this necessity that there sometimes exists an aversion to occupational programs. The "aversion" may be that the student is forced into decision-making before he feels ready to decide. Planners of occupational programs are urged repeatedly by students to try to reconcile the understandable need to teach the skills requisite for early employment with enough flexibility in the program so that the student does not find himself unnecessarily boxed in as his learning continues and goals change. Surely this is a worthy objective. At the same time, decisions cannot be postponed indefinitely, and no one has found a way to provide complete protection from the consequences of choices that turned out to be less than satisfactory.

Information about Options

The high school graduate comes to the community college and is confronted with a broad range of educational programs from which he has to choose. Chances are he has received some information in his high school days about four-year college programs, their requirements, and their characteristics, but the odds are against his having learned about postsecondary programs that prepare for early employment. College catalogues are available in the high schools. They present information about the college programs in the academic language which high school guidance and counseling personnel are accustomed to speaking, having come out of that environment themselves. The materials are easily available. However, information about occupational programs which require less or different training than the baccalaureate level is not as readily available.

The field presents difficulties to the counselor because of his lack of firsthand experience and the tremendous variety of programs, some of which represent recent developments and are in the process of change. Furthermore, many high school counselors appear to be overloaded, and it is difficult for them to keep up with information sources. And, occasionally, they have been described as "not oriented to the community college."

A big city community college invited high school counselors to the campus so that occupational programs could be interpreted. A career newsletter was published and distributed on a regular basis to neighborhood centers where young people and adults gathered. Counseling centers were established in various communities. At another college, this one in a rural area, high school counselors were brought to the campus for a two-week period to acquaint them with the college offerings. But there was more involved than college briefing papers. They were taken out to the hospitals to observe the training requirements for nursing. They were taken to food processing plants, to hotels and motels, to insurance offices, banks, and department stores so that employment opportunities and skill requirements could be observed and understood. The college paid the high school counselor for the two-week program. Established only five years ago, this college now works with a network of high school counselors who know the institution personally, who understand the demands and attractions of many occupations in their area, and who are able to interpret to their students educational and vocational opportunities other than those of the traditional four-year type.

It Is Easier to Establish a Transfer-oriented Institution

Another possible reason that community colleges give more attention to academic transfer programs than to occupational education may be found in the view of administrators that it is easier to start an institution with what is, in effect, a packaged curriculum determined largely by university transfer requirements. The programs are likely to be standard. Faculty members are readily available and prepared for this kind of teaching task. However, if an institution begins with an occupational base, local needs must be studied, employers contacted, and faculty trained. Seldom is it possible to find teachers who are suitably prepared by the state university.

Presidents said it was often necessary to find people with the desired personal traits who had been successful in their trades and to train them for teaching. Other problems in the occupational programs include the cost of equipment and the threat of obsolescence due to rapid change in technology. Furthermore, to occupational educators the requirements of accountability appear to be more stringent in their field. Success is measured in the forthright terms of getting jobs for the people trained—jobs related to their training. Follow-up studies are common and revealing. "On the other hand," commented a dean of occupational education, "the state university graduated 600 people in various teaching fields and to date only 25 of them have been placed. If that happened in our institution, they [the state board] would close this place down for us."

Occupational Programs or Academic Transfer Curricula First?

To evolve toward comprehensiveness, is it preferable for the institution to begin with emphasis upon occupational programs or the academic transfer curricula? Since it is not common for community colleges to open with a complete spectrum of offerings, this question is raised frequently. Financial limitations and the need for detailed information about the clientele to be served require priorities to be set for the initial programs in the college.

The state of North Carolina has chosen to develop comprehensive institutions on a vocational-technical education base. Several competent observers in that state, as well as in Wisconsin and other states, were sure that there was value in this approach. It is a good thing, they felt, for the original orientation of the institution to be toward students who have objectives different from the academic or university world. The stance of the college from the very beginning has been one of respect for and interest in students of this kind. Faculty are appointed who have the capacity to relate well to these students; moreover, most of them have worked in other than just the academic fields. A variety of programs, vocational and technical, is provided in recognition of different student interests and ability levels. And perhaps of major importance, the institution is basically "self-directed." Students may transfer to a four-year institution, but that is not their primary purpose for being there. They are preparing for employment. In that process many are taking mathematics, physics, chemistry, and other courses which are similar to those of students in the lower division of the university, but neither the programs nor the students are aimed at the universities. Rather, the four-year institutions, after becoming familiar with the programs at the community college, note how similar some programs are to their own and consequently give academic credit to the community college students who decide to transfer.

I think that if a community college has opportunity to choose its antecedents and if that institution is intended to be comprehensive, with occupational education as a respected part of the operations, then to start with an occupational bent would provide a good boost in that direction.

And this conjecture leads to another surmise: what if the community college concept was based on the assumption that most students would not transfer? What difference would it make in terms of faculty and student morale and measures of success? I am not suggesting that the possibilities of transfer be ignored, but I ask what would be the effect of concentrating on students who would be placed immediately in employment as a result of training. Most community college students do not transfer to four-year institutions.[1] A program that spotlights the transfer students could be run quite differently from the way it would be conducted if it concentrated on these other functions. Perhaps frustration would be less and faculty and student morale would rise.

The Comprehensive Institution Is a Relatively New Development

It is too soon to make conclusive judgments about the capacity of the community college to "do right by" occupational education. In some states the comprehensive approach was adopted only recently. For example, in 1964 there were only seven occupational programs in all the community colleges in the state of Iowa. Since 1966 more than eighty programs have developed. In Texas, a state considered a leader in the community college field, as late as four years ago the oldest junior college did not have any vocational programs. Their development in Texas was held back to some extent because only 60 percent state-level funding was provided as contrasted with 100 percent support for the academic programs. That picture is changing now and there will be no distinction in funding between the academic and vocational-technical courses. In Washington, another leadership state, new legislation has resulted in the absorption of the

[1] David S. Bushnell, *Organizing for Change: New Priorities for Community Colleges*, Chap. 5, McGraw-Hill Book Company, New York, 1973.

technical institutes and the postsecondary vocational schools into community colleges. The comprehensive community college with emphasis upon occupational programs is relatively new, therefore, in that state, and once-disparate educational elements are still in the process of coming together.

The state of Mississippi began matching federal funds to build facilities and matching other appropriations for expansion of occupational education in the community colleges in 1966. Only since 1964 in that state has there been any vocational education in the high schools except for the traditional home economics, agriculture, and distributive education.

Similar moves toward the comprehensive concept have taken place in a number of other states during the same period. It is not too much to ask that more time be provided for the difficult process of accommodating in one institution educational programs that not only have been separate traditionally but also have been characterized by perceived differences in caste, class, and social worth.

Does the Training Pay?

Are there jobs at the end of the training program? If there are, then are the rewards greater as a result of the additional training beyond the high school level? Students ask these questions. In some places a serious deterrent to interest in occupational programs is lack of provision for a person who has completed a two-year postsecondary program, for example a teacher's aide, to be paid any more money than someone with no training beyond high school. This is a problem in other fields. Until there is recognition in the form of additional pay for people who have taken additional training, the paraprofessional fields, as they are sometimes called, may lack attractiveness. The United States Civil Service recently classified job levels and requisite training to take into account the associate degree for salary purposes. But there is still need for a change in business, industry, and the health professions nationally so that the role of the semiprofessional is recognized. Pay scales should relate to various levels of training.

It's not just the pay that bothers students. They wonder if the college is training people for jobs that do not exist or do not exist in the form that the training implies. Materials and techniques are constantly changing. Are the colleges keeping up? Are industry and business involved in program development and placement of graduates? A former community college student in industrial electricity who returned to his college as an instructor was not enthusiastic about the relevance of occupational programs. "We are training students in jobs that don't exist or will not exist after their two years of training," he declared heatedly. He charged that the coordinators were not doing a good job in relating to industry and in their research into the needs for training in the area.

And there is another question: How much can one institution do? How many programs of quality can it provide? Perhaps the resources of a college limit the breadth of its services. If that is the case, said many students, let the college level with us. Tell us honestly what it is able to do and what it cannot do.

Whether the colleges deserve the criticism voiced here is not the important question. Many do not. This report, however, deals with perceptions of people. Perceptions affect behavior. Student perceptions of vocational-technical programs will influence them toward seeking opportunities for fulfillment offered there or in rejecting them for other avenues of learning which may be less appropriate and productive. So the questions raised should be heard and dealt with.

TO DEAL WITH THE DILEMMA

Educators and taxpayers have reason to be concerned about the discrepancy between the numbers of students expected to enroll in occupational programs and the smaller numbers who do. Why be concerned? Some reasons are obvious: skilled manpower may not be prepared for society's complex tasks. And the tone of our national life could be affected negatively if large numbers of college graduates are unemployed or underemployed. But of greatest importance are the possible adverse consequences to the student himself.

Opportunities for self-fulfillment and economic gain may be bypassed because of a false interpretation of the worth of vocations that do not require a four-year degree for entry. Some of the responsibility for a shoddy interpretation of occupational fields may be attributed to professionals within the educational community. Counselors, parents, employers, and teachers, however, need to acknowledge a common responsibility—the illumination of a broad range of educational opportunities as effectively as possible so that all students can make choices appropriate to their own objectives and resolves.

Education Will Include Employment Preparation

Changes in the patterns of formal education are now anticipated. There is a concept slowly gaining acceptance that learning should be lifelong and that educational opportunities should be available to an individual at any point during his life when the need and interest exist. The educational program may become more intermittent with employment experience or travel or national service. Larger numbers of people may move back and forth and into and out of education. Consequently there will be a mixture of adults with young people in our colleges. Reference has been made previously to this development. Combining job experience with the college experience will become more common. Career education, or occupational education as it has been more commonly known, will be viewed as part of the total educational experience for the individual, not as an alternative to secondary or higher education. Education includes preparation for employment.

Trends suggest a meld of education and training. For example, there are moves in the economy toward more service-type jobs and away from production-type jobs with the consequent need for emphasis upon personal, social, and communication skills. The president of an urban community college with a predominantly black enrollment agreed. "Technical training must be combined with liberal education in community colleges," he asserted, "in order to develop citizens who can think creatively and critically about the society and form proper standards of taste and judgment in connection with the culture around them."[1]

If students are going to be taught to "think critically and creatively about the society," does this mean that they will be required to take social science and English 101? Many enrollees in occupational programs told me they were sick of taking the same old high school courses over again in psychology, English, and health. They said these were boring and repetitive.

Students preparing for early employment often lose interest if they are required to take academic programs. They want to get to their destination as soon as possible, and the destination is a job. But in some states courses of this kind are required of all students. Accrediting organizations add fuel to the fire, in the eyes of some instructors, by emphasizing general education to the point of discouraging occupational students and reducing the effectiveness of

[1] "Occupations & Education in the 70's: Promises & Challenges," American Association of Junior Colleges, Washington, D.C., p. 35.

the training programs. They cite the difficulties in meeting general education requirements and at the same time preparing someone for job entry as a qualified employee in the limited time available. Federal programs have their effect, too. In some cases, community colleges, set up for the purpose of providing programs in vocational-technical education with arts and sciences as a "sideline," find that unless they are either accredited by a regional accrediting association or a candidate for accreditation, they are not eligible for certain federal funds.

Apparently a quandary exists. How does the institution meet general education requirements of federal agencies and regional accrediting agencies, minimize in the student's load those courses that the student feels have little meaning or utility, keep the student's options open as long as possible to go to work or transfer to the university, provide learning experiences toward informed citizenship, and prepare for early employment in a specialized field? Can it be done in two years or less? Only one satisfactory response can be made to these questions. The community college does not have to do everything, and everything does not have to be done at one time.

Other Institutions Play a Role

There are other institutions in most of the states that offer specialized programs to prepare for employment. Area vocational schools, publicly supported, exist in large numbers and have a rapidly mounting interest in postsecondary programs. Tensions exist in some states between the area vocational schools and community colleges as the latter expand their work in occupational fields. However, in other states the community colleges have been designated as the area vocational schools. The resources and common interests of these two types of institutions must be harnessed. Where the vocational schools exist and meet needs for job preparation at the postsecondary level, it would seem wise for the community college to avoid duplication.

Another kind of institution trains for employment—the proprietary school. Although the place of these profit-making colleges has been a matter of controversy, their potential in meeting significant national needs must be considered.

In the Commonwealth of Pennsylvania, according to a recent statement,[1] business and industry have looked at the proprietary

---

[1] Warren D. Evans, "State Recognizes Specialized Training Schools," unpublished paper, Pennsylvania Department of Education, Harrisburg, Pa., Jan. 27, 1971.

schools as valuable sources for trained manpower because these institutions have developed programs especially tailored to its needs. Students have enrolled in the programs of these schools because of the immediate career entry possibilities. The state board of education in 1969 established regulations for the approval of programs of proprietary postsecondary institutions. Students completing programs are entitled to receive either the degree of associate in specialized business or the degree of associate in specialized technology, depending on the orientation of the program. General education is the dividing line between these schools and a nonprofit junior college, a community college, or the first two years of a four-year college or university. The latter institutions require this part of the curriculum to have a liberal arts orientation. The more specialized proprietary schools require a minimum of 25 percent of the curriculum to be courses intended to support the area of specialization. Pennsylvania is one of the first states to give recognition to the proprietary segment of postsecondary education and the programs in technical or semiprofessional training. Also it is the first state to mandate an evaluation procedure in order for a proprietary school to obtain degree-granting privileges.

In a number of states I was told that the proprietary institutions would play a larger role, and in some cases discussions were under way which could lead to these institutions contracting with the public institutions to provide some services.

Community College Is Not a Panacea

The entire educational and training job does not have to be done at one time. I have referred to the probability of intermittent periods of education and job experience. If entry and exit arrangements can be established to facilitate the learning program of the student, some objectives can be deferred to another time. At some colleges there was talk about "front end load curriculum." Translated this means a program that emphasizes the occupational, that is, readies people for employment. At a later time, then, I was told, "You can throw in the humanities and general education." It even could be assumed that the individual, if properly conditioned and stimulated at college, could carry on his own reading program in the humanities or history or the arts after he secured employment.

At another college there were no semester requirements. The person could move at his own pace and "plug into" a program at almost any time. Manufacturing technology offered one example. A certificate of completion is given which, in the estimation of my interviewees, was more valuable than a diploma from the standpoint of job placement. An objective is to make it possible for the individual to move through the program as rapidly as he is able. In a number of institutions there was talk of the need for "mini" and "micro" units. A mini course in physics, for example, would relate specifically to preparation for an occupation, with the assumption that the student would be able to take further work in physics when there was a reason for it. It was estimated that in an inhalation therapy program no more than 30 percent of the usual physics courses were germane to employment entry; hence the mini course.

If the college had to do the complete teaching job and do it at one time, the tasks would be impossible. However, learning is not limited to the college setting. By linking to other learning experiences, and by making available to the individual learning resources as he needs them throughout his life, the specific task of meeting the student's immediate requirements while he is in the college becomes feasible. Some faculty members were aware of this and contended that there was a tendency to underrate students.

At an institution in Appalachia, a dean declared:

> We talk about these kids out of the hills; but they are well informed, and we must upgrade our estimate of student capabilities. They are more aware of the impact of the present. They are keenly aware of issues like pollution and drugs. They are alerted to these developments through TV specials. They hear them on the radio. They look around.

He joined others in recognizing the absence of a college monopoly on learning experiences. The college doesn't have to do the whole job.

Knowledge of Occupational Education Needed Earlier

Students ought to know something about occupational education long before they enter the community college. In several states children in the early grades, kindergarten in some cases, are learning about occupations. In the state of Illinois, for one, field experience is provided so that children, who seldom have opportunity to see how their fathers and mothers are employed, can become acquainted with ways in which society's tasks are accomplished. Programs continue at the freshman and sophomore levels in high school. Obviously the intent of these efforts is to develop in young people from the earliest years some understanding and appreciation for a variety of occupations in a postindustrial society where home, school, and work have become compartmentalized and separate areas of experience.

Toward Understanding within the College

How can the college itself bring together in a community of mutual understanding and respect the faculty and students who represent such apparently diverse objectives and fields of interests? The arrangement of facilities can help or hinder the process. At a west coast college, persons going to the educational resources center, and almost everybody does, pass a building with large windows that provide a view of the diesel technology shop. People slow down and take a look. The equipment is impressive. Surely a student who can plumb the mysteries of these technological beasts of burden has something on the ball. At another college, a shop for furniture repair is next to the counseling office. Students with growing interest in handicrafts and antique refinishing watch intently the labors of their colleagues. The results of this kind of exposure are unifying.

The economic pinch has resulted in a coming together of students and faculty in occupational and academic programs. A reduction of specialized courses has occurred. Mathematical programs for electricians are less often taught by electricians than by mathematicians. English teachers are teaching technical writing. Some resistance to these developments was reported and some anxieties expressed. "The mathematics department doesn't want technical math," I was told, "and the English department doesn't want to teach technical writing." Instructors in the occupational fields wanted assurance that the English, mathematics, and science instructors had an appreciation of the needs of the vocationally oriented students. Difficulties were acknowledged and apprehensions expressed, but the need to reduce splintering of personnel and programs was a common concern.

The college schedule is sometimes an inflexible and demanding taskmaster. It is difficult for students in the occupational fields to rub shoulders with those in the academic areas because of the traditionally large time blocks around which their work is organized. For example, in drafting or automotive technology three-hour sessions are common. Students were not able to suggest precisely how it could be done, but they wondered whether somewhat shorter periods would encourage enrollment in some courses by nontechnology majors even if it were no more than a student taking a class on how to repair his own automobile. Some pushed this position farther. Would it not be a good idea, they asked, for all students to take some occupational program? If certain academic courses are considered essential for all students, why shouldn't some kind of vocational-technical experience be justified as part of a common educational program? At an independent junior college something like this was being done. All students were required to engage in some form of creative production or performance. Many had never created something of their own or faced an audience. The faculty reported, "Students grow when they have an opportunity to do this sort of thing."

It will be done in many ways, and just how is not clear, but I believe the search is on to join the academic theory and application, the abstract and the tangible, the scholar and the craftsman. Perhaps in this process is found a basic difference between the occupational programs of the community college and those of the more specialized institutions.

Expectations are frequently voiced that occupational programs will have more appeal in the future. The reasons given may appear somewhat contradictory. The first is pragmatic and materialistic: jobs are available in many fields of technical and vocational specialization. The jobs pay well. The training period is two years rather than four. Consequently the paycheck will come at an earlier date.

The second reason is related to the values of the "counterculture." The anonymity and impersonalism involved in mass production are repudiated. The creative expression of the artisan and handicraft worker is respected and admired. Perceptions may be changing toward a greater appreciation of the work of the farmer, carpenter, mechanic, and chef. Vocational programs could possibly have a new respectability for the children of the GI generation, a generation of first-time college goers clearly bent on economic and social mobility with education as the means.

The Real Dilemma

Is there really a vocational education dilemma? What is the true meaning of what appears to be a negative attitude toward occupational education and the apparent attraction of academic fields and the bachelor's degree?

I suggest that basically the dilemma is in the mind of the student who faces an environment pressing him to decide—to determine his educational program—his occupational objective. What should he do? What will he take? Where will he take it? When will he take it?

He is uncertain. He wants to hedge his bets, to keep his options open. How can he do it? What are his chances of moving within an educational institution if he changes his mind, finds out what he thought was good is not for him? How can he make the move to another institution if that seems advisable? Where does he go for job information? How do college programs and job possibilities connect? How do his public school experiences and postsecondary work come together? What relationships exist among the educational institutions that will serve him in his postsecondary experiences throughout the rest of his life?

Put the pieces together and you begin to see the real problem—the need for reciprocal relationships among educational and training institutions and the world of employment so that the person emerging from the schools that served him through his youth is able to take his particular place in society. At the present time our society's approach is fragmented, competitive, and institutionally oriented. The student is the victim, and the institutions suffer because they are attempting to serve some individuals at the wrong time or for purposes that could be better accomplished by other agencies.

Some clues to the situation described here can be found in the sincere interest and mature motivations that frequently characterize people enrolled in evening programs in community colleges. On the other hand, many recent high school graduates are uncertain in their objectives and lack motivation for further educational work. The community college appears to be a kind of automatic extension of the twelve years of schoolwork already taken. Perhaps other learning experiences at that stage would be of greater value. But the question is, what kinds of experiences? And how do you move into them and back into education or employment when you are ready?

I am convinced of the need for a social instrument which could bring together the now separate streams of work and education and which would provide an organized way to relate those educational institutions that offer a variety of services and environments to the potential student so that information and counseling could be readily available.

Troubled by a growing dissatisfaction with piecemeal efforts to link school experiences to college programs, I was delighted to read an article by a former dean of the College of Education at Arizona State University in which he described effective transition of youth and adults from school to society as "an important and long-neglected social responsibility." The president of the university introduced me to the article as we spoke of the respective roles of community colleges and the universities in his state. It was asserted by the author that the transitional problem is not being adequately met by any single educational institution or social agency. He proposed that the junior college in Arizona become a community guidance center and "guidance and counseling of youth and adults be accepted as its primary and pervasive responsibility." He further suggested that "educational programs would continue to be developed and offered to meet the needs of individuals who have discovered through systematic guidance and counseling what their needs are." Among the services to be provided would be assistance in job training, in placement, and in finding other suitable experiences. These services are proposed:

1   Accept on transfer and maintain an active register of all secondary school graduates and school leavers until age twenty-five.

2   Assume as a primary task the assistance of youth for several years after each has left school with a comprehensive program of educational and occupational counseling, placement, and follow-up service. Some youths would be placed in part-time or full-time employment almost immediately. Others would enroll in the junior colleges or in other educational institutions part-time or full-time and remain for months or years.

3   Provide youth seeking admission to other educational institutions the full use of the guidance services in selecting institutions, planning programs of studies, gaining admission, seeking scholarships or other financial aid, arranging for living accommodations, and planning for recreational and other extra-curricular activities.

4   Assist youths seeking full-time or part-time employment to utilize the coordinated placement services of the guidance facility for help in initial occupational placement and in becoming participants in recreational, cultural, and community service activities.

5   Make continuously available to unemployed youths the counseling, placement, and follow-up services of the guidance program. The placement and follow-up services of the junior college would coordinate, or at least be in touch with, all job opportunity and employment programs at the community level and be fully informed of state and national programs.

6   Assist adults who are seeking further education or training for upgrading and advancement in employment or retraining for new employment to use the opportunities and services offered through the educational and training programs of the college and the guidance, counseling, and placement services.

7   Conduct follow-up and other types of research studies designed to evaluate, strengthen, and improve each of these essential guidance services.

8   Develop an expanded guidance facility and program to serve as the central agency of the community for coordinating the activities of public and private social agencies, service clubs, special organizations, task forces, and the Office of the U.S. Employment Service. Such a development could result in a united and cooperative community effort to serve youths and adults in the entire field of

educational, occupational, and personal planning and enable them to adjust progressively to life as citizens and workers.[1]

The author maintains that the demand for additional education and training beyond the secondary school and proposals for extension of universal educational opportunity beyond the high school point to the junior college as the most likely unit of the educational system to discharge what he describes as a "fundamental educational obligation."

Whether it be the community college or not, an integrated service to fill this need in our society should be made available to individuals as they experience the frequent transitions that a rapidly changing society makes inevitable. Perhaps the community college ought to provide this service. Some of the tasks specified are now attempted but without full acknowledgment within the institution or by the community that they are essential and appropriate. One thing is clear: education, training, and occupational experience have essential relationships which have not been fully examined. These relationships will be more productive and benefit both the individual and participating institutions if the transition from school to society is given the attention it must have.

SUMMARY

The public has been led to expect that the community college will provide comprehensive educational programs, including occupational education. Educational planners have seen such programs as a part of the community college's purpose. Social, economic, and educational factors all indicated that this made sense.

But, for a variety of reasons, there has been a discrepancy between what made sense and what actually happened. The main reason appears to be that prospective occupational education students have needed more information and more time for decision making.

To be entirely realistic we must acknowledge again that even the educational planners and the educators themselves have not yet developed all the information needed about occupational education programs in community colleges. This is on the work list of things that must be done. But, comprehensive community colleges are still relatively new creations in some states, and it will be several years

[1] H. D. Richardson, *Developments in Counseling*, College of Education at Arizona State University, Tempe, Ariz., pp. 24–25.

before the necessary experience and data about the advantages and problems of offering occupational programs and academic programs in one postsecondary institution will exist.

Several things can be stated, however. One point is that community colleges will undoubtedly have a key role to play in postsecondary occupational education programs, but they should not try to do these things that can be done just as well, or better, by other kinds of institutions, such as some existing technical institutes and the proprietary institutions. Another point is that occupational education in community colleges will probably enjoy greater success as the colleges are able to design curriculum content, admissions requirements, and calendar schedules in such a way that the immediate needs of prospective students can be served. This means breaking away from some traditional forms and procedures. But, it seems clear that seeking "academic respectability" through these traditional routes is not going to get us where we want to go. Rather, the name of the road we want to travel is *service*. If we can truly structure our occupational education efforts to serve the needs of the students, then the related problems will be easier to solve.

Part 3. Changes in Organization and Governance

Another conflict seems to be rising. It is the tendency of the state to centralize control. At the same time there is growing recognition by the community that this is indeed a community college. So there is a collision coming.   A Board Member

Chapter 7. Who Calls the Shots?

Who decides? Who calls the shots? Who will determine what students should be served by community colleges, how many students there can be, how much tuition they will pay? Who will determine the educational programs and learning strategies utilized? Who will establish teaching load and salaries? Who will determine the buildings to be constructed, their architectural style, and their location?

In his autobiography Lincoln Steffens describes a technique he developed for getting at the people who make decisions:

> I went to the newspaper offices, one by one, all of them, and I hit upon an approach which I have since used on all subjects—business, politics, reform. . . . The question I framed for the newspaper offices, as for the city, was directed to find the boss of the paper. Calling with my card at the editorial office, I would ask the office boy: "Say, kid, who is 'it' here?"
>
> "Why," he would answer, "Mr. So-and-so is the editor."
>
> "No, no," I protested, "I don't mean the front, I mean really."
>
> "Oh, you mean the owner, that's Mr. Blank."
>
> Feigning disgust and disappointment, I would say, "The owner, he's only the rear as the editor is the front. What I mean is, who's running the shebang? Who knows what's what and—who decides?"
>
> "Oh," he would exclaim—whether he was the office boy, a reporter or an editorial writer—his face lighting up with the intelligence faces habitually conceal—"Oh, the man you are looking for is—Nut Brown."[1]

[1] Lincoln Steffens, *The Autobiography of Lincoln Steffens*, p. 402, Harcourt, Brace and Company, Inc., New York, 1931.

The locus of decision making is the locus of power, the capacity to determine what will be done. Historically, boards of trustees, locally elected, joined with the president of the college to resolve such matters. A look into the future, however, reveals a more complex picture with a possible shift of power to administrative levels far removed from college and community.

There are many who would be party to institutional decision making. Among these are students, faculty, administration, local boards representing the community, state-level community college boards and similar agencies, coordinating boards for higher education, the legislature, and the governor's office. What is the forecast of their relative influence on the policy directions of the college?

Probably more of the decisions affecting the goals and priorities of community colleges will be made in the state capitols. The state legislature, the governor's office, and state agencies will play an increasing part in shaping the future of these community-oriented institutions. The move toward greater state-level power comes at the same time as a rising demand at the local level for the college to be more quickly responsive to community needs as well as to broaden opportunities for participation by faculty, students, and community representatives in goal setting and program development. The result is tension and struggle for decision-making authority among parties on the local scene and among those on local and state levels. Dominant among the state-level forces, in the eyes of most interviewees, will be the state legislature, which shows not only increased interest in educational matters but a new consciousness of its own role and responsibilities.

THE STATE LEGISLATURE

The 1970 session of the California legislature was the longest in history—229 days plus a 3-day veto session—and concern with education helped make it so. A near record number of measures was introduced—5,139. The governor signed 1,628 bills and vetoed 77. The office of chancellor of California community colleges prepared analyses for more than 800 bills which concerned education and other subjects of interest to community colleges. Some 200 measures received close attention and were supported or opposed with testimony and efforts to voice community college concerns.

State legislators are increasingly getting into the nitty-gritty of college operations, whether justified or not. Many feel they ought to call the shots—as representatives of the people—on all the issues. The chairman of the senate finance committee in one state told me that two universities were "crosswise" with his committee because the committee was asking for a master plan for capital outlay. The universities contend that they are constitutionally autonomous.

"They can be as constitutionally autonomous as they want to be, but they are not going to get money from us," he said. "They can be as constitutionally autonomous as they can afford to be."

In the same state the 1970-71 legislature established a minimum of fifteen contact hours per week for community college faculty teaching load. Hours were also specified for the state colleges. The legislature took further action to fix tuition in the community colleges. Previously the rates had varied throughout the state.

Surprise for College Personnel

The move of the legislature in setting the minimum contact hours apparently was close to a complete surprise to community college personnel. They became aware of developments almost after the fact.

In commenting on problems in the community college field, a legislator said, "Up until this last year we have let them go their own way pretty much on funding, but now we have written in minimums and maximums in tuition." He also expressed his concern with presidents who, in his view, want their institutions to become four-year colleges. "This we will discourage," he said.

I asked a president what his reaction was to the legislative determination of minimum contact hours. "There have been pressures by a few of the unions down toward twelve hours, so we did not resist the legislation although we didn't really like the idea of the legislature doing that." He described a problem now before the state in that some community colleges have contract arrangements with faculty based on the twelve-hour load. At the present the contract is honored, but what will be done in the future is uncertain since the contract provisions are in conflict with state legislation.

Who will determine faculty load? The state legislature or the community college district?

The head of a state-level coordinating board for higher education said that people in the legislature are "much concerned about community college growth. They feel that it is coming about without state guidelines or standards." He thought that "there is a hell of a fight coming" because people in that state will guard a kind of local control and autonomy but that more state control is inevitable. He looks for increased questions from state legislatures about facilities:

Some people feel that these colleges have a country club setting with a large campus, lots of space, and fancy facilities. One of the colleges began to bring on severe negative reaction with a kind of "astrodome" or some damn fool thing. The idea was to roof over a stadium, but right or wrong, this created a mind-set in those people who make decisions at the state level—the governor and others.

Salaries Are Another Bone of Contention

"If the local communities are going to pay big salaries up beyond what the state colleges are going to be able to do, the legislature will look at the support patterns," said the coordinating board chief, raising another problem. "They will look at the pay with regard to qualifications."

According to his figures, 50 percent of the faculty members at the state colleges hold doctorates. Of the faculty in community colleges 9 to 10 percent hold doctorates. So his question was, "Are you relating pay to qualifications for the job if community college faculty are paid more than state college faculty?"

I asked whether he was equating qualification for teaching with a doctorate. He replied that it was a matter of tradition. In the state, he asserted, people still pictured the university at the pinnacle with the state colleges somewhat lower down and the community colleges at the base. The reward system is expected to conform to that kind of pyramid.

Who decides what salaries will be paid in community colleges and how compensation relates to qualifications?

"Why," I asked a state legislator, "is there such an obvious interest in the legislature about education, and how do you account for the apparent similarity in developments among a large number of the states?" He replied:

The governors are meeting more often. They are serious about their work. There were thirteen governors knocked off during this last election, and to a great extent the reason seemed to be higher taxes for education. Also they have noted that a large percentage of unrest among the taxpayers has to do with educational issues. So the key word now is *accountability*, and they are going to look at education as it has never been looked at before. There is a taxpayer revolt, and we must be as alert as possible.

Politicians are much more interested in education than they used to be. The smoke on the campuses has had something to do with that. This has had a dramatic effect upon the legislators. Also there is the effect of negotiations. At the present time, only at the local level do the teacher organizations have negotiations rights, and there is fear in the local school boards about the future.

The governors are beginning to see that they have to reorganize so that the 30,000 teachers of this state, for example, negotiate with a state-level agency, or they will bleed each institution white.

He looks for statewide salary negotiations with perhaps a 10 percent corridor, as he described it, for more affluent counties. Negotiations would not be conducted at the local level with local boards but on a statewide basis between teachers and a state-level agency.

For whatever reason—the costs of education, unrest on the college campus, the rise of collective bargaining—state legislatures are demonstrating a keen interest in education from preschool through the university. Moreover, there are changes coming about in the legislatures themselves which have further implications for education and other state services.

The Trend to Beef Up Legislatures

A trend is apparent in strengthening state legislatures. Office facilities are being added and staff services expanded, including legislative reference services to examine the impact of legislation and fiscal services to ask questions about the impact of legislative measures. Salaries have been raised. Through redistricting in the states, legislators bring different socioeconomic characteristics to their tasks.

I was told:

There is an increasing number of young Turks, very bright. They want data. The staff of the legislature has been expanded and is making educational decisions. Salaries have been increased, and legislators need to justify that increase. The legislature is going to have much more to say about what the state is getting for its investment in higher education.

That the legislature is going to have much more to say is an assumption widely shared. However, it runs head on into strong convictions about the value of decision making at the local level:

"This board has a position with regard to local board control. We are in favor of maintaining it. We want to be able to determine who comes to this institution, the curriculum, the budgets, and the staff. We feel that this is the only way to really take care of local needs." This board feared that moves toward major financial support at the state levels would mean a kind of state control "which would be overbearing."

Concerns about the marked shifts of power toward state levels are many and acute. A state director of community colleges was troubled that legislators and other officials tend to look at the budget, not at the mission of the institution.

"They can cut the budget and distort the mission. The basic question seems to be What is it going to cost? not What is it that you are trying to do? or What needs to be done?"

The same official referred to another matter which has stimulated some anxiety among state officials, the rapid growth of community colleges. "Our enrollments will be doubling over the next ten years, and I know that this will scare the devil out of them."

It is conceded by community college personnel that in the past, with local control, it has been difficult for state-level planners to secure comparable educational data for purposes of evaluation and policy development. Now the questions are, How can such information be made available without establishing patterns of uniformity and standardization which discourage creativity? and How can vanguard institutions be encouraged to build on their strengths?

The Big Demand for Accountability

"There is going to be a great demand for the principle of accountability," said the president of a large institution. "I do not object to this as long as it is put in educational and nonpolitical terms. I am concerned, however, that at the present this has great political overtones. Legislators are talking in terms of output-input ratios and productivity figures. I am wondering how the legislature will define those terms."

The quality of the deliberative assembly will be crucial to community colleges. In some cases a large turnover has occurred in membership, and new personnel appear to be less than well informed about educational matters. It was alleged that they seem more interested in their own collegiate institutions than in the overall state program of higher education.

And another factor asserts itself, the frequently declared independence of the legislature from the executive office. In a leading state, legislation had been introduced to strengthen the state board of education in its planning and control responsibilities, but the legislature appeared reluctant to approve a move which in effect might tend to reduce their powers and strengthen the power of the governor to whom the state board of education is responsible.

A recitation of elements which enter into educational decision making would be incomplete without referring to the state in which it was proposed that an upper-level university similar to the Florida pattern be established. The institution would not offer the first two years of the college program because a well-established community college already existed in the area. Reaction in the state legislature and from the area under consideration was: "We want a football team—a good football team. We want a stadium—a stadium suitable for the university team and for professional football. So we want a complete university, not just part of one."

STATE AGENCIES

"California junior colleges have been insulted." "This is the most frightening thing I have seen." "What the hell are we going to do about the board of governors?"

Heated comments dominated a meeting of community college presidents. The object of their displeasure was a work program proposed for the staff of the chancellor of the California community colleges. The chancellor serves as executive officer for the board of governors, a new agency created by state legislation in 1967 with power effective in 1968.

Uncertainty reigned as questions were asked about a possible requirement that courses offered by the college be approved first by the state-level agency. Would it be courses or programs? All programs or just specialized programs? Is the board to be an approval or a service agency? Does it have a leadership role? What will be the powers of the chancellor and his staff in relation to the authority of local boards and administrators? California community colleges, with a long tradition of local control, sensed a threat from Sacramento.

The functions of the state board and the chancellor's office were not specifically indicated in the 1967 act. However, basic areas of responsibility were identified:

It is the intent of the legislature that the Board of Governors of the California Community Colleges shall provide leadership and direction in the continuing development of junior colleges as an integral and effective element in the structure of public higher education in the state. The work of the board shall at all times be directed to maintaining and continuing to the maximum degree permissible local autonomy and control in the administration of the junior colleges. . . . Commencing on July 1, 1968, the Board of Governors of the California Community Colleges shall succeed to the duties, powers, purposes, responsibilities, and the jurisdiction heretofore vested in the State Board of Education, the Department of Education, and the Director of Education with respect to the management, administration, and control of the junior colleges.

What Is the Role of the State Office?

It was the working out of those specifications in a detailed way which was leading to the apparent unrest and concern voiced by the administrators. Prior to 1968, state-level responsibility for community colleges resided inconspicuously in the state department of education.

The fifteen members of the new board are appointed by the governor. Repeatedly, the chairman of the board declared to me that the state board should not in any way dominate the local boards, that the local boards ought to be the primary locus of responsibility and control for the community colleges. He looked for leadership to continue to come out of the local institutions.

It is the chancellor's view that the board was established not only to support community colleges in Sacramento but also out of the legislature's desire that a state agency oversee its legislative stipulations. An example of this is the 1967 Construction Act which called for 10-year master plans which are updated annually. Since facility plans have little meaning without relation to educational programs, the effect is a requirement that 10-year program plans be updated annually.

Regardless of statements from the chancellor and the board to the contrary, there is widespread apprehension on the part of administrators and local board members that power will be centralized in the chancellor's office. They expect increasing state control, more power over what they can build, the equipment they can buy, and how they staff the institutions. When a new facility is proposed, not only does the board of governors appraise it, but also the department of public works and the department of finance do. Several years may pass from the time of identifying need for a building to completion of construction.

In another state a president reported a trend toward centralization at the state level.

Almost nothing was written down at the state level a few years ago, and you could do almost anything. Now new programs have to be based upon local surveys with participation of advisory committees, approval by the local board, then approval of the curriculum by a commission at the state level and finally by the board of higher education. Recently I had two programs that were tabled briefly by the board of higher education, and I had to conduct a kind of seminar with the board on what a community college is all about, before these programs were approved.

State-level community college officials say they are pressed by the governor's representative and by other agencies to look more closely at the details of community college budgets and proposed programs. They have a sense of mandate from the legislature. "We may not want to do this, but we are forced to." Comments from one state seem generally representative.

> The matter of construction and approval of new buildings used to be pretty much of a rubber-stamp operation by the department of education. Now there are examinations of the preliminary drawings, equipment lists, etc. The department of state planning gets into this because they look at all proposed buildings from the standpoint of general state planning. This agency reports to the governor. Also, the department of general services gets into the act. They are concerned with the architectural and the engineering facets of the building plans.

An increased flow of power toward the state-level community college agency, often under pressures from the state legislature to ascertain what is happening in these institutions, elicits mixed feelings from presidents and local boards. A stronger voice in the state capitol is sought, for purposes of legislation and appropriations. At the same time, misgivings are expressed about state-level leadership that might encroach upon local decision making: "We want more status for community colleges at the state level and broader services. We have not had the quality of personnel to do that job. On the other hand, maybe we are lucky if we are left alone."

Community Colleges Will Not Be Left Alone

But community colleges are not going to be left alone. Budgets are too big for that, and generally they become a matter of more than local concern. As enrollments rise and costs go up, the search for funds leads increasingly to the state level. The state wants to know what it is getting for its money. The legislature has little desire to deal with dozens of community colleges. It will look to a state agency as its point of contact. The quality of that agency will be of critical importance in maintaining a constructive tension between local and state forces. State-level leadership is required which has high respect for the capacity of the local institution to identify and respond to community needs, a leadership which exercises its authority more through persuasion than through regulation and seeks full discussion and involvement by those who will be affected by policy determinations.

A professional leadership is required which talks the language of the community college field and is at the same time sophisticated in matters of finance and legislation, which are the business of state capitols. To operate by the book, to want the same things at one college as at another, is to yield to the ever-threatening rigidities of bureaucracy. Frequent utilization of ad hoc advisory groups and people who can be pulled in from their institutions for a short time to work on problems could help keep the waters fresh and broaden the process of involvement.

The profession of state-level community college administration is relatively new; with a few notable exceptions, it is a product of the past ten years or less. With a shift in locus of power toward the state and with the consequent tensions already mentioned between local institutions and the state, plus the often competing interests commonly found in state capitols, expertise of the highest order is needed for difficult and complex administrative tasks.

BOARD POWER

I listened to members of a community college board discuss the future of their institution. The way they were talking, I told them, one would assume that they felt they would have a great deal to say about the direction in which the college would move. "You are damn right," they responded. "We don't need people in the state capitol or in Washington telling us what to do." "It is a bunch of egotists like this that contribute toward the inability of this state to come up with a master plan for higher education," the chairman of the board declared. "It is great to have more financial support without surrendering your power. But, can it really be done?"

Are boards surrendering their power? Developments in state capitols may indeed hold implications for future board policy determinations. What I see happening though, even in the face of possible limitation of power, is more active exercise of board authority than previously has been the case. The threefold adage about the president—the board is to hire the president, support him as long as it can, and then fire him—which at one time allegedly described the major role of the board, will not hold true.

Reports of student dissent and protest, whether at the local institution or not, plus community concerns about the tax dollar have resulted in mounting pressures on local board members. Constituents are asking questions. They want answers from the board. People who in former times may have enjoyed the honorific aspects of board membership are compelled now, in their own defense, to have up-to-date, comprehensive knowledge about the institution and its programs. Another reason for stepped-up board interest and participation is the number of educational matters now adjudicated in the courts. The board, as the legal entity for the institution, is involved whether it wants to be or not.

Actually, the community college board member is a relative newcomer to a field of activity long occupied by public school boards of education and the regents and trustees of the college and university world. Not until 1967 did the community colleges in the state of Washington have separate boards, distinct from high school district boards of education. And in Illinois the process toward community college boards was given impetus under the higher education act of 1965. Until 1969, Florida institutions were under county boards of education with community college advisory councils. In Maryland, county boards of education had jurisdiction until recently. The same thing would hold true for other large sections of the country. So, in fact, the identity of the community college board member has been established in a number of states not much more than five years ago. Add the fact that 200 to 300 new institutions have been established during that same period of time, and the result is several hundred new trustees seeking to determine the suitable role of the community college board as well as their own responsibilities as members.

A State-level Community College Board Is Created

At the same time, another new entity, the state-level community college board, was created in several states: California, Arizona, Illinois, Washington, and Maryland, to name only some. Now there is a problem of sorting out respective responsibilities and authority between state and local levels. There will be more state-level boards, for reasons given previously. Local boards are apprehensive that this may mean decreasing community orientation and the capacity to respond easily and quickly to local needs. Where local boards exist, often there is a strong sense of community loyalty and faith in the merits of localism.

In seventeen of the twenty states included in field visits, the pattern of local boards existed. However in Tennessee, Massachusetts, and Virginia there are no local boards, or they are used in advisory capacities only. Where administration is predominantly under a state-level board there are recurrent calls at the local level for a means by which the different needs of community college areas can be recognized. Constituents ask for a mechanism by which the state board can be held accountable to each community college area as well as to the state as a whole.

How to Appoint Board Members?

One matter at issue is the process by which board membership is determined. In places where board members are appointed, that arrangement seems to be favored, although a question long debated but not answered is how to keep politics out of the appointments. In one state where the governor appoints, his designees are ostensibly recommended by the senator from that area sometimes with support of a local political committee. People in the community, it is reported, frequently wonder what the "payoff" is for. Not much respect is noted in the college community toward the board. One of the governor's choices indicated that he was not looked to by the community as someone to participate with others in developing policy but rather as a "prod" to get things done. If a student who flunked out of the university wanted to get into the college, the board member was called upon by the parents to put in a good word for their son. In his position, people in the area gave little thought to the policy-making responsibilities of the board but suggested to others, "If you have a problem with the college, call up that guy Fisher, and he will fix things up for you."

The president of this college reported direct contacts by board members with college administrators and faculty in order to have favors done. Interviewees reported a tendency for the board to "get involved in every detail." Are the characteristics of this board a function of the system by which members are selected, or are there environmental factors to consider? The director of the community action program for the area described political action in that county as "very direct and sometimes very messy." He did not think you could eliminate politics. His advice: "You can't afford to have vested interests in your job as college president. You make the decisions you think are best, and then you get grabbed by the political arm. You need to have other expertise so that you will have something else to go to."

In another state, three board members are appointed by the governor and six by the county commissioners. The rationale given for gubernatorial appointments has to do with the state's share of financial aid to the institution. The board chairman in this case favors the appointive approach and believes there is a difference between elected and appointed trustees. "If you are elected you have some sense of obligation to those who elect you and you are probably more aggressive with regard to your stance toward administration."

A leading industrialist commented on the makeup of that board: "In the beginning they seemed to be quite ordinary people. They had not been greatly active in city affairs, but they turned out to be superb and dedicated to their tasks."

He felt that the appointments had been good, and he would favor this kind of appointment by a local body (county commissioners) rather than by either the governor or popular election.

And in still another state, a board member appointed by the governor saw the governor as being too far away from the local situation. He wondered if at least one of the five board members could be selected by local people. At present he feels that the local people "have no say." He added the comment that a Republican governor seems to select Republicans as board members, which certainly isn't surprising in this era of political influence and power.

In several states where the common practice is for board members to be locally selected, governors are revealing a new interest in making appointments of at least part of the board based upon the larger share of the financial load carried by the state. In those states where costs are met by state, local district, and students, the question is bound to come up of whether this line of reasoning would lead toward student representation on the board.

Board Behavior Varies

To anyone taking a national look, board behavior shows remarkable variety. This may be a phenomenon of the particular political modes of state or region. One element of difference is the degree to which authority is delegated to administration. Faculty members in an Eastern college said that they could not understand why seven political appointees to a board that meets five hours per month need, apparently, to make all the decisions. The president, they said, must have authority delegated to him. They reported additionally that during the past two years there had been almost 100 percent turnover in the board. They were concerned because they had a salary package coming up for consideration which represented a great deal of work on their part. And a new board member, one who had not attended any previous sessions, was to be at the meeting. The faculty were of the opinion that he knew nothing about the college and its program, but he might cast the deciding vote. There must be a better way, they said, of selecting board members and relating the board to faculty and administration.

I sat in on a board meeting in the South. There were no

students, faculty, or community representatives present, just the
president, a few administrators, and a newspaper reporter. Among
brief presentations made to the board was a college "master plan"
required by a state-level agency. The president asked an administrative assistant to make the presentation. Posted on the wall were a
number of drawings to show placement of proposed buildings. No
questions were asked about program planning which might have led
to the determination of the facilities or their placement. The college
gets "points" toward possible federal grants if a master plan is
approved by the board. Among the facilities described were a new
administration building, a gymnasium, wings on the technical
building, and parking lots.

At the close of the presentation the president commented: "In
addition we will need to provide some program material and a little
later on some examples of how we are serving the disadvantaged."
One board member asked, "Do you have an estimate of the number
of students we can handle with those facilities?" The president
responded, "Well, we haven't got that yet, and of course this plan
can be changed as we get closer to doing some of the buildings. Also,
it will make quite a difference if we can get the youngsters to come
in the afternoon. Now all of them want to come in the morning."

A motion was made to accept the presentation as a master plan for
the college. Elapsed time: fifteen minutes. Obviously, board members in these two institutions did not have the same views about
delegation of authority to the president or policy responsibility of
the board.

Who Speaks for the College?

Who speaks for the college—the board or the president? is a related
question. In one state, board members from two institutions who
were elected by their constituents likened elected board members to
the office of United States senator. The president of the college, they
stated, has a role similar to that of the administrative assistant to the
senator. As they see it, the community college president is to the
locally elected board as the administrative assistant is to the senator.
And so who really speaks for the institution? Is it the senator or the
administrative assistant? Is it the board member or the president? It
is the board member, they would say, for it is their view that they
operate under a mandate from the citizens who elect them.

But in a community college located in a large city in another state,
the chairman of the board said the institution needs a strong
president. He needs to be looked to as a leader. He did not for a

moment agree with the definition of the respective roles of trustee and president described above.

Board members need understanding of what goes on, and it seems that there are so many high-priority crises. Just as you are about to get to some kind of an evaluative look, another crisis changes the priorities. Curriculum, for example, does not get to the board. By the time we hear about it, all the processing has taken place, and it is just presented for adoption. Answers that we request seem to get lost in the computers. So we really don't quite know the score.

He was not expressing bitterness, but almost wistfully seemed to be saying, "We would like to know a little more about some of the really important matters, and one of these is program, and another is students. Yet we spend most of our time on buildings and crises."

The call for more board time on institutional purposes, goals, and evaluation of policies was sounded in a number of places.

One trustee commented:

Five years ago we had kind of a "ho hum" board, but now people have found that one of the ways to get things done is by being militant, and this is the kind of approach they make to the board. Without this kind of pressure, unfortunately, the board would probably not have gone as far as it has gone in responding to needs.

Other comments were in a similar vein:

Waves of community concerns and feelings wash over and through the college.

Constituents call you up and want to know what is going on; you have to find out. You had better know.

In former days the board would appoint the president and keep hands off, but no longer. We need to know what is working and what is not working.

Frequent reference was made to the "review and evaluation" function of the board. After a board approves policy recommended by the president, they want to know what the effect has been of the policy adopted.

Board Power Is a Fascinating Anomaly

A trustee in a paper on board power described the "fascinating anomaly" of a group with almost absolute authority and responsibility de jure, which has almost no authority de facto. He maintains that

the legally vested power is greatly restricted by (1) a dependence upon administrative and faculty expertise which results in boards ratifying the decisions of others; (2) a lack of basic inside information about the operation and ideological direction of the institution; (3) a tradition of delegation of authority for administrative and curricular decisions which determine the basic character of the institution.

Much of the current faculty, administrative, and student attack upon governing boards has its seeds in the board attempt to recapture authority over college affairs commensurate with the legally established responsibility imposed upon the board.

He proposes that if the board is to effectively exercise its power as a legislative body developing policy and evaluating college practice, it must be properly staffed. He further maintains that a board member should consider it his responsibility to criticize judgments on "educational matters" which do not jibe with his view of the social obligations inherent in the community college.

To even suggest that the board have its own staff for review and evaluation and not rely entirely upon the president's staff is so contrary to administrative mores that a former president trembles to see the words appear on paper. Nevertheless, evidence is substantial that the legal responsibilities placed upon those boards of trustees which function in an environment of rapid, sometimes revolutionary, change will require them to be more involved in the conduct of the institutions than generally has been true in the past. The press for tax dollars and consequent demand for more accountability by institutions to the funding sources further commits trustees to a knowledge of goals and performance that cannot be achieved by simply reading college brochures, the president's annual report, or even the usual college budget. But the need is not for boards to do the president's work, but rather to insist upon the exercise of its own full legislative authority with the support of an executive who is equally clear as to his role.

Board members should be prepared to deal with change, so that when change is forced, it is probed for its possible values rather than dealt with as a threat. A board needs to develop a sense of past and future and the capacity to perceive issues in a conceptual framework so that they are dealt with other than on an incremental basis, from crisis to crisis. They need to understand the frustration of community groups who find it impossible to deal with the Pentagon or even state colleges and universities because of the insulation of layers of administration and control, but who will exert their power to get things done at the local level because the community college board is there. The local board fulfills a principle long honored that government should be as close as possible to the place where action is taking place. In many parts of this country change will be demanded.

Will the board use change creatively and constructively to come up with wise policy?

Board Responsibility Grows

In many metropolitan areas and other large community college districts, boards may carry responsibilities for several colleges or campuses. The multiunit district organization has evolved largely during the past ten years. It has the value of broadening the financial and population base so as to make possible a greater diversity of educational programs. Moreover certain economies are gained through central purchasing, financial administration, facility planning, and computer operations. Now, board members are facing many questions about this organizational form. The board and district administration are perceived to be far removed from some of the communities. Students say, "Each campus has to be able to adjust and accommodate to its own service area. It has to be alert to those factors in its primary service zone and adjust to those. It cannot have the district establishing or superimposing a system to make these campuses duplicates of each other. Each campus must be unique." Students and faculty show impatience with layers of administration. And citizens claim the district board is distant and remote from the real local problems that the students and community face. A common charge is that the board is not truly representative of some communities. Board members themselves are wondering what kind of organization it takes to move effectively in districts served by several college units.

One big-city board has committed itself to an examination of alternative organizational patterns. Under consideration is the use of appointed councils or committees called college community boards. Each college in the district would have an appointed community board which reflects the communities and neighborhoods of the college both socioeconomically and ethnically. In effect, these community boards would be interposed between the existing district board of trustees and the colleges themselves. At the same time, the district board makes clear that it will not abrogate its legal responsibilities. It will continue to review those matters which it is charged by law to consider, ratify, or reject. The board has further declared its interest in "furtherance of creative state legislation that permits even more effective means of achieving genuine community control and participation by the citizens and students that the colleges are philosophically committed to serve."

Other concerns are voiced about district organization, about its capacity to make decisions that are timely and take into account the individuality of the various units. There are calls for a greater degree of independence among the units. Change is described as more difficult because of the complexity of the district operations. Faculty asked for more campus autonomy so that action could be taken more quickly when such action is indicated. "Bringing about change here is about as hard as moving a pyramid," they claimed. "And if X campus gets electronic pianos, then Y and Z campuses must have them."

Approximately three-fourths of the community colleges recommended by the Carnegie Commission for establishment during the next ten years would be in metropolitan areas. There is continuing need to clarify responsibilities of district administration in relation to unit administration and to determine what functions are most suitably decentralized.

FACULTY POWER

Faculty members are seeking more power in the governance of community colleges, and there is general agreement among board members, administrators, and faculty that this constitutes a trend. How far this trend should go is a point of disagreement.

Community colleges do not have the tradition that the locus of power is in the faculty. It is not uncommon for change to be initiated by the faculty and sanctioned by the administration in four-year colleges and universities. This is not so in community colleges. Administration is often strong, forceful, and aggressive. Faculty members appear to be awaiting directions from above before responding to critical problems of curriculum or learning strategies. Furthermore, divisional chairmen have been appointed by the president. Frequently college councils tend to be advisory to administrative personnel, with administrators possessing the right of veto. These practices are changing.

What accounts for the change? The reasons are many. Among them is the social mood which challenges authority. Another factor may be the recruitment efforts of faculty unions. Perhaps the age of community colleges has something to do with a more aggressive faculty stance. The pace of development in the initial years of a new institution offers little time for other than the tasks immediately at hand. In institutions now several years old, faculty are aware of developments beyond their classrooms and laboratories. The frustration of working with students for whom the usual instructional strategies fail may also prompt the teacher to insist that the ways of the institution need changing. And another element may be the fact that some administrators invite participatory forms of administration.

The Faculty Want a Greater Voice in Decisions

Whatever the reasons, faculty members are asking for a more definitive voice in what is decided. They suggest the need for a climate which would encourage people to participate more, to exchange ideas, and to experiment without a defensive reaction from the administration. In a large institution described by faculty and students as autocratic, the longtime chairman of the board opined that the next president will have to be more responsive to faculty. It is his view that faculty should feel that they can be heard but that they should not make policy decisions. "Perhaps," he said, "we should even ask them for their ideas and consult with them more."

Acknowledging exceptions, I have a distinct impression that many faculty members to whom I listened feel that they are not involved in determining the educational philosophy of the college or in shaping its program. They report that recommendations by which instruction could be evaluated, for example, were rejected out of hand by administration. After participating in the development of salary schedules, faculty found little attention given to their work and that the president still evaluates with regard to merit. "We spend our time on things which the administration rips up in five minutes, something we have taken five months to do, and they don't really tell us why."

In several states, the desire of faculty to be directly involved in policy making has led to action by the state legislature. For example, in California the establishment of faculty senates is mandated. In Washington, Michigan, Pennsylvania, and New York, among other states, professional negotiations acts have been passed. In the state of Washington, faculty described the act as granting them the right to organize and negotiate with the board of trustees on policy decisions.

Before the negotiations act was passed, the faculty found themselves in the same position as students are now finding themselves in, the position of noninvolvement in college decision making because no law protected their right to bargain with the board of trustees. Feeling they should be directly involved in policy making, teachers organized politically to achieve their rights.

Presidents expect further movement toward faculty unions, although in only three of the twenty-five institutions I visited was a faculty union recognized for bargaining purposes. However, this number corresponds to the percentage of institutions nationally which engage in collective bargaining. As indicated in a previous chapter, the patterns and procedures of collective bargaining were thrust upon community colleges when just a handful of people in the institutions knew anything about negotiations, arbitration, and mediation. The effect was stress between the adversary parties which still remains intense in some areas. Without judging the issues in conflict, I can describe concerns that bear upon the question of who will be influential in determining the policies and program of the college.

Administrative personnel have described as "ridiculous" demands by some unions for a faculty load of no more than twelve student contact hours. They maintain that if faculty push for higher salaries and reduced teaching loads to the exclusion of other financial needs in the institution, then the faculty is indeed "calling the shots" with respect to what students can be served by the college and how they are served. It comes down to a matter of money. It is further reported that in some places counseling services, learning laboratories, and community services have been cut back in order to meet the financial costs of the union contract. The chairman of the negotiating team in a Northwest community college was aware of this problem. He believes that the choice of who is to represent the faculty is critical with regard to negotiations. He does not favor an outside negotiator. He asserted that you need someone who has a stake in the institution because teachers may be willing to forego some money if the funds are to be used for another good purpose within the institution. He wants the president to represent the board. On the other hand, a number of presidents say that negotiations are extremely time-consuming. One had spent several months trying to come to agreement on a contract and urged that someone other than the president should lead the process, for if the president does, he will have little time to do anything else.

Are Faculty Concerned with "Bread and Butter" Issues or Big Issues?

It is conceivable, unless faculty are attuned to the purposes of the institution, that agreements on salary and working conditions could reduce the resources needed by the college in order to serve all its students. And this raises another question. Where faculty members are responsibly involved in policy and program development, are they inclined to push for contract levels that jeopardize other essential services of the institution? Do faculty concentrate on the "bread and butter" issues when they do not have a sense of responsibility for broader matters? A director of community services responded in part to that question: "A major reason why faculty have not accepted either the diversity of function or the community centeredness is that they have not been involved in developing these goals and directions in any kind of significant way. They have not been placed in a position of either sharing in control or in responsibility for decisions."

There are indications that unless personnel of the college can reach a level of accommodation which enables the institution to pursue its goals, the bargaining might take place between the faculty unions and a state-level agency, or the legislature itself could determine salary and load. In Chicago, where the twelve-hour student contact load has been adopted, there are reports that the legislature is "ready to get into the act" with a bill which would specify class load and the number of hours an instructor is required to be on campus. As reported earlier in this chapter, similar legislation has been adopted in other states. In fact, state legislatures could supersede in those matters now covered in master agreements. As one dean expressed it: "You could take care of all of your bargaining problems with the faculty by just handing them a copy of the state law." He said that probably this would make things easier for the administrators, but he was opposed to it. He did not want the state capitol making determinations of this kind.

In contrast with his views, however, is the situation in another state. Bargaining began two years ago, and agreements were worked out on an institutional basis. The presidents favored that approach. Now the majority of them are interested in turning the process over to the state because "we are whipsawed by negotiations conducted by each institution. We don't have the time to work on these things, and we feel the state is obliged to find the resources to fund the agreements."

Looking to the future, I found general agreement not only that the faculty of community colleges should be more involved in those decisions that affect them and their work but that such participation was likely to occur. The nature of that participation is of crucial importance in fulfilling college purposes. For the faculty member is in direct contact with the student, who is the focus of all efforts of the college. Plans, programs, and administrative structures all have their ultimate expression in student-teacher interaction. Will the organized power of faculty, which is taking a variety of forms throughout the nation, be utilized predominantly to make secure the place of the faculty member within the institution? Or will it have broader reach toward institutional goals? If the latter, it will not be enough to develop a deeper understanding of respective roles of faculty, board, and administration, nor to achieve greater skills in relationships. Beyond these, new patterns of organization may be required which are more suitable to the ends specified above.

STUDENT POWER

Characteristics of the local culture rather than a national student culture or movement seem to affect the degree of involvement of community colleges in institutional decision making. For example, in California students are organized in the California Community College Students Association with a paid executive director and a legislative program. They have equal representation on the Board of Directors of the California Junior College Association along with presidents, trustees, and faculty. A student sits with the Board of Governors of the California Community Colleges and has a voice in their deliberations. Many institutions provide for student participation on councils and committees. In one college, the curriculum committee is made up of eight faculty members and seven students.

Yet, in another state, members of the college board reminded me that they were all appointed by elected officials and that they are not ready for unions or for students to "run the college." They agreed that the wise administrator will consult with others, but they felt that there would not be any marching on their campus. "Our students are close to their church, to their family, to their friends, and their parents would not permit this kind of behavior. They are serious about getting an education, they have a good Christian background, and they are not going to cause trouble."

In another college there had been some discussion about a student on the board. With some heat the board chairman addressed the student making the appeal saying, "You want to be on the board? I'll help you prepare a petition. You run for board membership the way I did."

Although there are a growing number of community colleges where student participation exists, I found that student desire for a voice in the operations of the college was often perceived by the board and sometimes by administration as protest or disruptive dissent. On the other hand, there was acknowledgment that the right to vote at age eighteen represented a recognition of maturity which suggests appropriate involvement and consultation with students.

Students point to the difficulties of getting more than a comparative handful of their number interested in a say about what is done and how it is done. In some cases where the college senate has provision for student participation, it is reported that attendance by students has been "unbelievably poor." "At the council meetings and other committee meetings you tend to see the same people, faculty and students, carrying the responsibilities." Students say that it is a problem of finding the people who have the time. Faculty and administrators, they point out, are paid by the college and devote all their time to the college, but students have other demands upon them. For example, many students have full- or part-time jobs. With a commuting population it is hard to get people together. Some students seem to get involved only on a crisis level and then their participation has a negative quality rather than one of ongoing constructive participation. That only 5 to 6 percent of the students are really involved in student government is a frequent complaint. They have jobs and families. They come to college two or three days a week and have to leave in order to get back to the job or back to their homes.

The student government president in a large community college said: "You need to remember that we have a 70 percent turnover each year, that only 30 out of 100 students entering the first year are back the second year, so there is a real problem in continuity. We still have some people who break their backs to participate."

Is Student Participation Only Window Dressing?

Where student representation does exist on boards and committees, occasionally an element of cynicism is encountered. Is this just "window dressing"? Or is the student sitting in a peer relationship with those who respect his judgments and wish to draw upon his experience in determining policies and programs? "We have made gains in the structure but not in the process," is the way reservations are sometimes expressed. With regard to the board:

They seem to listen, but they don't really seem to hear what we are saying. They don't take into consideration what the student says, and then the administration simply states that, after all, this is a board responsibility or the responsibility of administration, and this is the way it has to be.

Students describe this means of closing off any further consideration as a "cop-out."

There is a widespread view by students that "deans and administrators don't really trust students." On one campus there was the incident of the rocks. A large supply of decorative rocks was used in landscaping the new campus. Somebody became nervous about the proximity of the rocks to the vast expanse of plate glass used in the newly completed buildings. The insurance company apparently joined in the concern. Trucks were brought in, late one night, to move the rocks. The president of the student association said that he heard about this some two days later and that it was embarrassing to have students ask him about it when he didn't know it was going to be done. He said, "If they had just said, 'look Bill, we are taking the rocks out, and we would like you to know about it in case anybody asks you.' "

In an institution where an all-college senate has been formed, students report that students and faculty are working together and in "the right direction." They were quick to say, however, that they could not recommend their system for every institution. The system, they maintained, needs to be relevant to the institutions.

Our college has the idea of change. We have an open-mindedness upon the part of administrators and students. We don't know whether the college senate will work, but at least we can try things out. This concept has failed in some places. But if students are not given power, they don't learn responsibility, and they move out into community life or into the world of jobs without the capacity to exercise initiative and responsibility. This is not living.

To what extent will students call the shots in community colleges? The answer will vary according to the social and political makeup of the area which the college serves. In view of the goals sought by community college students as well as their other characteristics previously described, I think it unlikely that they will seek to "run" the institution. It is true that they possess an ultimate "weapon" in that they can decide whether to enter the college or not and for what kinds of programs they will sign up. However, this element of choice may be limited if society continues to demand postsecondary training as a qualification for employment and if alternative educational or training opportunities are not readily available. Most important, though, is a basic question of whether the community college is viewed as an institution designed to process academic products, or of whether an important goal of the college is involvement of faculty, administrators, and students in a learning process not limited to the classroom which encourages participation, interaction, and shared responsibility. If the latter is the case, then goals of learning such as self-management, ability to relate effectively to others, and capacity to exercise initiative and to assume social responsibilities can be realized by exploiting the learning opportunities implicit in the total operation of the college. And not insignificant is the residual benefit from sharing in appropriate discussion with other participants in policy making: commitment to implementation of ultimate decisions.

A community college seeking to carry out a program of this kind faces numerous obstacles. Among these are the great range of ages, broad spectrum of educational and vocational interests, differences in motivations, and a commuting student and faculty population, as well as the factor of student transiency. If students are to be more involved in institutional decision making, administrators and board members will need to encourage that process. Contravening forces are better organized to condition the directions of the college and hence possess more relative power. No great change is expected with regard to "student power" in the community college unless deliberate measures are adopted by the college to encourage that development.

POWER VIEWED IN PERSPECTIVE

Continuing tension exists between the need to meet statewide higher education requirements and to leave local institutions free to pursue their own educational objectives. As this issue is viewed in its proper perspective, it is not a matter of either/or but one of trying to carve out the appropriate role for each decision-making body to ensure that the public interest is met, scarce resources are allocated optimally, and those affected by the decision-making process (e.g., students, faculty, administrators, and taxpayers) have an appropriate role in shaping such decisions.

A division of labor should exist among those responsible for the management of local institutions, those at district levels, and those at state levels. The task at the local level is to identify needed resources and implement programs specified at the district level. The district-level task is to differentiate and specify the roles of its institutions. And the statewide agencies' major task is to specify the goals and priorities for districts so that statewide needs are adequately met.

"Their College" Needs Local Control

The mission of the community college will be more difficult to maintain as it is further removed from local control. To accept some shift in control as a fact of life is also to acknowledge the care required to ensure that within future structures the basic mission is not altered. There is value in local control. Decisions should be made as close to the source of action as possible. Local people usually have a feeling of what the community needs. A quick response is possible. Impetus for growth and change in postsecondary education in several states has come as a thrust from the community college. There has been enthusiasm and excitement. People feel it is "their college." There has been a sense of local involvement, local autonomy, and pride. To move more and more responsibility to the state levels might smother feelings that are important to the quality of community life.

On the other hand, what kinds of decisions need to be made at the local level for the institution to be truly community-centered? How often does the rhetoric of being responsive to community actually mean responsiveness to local politicians or powerful interest groups? How does the local institution pull itself up above the borders of its own district to take a look at the larger environment as it shapes its program? What does community control mean in a time of increasing mobility and social and technological interdependence?

A competent observer reported to me that when the Head Start Program was initiated in some Southern communities where local control was largely in the hands of parents, they tended to emphasize the conventional wisdom that academic orientation was to be stressed for their offspring, e.g., the development of reading skills. The program quickly deteriorated in terms of its ability to serve the needs of children effectively. At the other end of the continuum, the lack of awareness of what educational skills are needed in a complex technological society leads some groups to stress practical skill development to the detriment of an open, more liberally oriented learning experience.

The influence of an agency external to a community may be salutary in attacking problems at the local level. State regulations and standards are frequently cited by administrators to the board or to the community in support of measures considered essential—in building construction, program development, or conditions of faculty employment. A university president spoke to me about this kind of need in response to a question about the educational mission of his institution.

The key point is this. Does anybody think that I can really write a charter for this institution? That I can make a break? We need some external group to say some of these things. There are endless constraints on an institution as a whole to try to get a clear role definition vis-à-vis the role of other institutions. This really needs to be mandated externally. I know that this is heresy, but that's the way it is.

A state has responsibility to its citizens to see that educational opportunity is provided to all. If local control appears to lead institutions in directions that are contrary to this goal, then the state must exert its influence. With what appears to be an inevitable move toward a greater proportion of financial support from the state, state agencies will appropriately exercise review and evaluation functions. They will insist upon coordination of institutional effort and high-level utilization of educational facilities. In the words of a legislator, "We want the state community college agency not to make the colleges alike but rather to give some assurance that they will be different."

Clearly there is need for overview, coordination, and rational decision making at the state level. At the same time there is need for local involvement and for decision making at the local level. The problem is to combine the best of these ideas. Strong state involvement, strong local boards, and a strong presidential system promise a wholesome pluralism with checks and balances.

SUMMARY

A great deal has yet to be determined in the nation's community colleges on who will make the decisions about who enrolls, who teaches, who pays, and who governs. The makeup of the curriculum, the extent of the services to the community, the number and locations of colleges—these are decisions that must be made every week which shape the institution. The decisions are being made. But the number of persons involved in the decision making is getting larger, and the proper role for each participant is still being defined.

The picture varies from state to state and from college to college. But the trend is for increased involvement by state-level officials, most notably the governors and the legislators and agencies set up and acting under their mandates. The reason for this increased involvement is the mounting investment the states are being asked to make in community college education. State officials want to know, and must know, how state funds are being spent. Review of educational programs at this level can be advantageous. The kind of coordination that prevents unnecessary duplication and promotes efficiency and cooperation within a state can benefit the institutions and the public. A key element here will be the development of a new kind of professional: the state-level administrator who understands community college education, the educational needs within his state, and the political process in which he works and possesses the abilities to facilitate sound growth and development.

On the campus there is more participation by trustees, faculty, and students in decision making. Who calls the shots in this milieu is certainly an open question. Changes in local decision-making structures are taking place because of new developments such as collective bargaining, growth of multicampus districts, and the increasing maturity of the student body. The end results of these forces and their effects of governance patterns remain to be seen.

There is an increased willingness on the part of the traditional policy makers, the presidents and the board members to accept the idea that all groups affected by a decision should participate, to some degree, in the decision-making process. If for no other reason, this modus operandi is being adopted because it helps ensure that the decision will become operational after it has been made. This same pragmatism will no doubt govern in the period ahead as there is probing and testing to find appropriate roles and degrees of involvement for all the participants in decisions affecting community colleges and the persons they serve.

Part 4. Shifts in Financial Support

What the state is willing to pay for is going to have a lot to do with the kinds of programs that are going to be offered by these institutions. A Community College President

Chapter 8.
Who Pays
the Bill?

Americans are being called upon as never before to pay for the high cost of government, for the accelerating costs of living. They find themselves taxed to feed and clothe the poor on the one hand and to support war on the other. The educational sights of the people have risen as schooling and going to college have been equated with the attainment of the good life. But Americans have had to pay for it. And they are being asked to pay even more bills with the growth and expansion of the community college.

For community college services, like other services, require funds—heavy support. The money has to come from some source. That source is usually the people.

How much financial support can community colleges expect if they offer the services that are needed? Where will this support come from? Who will pay the bill?

"Of all the problems we face, finance heads the list," asserted the chairman of an ad hoc state committee for community college finance. Just over 30 percent of the financial support for operating budgets of the community colleges in his state comes from state-level sources.

It is the same in other states. Primary reliance is on revenues from local property taxes. For community college administrators the local property tax, which often requires a vote of the citizens, is something close and concrete compared to the more nebulous federal taxes.

On the other side of the picture, the local taxpayers, while declaring support for the community colleges in the area, voted down increased levies for the operating costs of the institutions as well as for new facilities. They are becoming increasingly vocal in their protests about mounting taxes from all levels of government.

Inflation complicates the problem. It has taken 5 to 10 percent more money each year just to stand still, and society's expectations of community college services require that more be done than that.

With a tax rate related to assessed valuation, another problem appears: the rate of increase in the assessed value of properties is leveling off in many areas. And so there is little available to meet the higher costs incurred through inflation and demand for more educational services.

Community college personnel look with ever more critical eyes toward the public colleges and universities, 80 percent state-supported in some states. For although they utilize all permissive taxes, still things are getting tighter. Questions have been raised about what the institutions can afford to do.

"We may have to limit enrollments, and I'm not sure we can afford the open-door policy," said a Pennsylvania college official. "One of our districts has turned down the proposed budget; another passed it very reluctantly."

The only hope he saw was for an increase in tuition. But he wondered if that happened, whether it would be possible to fulfill one of the stated missions of the college, service to the financially disadvantaged. As he spoke, I noted a newspaper on his desk and the front page story: Philadelphia schools were closing down because they had run out of money.

PROBLEM OF INSUFFICIENT FUNDS

The problem of insufficient funds does not stem from just deficiencies in local property tax revenues. Community colleges in the state of Washington abandoned local sources of funding in 1967. But according to spokesmen for the state board of community colleges, proper arrangements were not made for replacing those funds. The community colleges in that state faced severe economic problems. Funding would be cut to the bone. The four-year institutions were similarly affected, but their financial stringencies compounded the problems of the community colleges, because limitations in enrollments at the four-year institutions resulted in pressures on the community colleges to pick up the slack. The result? The community colleges would be hard pressed to achieve their goals. Pressures and temptations would be great, said community college leaders, to go increasingly toward the university-parallel courses and the less costly students.

The state of Washington was experiencing substantial changes in its economy in 1971. Many were unemployed. There was great need for retraining services. Large numbers of veterans and other adults wanted first-rate occupational programs. But under the financial cutbacks facing the community colleges, the pressures were on to take university transfer students in the name of economy for the state. There was no denying that a financial crisis existed. The governor canceled all out-of-state travel for educators. Colleges and universities were required to *return* funds to the state treasury, in the case of community colleges some $900,000. (Actually it was withheld from budgets for the following year.)

Loss of Faith in Education

Education is not the only public service to feel the sting of financial limitations. But the experience has been bitter because along with the financial squeeze there seems to be some loss of faith in education as a means toward personal achievement and the solution of almost all problems, social or technological.

New social needs come into view. Said a commissioner for education: "Our principal problem in this state now is welfare. For the last fifteen years the big thing has been education, but now people are a little tired of hearing about it. Now there are going to be other social concerns, such as welfare, which are going to take the spotlight."

To talk about removing tuition in his state, he said, is like whistling in the dark. The whole tax structure, he declared, needs examination.

"Property tax is overloaded. People are dead-set against any increases. More of the income tax revenues need to stay at home. Maybe this involves revenue sharing or some other plan. But some of the money needs to get back to the local community."

I asked another state official what needs to be done. It was his feeling that the state had waited too long to solve its financial problems and that all these were coming home to roost at the present time. He reported school districts not far from bankruptcy. A big city newspaper in his area raised questions about how much the taxpayers were getting for the large amounts of money channeled to education. The state financial picture was not good, the editorial claimed. The state budget deficit would be large.

The Bill for Social Services

Of all the impressions I had from talking with hundreds of people, the most forceful is a concern by those people who carry public responsibilities about how society will pay for an increasing load of social services. The present financial structures may not fit the needs. For example, the director of finance of a Western community college reported that under the law the $1,750,000 which comes to the college from the local area can increase at an annual rate of no more than 6 percent.

"If we could just stabilize," he said, "things would probably be all right, but our enrollment has been increasing at a rate of 50 percent each year. There should be some leveling off, but it hasn't started yet."

Another factor to consider is that the cost per student for transfer work at one fairly typical community college is about $825 per year; for vocational-technical programs it is $1,200 per student. The latter figure does not count the higher equipment cost for the vocational-technical programs. In the name of economy, the direction is certainly toward the academic or transfer programs.

Financial support patterns are important. The "reward" system, or the basis upon which funds are made available, can advance or retard the institution in reaching its goals. The present crisis is more than money. There is the urgent necessity to determine whether financial support patterns facilitate the achievement of community college goals. There is a good deal of evidence to suggest that they do not.

PROPERTY TAX HAS HAD IT

Property tax has had it. That was the message that came through to me in the early months of 1971. The states were in a serious financial plight. Although other social needs vied for attention, education still took a big part of the public budget, and local property tax revenues were the main source of support. I had the feeling that the balloon was about to burst.

The financial needs of the schools, an inflationary setting, and public resistance to the traditional tax ways were interacting, and the atmosphere was heating up. And then the balloon did burst.

In late 1971 the California Supreme Court knocked down the state's reliance on local property tax for schools. *Serrano vs. Priest* resulted in a ruling that the use of local property taxes as the major source of funds for public education was unconstitutional. The court held that the property tax system discriminated against children who happened to live in poor districts with meager property tax resources. Somewhat similar rulings followed in Minnesota, Texas, and New Jersey. Unless appellate courts rule otherwise, it appears school districts will be required to find some equalization formula which will diminish the importance of the property tax.

In states where community colleges received part of their support from these local sources, they were greatly affected by the court actions. And in those states where the major support has been from the state level, there are new questions about the equitable distribution of state-level funds, not only among colleges and universities but also among the schools as well. Now who is to pay the bill?

SHOULD THE STUDENT PAY?

I found a general reluctance to increase educational costs to the student. However, one of the presidents most opposed to tuition confessed that even he had given thought occasionally to what $100 per student would do in aiding their budget. Tuition should be kept as low as possible. That was a prevailing theme. But, what would be possible was an open question.

In the community colleges of California and those in the city of Chicago, for example, no tuition was charged to in-district students. In other areas the average tuition charge was about $300 per year. It is common practice to require much higher payments of out-of-district and out-of-state students. However, in states where community college systems are well developed, a "charge-back" arrangement exists. The district of residence of the student will make a payment to the community college in which the student enrolls. Now the policy of out-of-district charges to the students is open to judicial review. Just as the Serrano-Priest case has opened up the issue of heavy reliance upon property taxes, the ruling of a Kansas judge in early 1972 held, in effect, that the eighteen-year-old vote wiped out a minor's legal subservience to his parents and with it the traditional views tying his residence to theirs. In the judge's view, when a teenager registers to vote in the community where he attends college, he becomes a resident of that community and thus immune to nonresident fees. This appeared to be another question destined to be taken up by state courts and ultimately to be decided in federal courts.

What are the arguments for keeping as low as possible the tuition and fees paid by the student? One argument frequently heard is that of social benefits. In addition to the values which accrue to a democratic society through a more enlightened citizenry (and enlightenment is presumed to be one effect of further schooling), there are the financial benefits of added training. If attendance at a community college enables the average student to get a better job and earn a higher income, then the cost of that education will be counterbalanced by the greater taxes paid by community college graduates. If their average income is increased enough, they will more than repay the cost of their education. Most studies have indicated that education is a sound investment and that well-educated citizens repay much more than the cost of their education.

Community College Helped Raise Local Economic Level

A judge in a Southern community gave the community college credit for raising the educational level of his part of the state and thereby contributing greatly to raising the economic level. He referred to the associate degree program in nursing and the licensed practical nurse program as well as the preparation of people for employment in industry.

"All of these," he said, "have contributed greatly to economic development. The hospitals were badly in need of more nurses, and they have them now. Factories are able to get foremen who are graduates of the community college."

Another civic leader commented:

> There is a need for better-qualified people at the local level. Many of these graduates from community colleges will stay in the area. They are the backbone of the home front, if you can pardon that mixing of metaphors. If students go out of the state for four or five years to go to a college and university, they are gone forever. In the senior colleges you have the people who are foreign to the state. They graduate and they leave. When it's over they are gone. But community colleges are made up predominantly of native people.

A state commissioner of education said he had mixed feelings on the question of whether students should carry more of the financial load. He was looking for a philosophical base. It was his impression that in this country we have tended to conceive of educational experience beyond the high school as a privilege. But he believes there is ample evidence of movement toward the concept that such experience is a right. And he questioned whether you can ask people to pay for something which is their right.

He said:

Within our lifetime or our children's lifetime, I think we will see postsecondary education as a right, and the implications therefore are for free public higher education. But we haven't answered these kinds of philosophical questions yet. Is education beyond the high school unique? Is it special? Should it be available to everyone? If the answer is that it should be available to everyone, then it is not special, it is not unique, and tuition should not be charged. It should be a matter of public responsibility.

A director of financial aid felt that increasing tuition would discourage many part-time students or those who are working part-time. In her opinion one important aspect of the mission of the community college is to "get across to the student and to the community the value of education. As the price goes up, it is perceived more and more to be just for the elite." She was concerned about tendencies toward elitism in education and that many students will consider education unattainable as it becomes more costly.

"But," she said, "if they can just get a taste of the community college experience, there is a good chance that they will keep coming and might even go on to higher levels of educational attainment."

Open Access Is Vital

State-level public officials in California thought that both the governor and the various legislative committees were not inclined toward tuition in their community colleges. They felt it essential to have one category of postsecondary institutions with open access.

Personnel in other states who favored no tuition on the basis that two years of education ought to be recognized as a public obligation expressed doubt about the feasibility of such a policy now. A highly placed spokesman in Illinois questioned whether a nontuition policy at this time was realistic, adding that there would be pressures for tuition to be charged even in the city of Chicago.

Those maintaining that no greater obligation should be placed upon the student reported at the same time that county or local district budgets were strained and that the states were not in much better condition. Where the money was going to come from they did not know.

"Anybody who really wants a college education can get it," goes a familiar refrain. I asked a financial aid director for his reaction. He replied:

> *Really wants* is the important term. One would raise the question whether it is wise to take money from other family needs in order to provide this opportunity. Or, should these students have to take eight years when it might be better for them to do it in four years and become more useful citizens in a shorter period of time?

He also reported that the number of financial-aid recipients had doubled that year. There were almost 500 students on welfare, and a welfare office had been opened on the campus. It was his impression that a much larger percentage of students were relying upon financial aid now than in the past.

A number of legislators referred with favor to new programs of tuition grants to students going on to private institutions. A few felt it would be better to give the student the option of utilizing the grants at the institution of his choice, although these usually turned out being within state.

Another factor, perhaps related to the eighteen-year-old vote, is under consideration. Where scholarships or tuition grants are related to family financial means, there should be recognition of the need of students whose parents may be well-off but who want to be independent of their parents and whose eligibility and need should be considered on the basis of their means, not their parents'.

The issue of tuition will not be easily settled in the near future. There are some who believe that even if the financial resources were available from public funds, some student participation should be in order because "Human nature being what it is, it is better for the person to contribute something directly. He appreciates it more." Others will point out that even if no tuition is required, the student may be contributing a great deal in deferred earnings, cost of transportation, and fees. At a low-tuition institution in Wisconsin additional fees ranged from $10 to $200. The person preparing to be a welder pays $190 for materials. Some may ask about the utilization of loans. In Chapter 1 there is reference to the problems many low-income students have with regard to loans. Students suggest that loans be on a voluntary basis with other provisions for people who feel it inappropriate to borrow the money.

Planners Look at Students and Finance

Just as the curriculum planner examines the characteristics of students in shaping educational programs, so in seeking answers to questions of financial policies the financial planners must take into account the kinds of students the institution is to serve. Those engaged in that kind of process throughout the country now seem to be saying that in community colleges no more than a minimum financial burden should be placed upon the student. Tuition should be kept as low as possible. And when society sees education beyond the high schools as a right, then the cost of such education should be considered a public responsibility.

It is possible that a substantial difference will exist between what should be and what is likely to be, however. Perhaps the easiest element to deal with in the college income mix is tuition. Up to the present, property owners and the state legislature appear to be much better organized in advocating their viewpoints about contributions toward the cost of college than the students. With property owners crying for relief from taxes and the legislature besieged by many interests, each convinced of the supreme value of its cause, the student may seem the lesser of the powers to be dealt with. There is some evidence, despite professions to the contrary, that the student's part of the financial load is increasing.

Assuming his post after experience in another state, the head of a state coordinating board for higher education was amazed to find that at least one public, large city community college had just adopted a tuition fee of $42 per semester hour for out-of-district students. He declared that it just is not possible to achieve an open-door policy with that kind of charge. He asked: "How can people at the state level allocate students, the disadvantaged especially, to an institution with those charges?" He further reported that the private colleges and the state university had strong financial aid programs but that the community colleges did not. In his estimation community colleges were pricing themselves out of the market they should be serving, and a good deal of the responsibility was attributable to the inadequacy of state resources.

THE LOCAL DISTRICT

The problems of relying upon financial support from local tax revenues are so numerous that they now draw national attention. Local taxes for the schools, almost without exception, mean property taxes—sometimes referred to as ad valorem taxes—and the common view is that "they are overloaded."

One prominent state legislator pointed out that in the area where he resides there is a mosquito district, a navigation district, a hospital district, a school district, a junior college district, and a flood control district. All these have taxing authority. Retired people with fixed incomes, he said, cannot afford to pay the growing amount of taxes levied. They sell their properties and move out. Moreover, properties don't increase enough in value to provide the additional revenue needed. He insisted that alternatives are needed.

A legislator in another state concurred. "As far as taxes are concerned at the local level, people really have had it. It is not possible to count on this as a source of continuing support. The local community is fully taxed. So, if the local community is fully taxed and students are economically deprived, this leaves growing responsibility at the state level." He reported that he was going to push for an increased income tax with the hope that property taxes could be lowered as a result of increased revenues from other sources. He wanted a maximum established on the millage levied on property taxes.

Beyond what is described as the "burden" of property taxes, this method of securing revenue is criticized on additional grounds. Taxing units often vary in their approach to setting valuations on property. And the strongest criticism is leveled at its inequity. For example, in one state 56 out of the total of 82 counties had assessed valuations of less than $25 million. One county, call it X County, and the three other counties that make up the X County junior college district represented an assessed valuation of $449 million. On the other hand, Y junior college is located in a five-county district with an assessed valuation of $70 million. X college will get over $400 per student from local sources, Y college only $186. X college will end the fiscal year with a surplus. Y college will not. A rate of only 0.5 mill is required for capital outlay in X County. The maximum rate allowable, 3 mills, is needed in Y County. The president of Y County college asked why taxpayers should carry unequal loads in these two different junior college districts.

Uneven Income Distribution Creates Problems

"How can you achieve similar quality in these various counties with their uneven financial capacity?" I asked several legislators.

There was some hesitancy in the responses. One legislator felt it would be ten to fifteen years before a foundation program could be developed which would equalize the financial burden in the 82 counties. Another senator said that he thought that move was just one lawsuit away. These men, who knew their state well, referred to the 82 counties in the state as having 82 different economic levels. They called for more state financing "to get the money where it is and to spend it where the needs are." They were of the opinion, though, that a move in this direction "would be real tough to get through the legislature."

What accounts for the apparent reluctance to establish measures for equalization of educational opportunity and financial load? There is a deep rooted concern on the part of educators and some state legislators that the price of equalization will be lessening of local control—the fiddler will call the tune. The agent for equalization is the state government through its fiscal services; hence it would be the "fiddler."

"There are forces that want to take over the junior college in this state," said a president. "They want to move it from local to state control, and once you start a major overhaul, then you begin to get amendments tacked on which could very well lead to this kind of change."

Although his institution was in one of the poorest districts, he was not sure he wanted the alternative he saw: more state control.

Some areas have been denied community college services entirely because local voters, required to express themselves both in favor of establishing a community college district and to approve a tax rate for support of the college, have rejected the proposals on the basis that they wanted no increase in taxes. In some areas, Austin, Texas, and Detroit, Michigan, among these, the proposal to establish the community college district has been approved, but the financial measure was defeated. Elections for tax levies have become increasingly traumatic in their effect upon community college operations. Uncertainties prevail. Community tensions and concerns about matters sometimes only distantly related to the tax election more often are affecting the vote. And with respect to recent bond elections, in one state more than 60 percent of these had lost. Without question, therefore, the trend line is toward a greater proportion of financial support from the states.

How much support? There would be almost unanimous endorsement of a provision that no less than 50 percent of the operating budgets to be met by state-level contributions. Concerns about declining local involvement and control slowly begin to rise with the increase in the proportion of state support. In most areas some local contribution is considered desirable.

There are presidents and board members who maintain that if the local area does not put some money into the college, it then cannot really be considered a *community* college. People in the community ought to show their interest through some local funding.

A modest contribution at the local level, some felt, would give some discretion at the local level on the part of people who know the institution and the community best. And a university president, formerly a community college president, now caught up in vigorous competition for funds at the state level, contended that he would take his chances on selling his program to the local voters rather than to the state legislature. He looked back with favor to his community college days when a third of the support was from the local district. To community college presidents he said, "By all means do not give up the ad valorem tax, or they will really kill you."

What the effect will be of the court decisions with respect to financing public education is difficult to assess at this time. However, there is a strong sentiment among community college leadership to retain some local capacity for college support. In one large state, the governing board for higher education was recommending that the state assume instructional costs with the local area having financial responsibility to provide the physical plant, its operations, and its maintenance. One advantage of this arrangement, said a planning official in another state, is "that the local district could get as fancy as it wanted." He had expressed concern at the unexpected high costs of community college plant construction and what he considered the "grand facilities." In this state three-quarters of the capital outlay is paid by the state, and he wondered if some procedure ought to be required for taking a hard look at some of the proposed designs.

There appears to be an almost inevitable trend toward major financial support of community colleges at the state level. Can decision making still be retained at the local level? The same concerns expressed by the states with regard to revenue sharing by the federal government characterize the views of community college leadership as the locus of revenue authority moves out of the local environment.

THE STATE—A SOURCE OF FINANCE?

The community college, largely dependent upon local tax support in the past, now looks to the state for the major share of its financial means. What the state is willing to pay for should have a lot to do with the kinds of services offered by the institutions. And there are numerous examples of financial support patterns that impede rather than encourage movement toward the generally perceived goals of the community college.

For example, in one state reimbursement is paid only in the case of full-time students. A full-time student is defined as one taking twelve semester hours or more. But college and community expectations are for many more part-time students; indeed it was stated repeatedly that the majority of community college students in the future may be those who are not carrying a full-time academic load. Part-time study associated with job experience or other responsibilities such as family or military service were judged to be a significant part of the community college mission.

In another state, institutions receive state aid on the basis of the semester hours recorded. A criticism leveled at this method was that all the funds might very well be used for support of faculty and instructional purposes with no assurance that some would be set aside for counseling. And it was the impression of observers in that state that a number of the community colleges provided little or no counseling service.

Faculty members in yet another state reported that transfer programs and occupational programs qualified for state-level support, but not the kind of programs designed to bring the student up to the level of "regular" courses. Such developmental services were dependent upon local community services money. The faculty emphasized that these programs were just as legitimate as the others, but their legitimacy and importance were not acknowledged in the state's financial patterns.

What is the effect of placing a dollar amount or percentage ceiling on the state's share? There is a possibility, according to experience in some states, that a ceiling of $600 per student (one-half the cost of instruction), for example, may lead to a tendency to concentrate on lower-cost programs—the academic rather than vocational-technical—in order to live within the budget.

Apportionment of State Funds Restricts Institutions

Procedures and definitions used in the apportionment of state funds can have the effect of restricting flexibility and adaptation of institutions to new knowledge. For example, apportionment for community colleges in California has been based upon the average daily attendance units accumulated during the school year. This number is based upon a summary of the total number of *student contact hours*, a term used to identify the number of hours students are "in contact" with instructors in the classrooms of the college. Student contact hours are converted to units of average daily attendance. The California Junior College Association and the California Community Colleges' Office of the Chancellor saw the critical need for the development of new, coordinated instruction systems which combine classroom lecture with modern technology to improve the instructional programs. Methods would include computer-assisted instruction, utilization of television, individualized computer assistance, and programmed or automated slide-tape systems for instruction. Standing in the way was the state requirement that average daily attendance included only those hours in which a student is in the classroom under instruction from the teacher. Action was taken to modify the education code to develop support for new kinds of community college instructional systems which have proven their worth. Obviously, the former "reward" system was not designed to facilitate the utilization of new technology in learning strategies.

Another lack of consistency between goals and financial facilitation is found in those states that assign high priority to community services programs in community colleges but provide no funds. In the state of Oregon, for example, board members declared "ten years from now the community college is going to be primarily a community service institution." However, no state funds were available for that function, although the state department of education in a community college plan was to recommend that assistance be provided for such programs.

This brief review of elements in patterns of financial support programs is by no means complete. It is intended to highlight an essential principle. In order to determine suitable means for financial support of community colleges, the states must first ascertain what it is those institutions are to do within the state system of education. A notable deficiency in state plans for community colleges now is that the financing patterns for public community colleges often are not expressly designed to facilitate the achievement of institutional goals. The specificity required with respect to institutional goals is essential, of course, with regard to the growing demand for accountability by educational institutions to those served and to the agencies providing financial support. Perhaps some of the inadequacy of present financial structures can be attributed to the deficiency in stating goals precisely and clearly. These times of financial distress may result in better statements of institutional purposes than were demanded in the past ten comparatively fat years.

Ohio Seeks New Approach

One state seeking new approaches to the support of postsecondary education has achieved a good deal of attention. The Ohio plan provides that students attending public four-year universities and graduate schools be obligated to repay to the state the amount of the subsidy the state has provided for them to attend that institution. In the case of a student studying for a bachelor of arts degree this would amount to approximately $3,500 for the four-year period beginning in September 1971. Other programs would be somewhat higher. Repayment of this obligation would not begin until the student finished school and earned at least $7,500 per year. At that income, his yearly payment would be $50. Repayment would follow a sliding scale up to a yearly payment level of $2,000 at $110,000 annual income. Students who attend a private college or university under the contract-for-services proposal would be obligated to repay to the state the amount of the subsidy the state provided to that private institution for their education. Students who go to two-year institutions would not have to repay the subsidy. The intent and the effect of this, according to an aide to the governor of Ohio, is to encourage students to go to the two-year institutions first and then transfer if they are going to continue. He believes the four-year institutions are too large.

After some initial flurry of interest, little has been heard about the Ohio plan. However, recent court decisions regarding property tax and residency requirements may very well press on the states the necessity to examine this and all other possible ways to meet the costs of college and university services.

THE FEDERAL GOVERNMENT

Community college leaders apparently are not yet looking to Washington for a solution of the money problem. I did not hear much talk about financial help from the federal government when I talked to people on the campuses. Local administrators seemed to be looking more to the state capitols for help with their money problems.

But in the state houses the people were saying the states were practically broke. State-level planners and administrators, therefore, often spoke about the need for additional financial help from the federal government.

One highly placed official suggested federal assistance in other fields of social need which would, in his opinion, permit the state to handle its educational problems. He was interested in the "federal umbrella" in certain costly areas of social welfare and medical needs. Higher education, he maintained, was not nearly as critical an issue as welfare. He referred to substantial migration throughout the country by persons searching for better welfare and medical programs.

"Let the federal government do something about equalizing the quality of health and welfare programs in the various states," he said. "Then we will have the resources to do a better job in meeting the state's higher-education needs."

When community college people did speak about federal support, they often mentioned the difficulty of working with the various categorical programs. And they spoke about their distaste for the grantsman syndrome and the lack of continuity and follow-through in program funding.

As this is being written, there are signs of change in Washington. Most of the hoped for changes are additions to the array of existing programs. These, for the most part, will be continued with minor changes. Among the new programs possible is some form of general institutional aid—money which institutions could add to their general operating revenues for whatever purposes they would choose. AAJC and several other education associations have for years been very much in favor of this approach to federal funding and would welcome its initiation, even on a limited basis at first.

Another possibility is a particular program for the establishment and development of community colleges, based on a bill originally introduced by Senator Harrison Williams of New Jersey in 1969.

While there is some uncertainty about these kinds of federal programs funded through the U.S. Office of Education, this represents only about 18 percent of the total United States support to higher education. Other agencies in the department of Health, Education, and Welfare (particularly health-related), as well as the Veterans Administration and the Departments of Defense and Justice, among others, account for the remainder.

GI Bill Provides Big Student Aid Package

Of the $7.4 billion total estimated United States outlays for higher education for fiscal 1973, the largest single portion comes from the

Veterans Administration as assistance to student veterans under the GI Bill of Rights. This is a whopping $1.8 billion, of which $683 million, about one-third, will go to veterans attending two-year colleges. This enormous student aid package is often overlooked in discussions of federal support for education.

It is estimated that two-year colleges will receive a total of $1.158 billion in fiscal 1973: this is 16 percent of the $7.4 billion total. The U.S. Office of Management and Budget estimates that federal support will approach 20 percent of the total expenditures of colleges and universities in 1973. Since two-year colleges do not tend to receive large research grants, their percentage of federal support is considerably smaller. Unfortunately, we do not have exact figures for this; the most recent estimate available (1968) places federal support at 5.76 percent of two-year college current funds revenue.[1] It is probably slightly higher now as an overall figure. Of course, the level of support to individual colleges varies greatly, from as high as nearly 30 percent in a few instances to almost nothing in others.

While 16 percent of total federal higher-education outlays are slated to go to two-year colleges, it may be more meaningful to look at the two-year portion of the combined two-year–four-year college total. In this case, the two-year college percentage is about 29 percent (excluding graduate and professional students, two-year colleges enrolled about 33 percent of all students in institutions of higher education in the fall of 1970).

Of the $1.158 billion estimated federal outlays for two-year institutions in fiscal 1973, by far the greatest portion, $915 million, is for student support. Of this, $682 million will support veteran educational benefits under the Veterans Administration. Other major sources of student support include the U.S. Office of Education's work-study, educational opportunity grants and loan funds ($141 million), assistance to nursing and allied health program students under the National Institute of Health ($21.5 million), student benefits from the Social Security Administration ($58 million), and law enforcement students under the Department of Justice ($11 million).

There is no reason here to outline all the federal higher education assistance programs: there are some 100 of them, and many of them do not even appear in the 1973 estimated higher education budget figures being used here, merely for guidance as to program

---

[1] *Current Funds Revenues and Expenditures, 1968-69, Financial Statistics of Institutions of Higher Education*, U.S. Office of Education.

magnitude. However, it may be instructive to point to a few major programs in the U.S. Office of Education and elsewhere.

Vocational education is the largest single form of program support available to two-year institutions. In fiscal 1972, an estimated $117 million went to postsecondary institutions through grants to state agencies. In many states, community colleges receive significant assistance from this program.

Help for Developing Colleges

Another important and increasing source of support for some colleges is the developing institutions program, designed to give general assistance to colleges "isolated from the mainstream of American life and struggling for survival," which has been interpreted broadly to include colleges serving large disadvantaged or minority populations. Two-year colleges by law receive 23 percent of total funding for this program (which may increase to 24 percent under the new legislation). The level of funding of this program is due for a substantial increase, since both the administration and Congress agree on its importance. In the past two years two-year college funding has been about $8 million.

The program of aid for the construction of academic facilities which is due to increase in the new legislation has been very helpful to two-year institutions. The current administration has preferred to subsidize the interest above 3 percent on private-market construction loans rather than to give direct grants of construction funds. The Congress, however, has refused to cut out the grants entirely—in fiscal 1970 and 1971 its $43 million appropriation of grant funds was entirely for public community colleges, a feat which is unlikely to be repeated. In any case, for various reasons the level of federal support for construction, especially grants, is not likely to increase.

Within the U.S. Office of Education, two-year colleges have also looked for support of such programs as library acquisitions assistance, institutes and training programs for faculty and staff, special programs for students with academic disabilities, and assistance in the purchase of instructional equipment.

Health-related programs administered by the National Institute of Health have provided major assistance to two-year college nursing and allied health programs. In addition to student assistance and a new program of "capitation grants" for schools of nursing, support is available for such activities as construction, enrollment expansion, curriculum improvement, research, and pilot projects. Program support was $6 million in fiscal 1971, and it is expected to reach $20 million in fiscal 1973. A developing but still small ($1.3 million) field is the training of mental health workers under programs of the National Institute of Mental Health.

Mainly through grants to states, the social and rehabilitation service supports training programs for a variety of social service workers, including services to older Americans. Also primarily through grants to states, two-year colleges can participate in noncollege "basic education" programs for adults.

Colleges located in areas served by one of several regional commissions—the Appalachian Regional Commission is a notable example—can get help from or through these various agencies.

Two independent agencies, the National Science Foundation and the National Endowment for the Arts and Humanities, support programs in their specialized fields. Funding the latter agency is very much on the increase, and the humanities endowment in particular has a very sympathetic interest in two-year colleges. For example, a program of fellowships was awarded in 1971; in 1972 79 awards were made.

Manpower Programs Are Huge but Untapped

Manpower programs under the Department of Labor represent a huge but largely untapped source for colleges able to perform the required services for this special clientele. At present institutional manpower programs are under joint authority of the Department of Labor and the U.S. Office of Education, which selects the training sites. This arrangement may change under new manpower legislation, but the issue is very much in doubt. Regardless of the administrative arrangements, however, two-year colleges should give manpower programs serious attention. Some already have. In Oregon, for example, almost all MDTA (Manpower Development Training Act) institutional programs are run through community colleges. Manpower programs are one of a variety of agencies able to fund career education, new careers, employee upgrading, and paraprofessional and aide-level training programs, many of which can most appropriately be conducted by two-year colleges, often in cooperation with employing industries or agencies. The pressures are strong—and in view of our seemingly chronic high level of unemployment may become irresistible—to make permanent the "emergency" public service employment act of 1971. Not only will this fund some of the colleges' own employees, but it will also provide many training opportunities for public service employees.

Agencies such as the Environmental Protection Agency, the Department of Housing and Urban Development, and the Departments of Justice, Transportation, Interior, and Agriculture, as well as the Small-Business Administration and the Office of Economic Opportunity, all have funds for certain two-year college activities. Even the U.S. Civil Service Commission, under the Intergovernmental Personnel Act, can be tapped by public colleges for personnel exchanges, temporary expert personnel, or training programs for public employees. A system of exchanges between college and governmental personnel would probably be refreshing and enlightening for all parties concerned.

Federal programs are for the most part categorical in nature. It is in many ways an unfortunate situation, for it requires a great deal of energy and time, first to learn what the program possibilities are and then to follow through and get the grants. Much to the consternation of some members of Congress, the new and relatively highly paid occupation of grantsman has developed. He is the expert who knows where the money is and how to get it. Grantsmen are not unique to educational institutions, of course, but sadly those educational institutions which employ or make use of grantsmen by and large are the ones which get the grants. This is one of the reasons two-year colleges have tended to get less than what might be considered their proportionate share of federal funds, for they discovered the need for a resident grantsman long after their four-year college and university colleagues were well into the game.

Perhaps if the concept of general institutional support were adopted and adequately funded, the federal emphasis on categorical programs would decline somewhat, though it is unlikely to disappear in the foreseeable future. President Nixon's proposals for revenue sharing would, if adopted, reduce the number of categories and broaden the scope of those which remain. However, Congress is very jealous of its prerogatives and has until now been rather cool to the idea of revenue sharing.

In the meantime community and junior colleges should understand the variety and possible magnitude of federal assistance which is available to them. Some two-year colleges have found it well worth the effort and have been able to fund many of their activities with federal assistance. Colleges which are small or otherwise unable to employ their own federal-programs expert might usefully consider other approaches, which might include giving a staff member this responsibility along with others, joining with neighboring colleges in employing one person to serve the group, developing a statewide federal information system through the state director's office, or a combination of the three.

SUMMARY

It appears that society is inclined to give community colleges—and that community colleges are generally ready to accept—a large and difficult assignment. But, for community colleges to provide the services needed, financial support must be assured. The present situation is this: the assignment is coming into sharper focus, but the sources and patterns of funding are less clear. Many persons in the field see a financial crisis arising out of this situation that could develop into the greatest problem facing community colleges. In some places this is already true.

The philosophy that community colleges should have low tuition or no tuition at all and that the primary source of funding should be taxes paid by the locality served is severely threatened by this looming crisis. Local districts are turning to the state capitols for increasing financial help. And the state-level people are beginning to see empty coffers and are turning their faces toward Washington.

Adding to the complexity of this problem are the so-called taxpayers' revolt, court rulings affecting the property tax upon which education has tended to rely, and inflation that continues to eat away at budgets.

Several things must be done. The first thing that suggests itself is improved management practices to assure the most efficient possible use of the resources that are available.

Systems analysis may provide some answers by tying inputs to outputs, making it possible to evaluate the impact of learning experiences on student performances. Combined with objective-oriented management, the systems approach concentrates on what happens to individuals as they are exposed to the educational process. Use of such procedures may result in two benefits: (1) aiding in the primary task of educating people better, and (2) assisting in pointing out inefficiencies and waste in the system.

More basic, perhaps, is the need for society to understand better what community colleges are capable of doing, to decide more precisely what it wishes to ask community colleges to do, and then to make a commitment to support the colleges in that work. Obviously the community college cannot do everything. In a pluralistic society, the contribution to be made by each part—family, church, business, military service—must be kept in view. This is a difficult job of interpretation and interaction, and the community colleges themselves must take the leadership in seeing to it that such a dialogue takes place.

Community colleges have tended to look to four-year colleges as having a great deal of influence in their destiny. But it appears there is a growing realization that community colleges will have their role determined to a great degree by the secondary schools. Community colleges need, in this regard, to redirect some of their attention. They need to turn around and look at the schools that are preparing the students that come to them. This is a matter of self-interest, no doubt about it. The stake of the community college in how well their students are prepared is very large. Whether community colleges are going to be asked to make up the deficiencies of a much larger and earlier system or build upon an effective educational foundation already laid in the secondary schools will make a great deal of difference in terms of finances needed.

Here, as in earlier chapters, we see once again the importance of community colleges not trying to go it alone. They must see themselves as part of a system of education and work to make the system effective as a whole. One of the most important steps in the effort is for each part of the system, including the community college, to have a sharply defined and well-understood function. And, when that is done, it is hoped that taxpayers will be ready to support the various agencies in their mutually agreed-upon and assigned functions.

As to who pays the bill—student, local district, state, or federal government—the answer is likely to be that all these sources must contribute if community colleges are to provide the services they have already been assigned. The real question is what portion each will be asked to pay. The answer will be worked out state by state. It is also to be hoped that the principles of extending educational opportunity and identification with the local community will not be sacrificed in the quest for increased help from state and federal government.

Chapter 9.
The College in
a State System

The community college affects and, in turn, is affected by other educational institutions within the state. Increase the retention rate in transfer programs, and the upper-division opportunities must be expanded. Limit enrollments in the four-year colleges and universities, and more students will seek admission to community colleges. Raise fees in some colleges, and students will be diverted to other lower-cost institutions. Build public, tax-supported colleges in an area served by privately supported institutions, and the composition of their student bodies will probably change. Policy determinations in one institution, or even unplanned occurrences such as dissent on the campus, will work their influence on other institutions in the state. It is time to acknowledge the reality of this interrelation of institutions and the need for a "system" approach to statewide educational planning.

WHY NOW?

More compelling than all other factors at the present is finance.

"These facilities and services need to be shared, whether we want it or not," I was told in one interview. "We are in a hell of a financial bind in this state, and only through movement in these directions is the problem going to be solved."

It is not simply the dollars required for education; programs of health and social welfare have reached cost levels in some states where they share with education the spotlight of taxpayer and legislature interest.

"In the future," I was told by a governor's education aide, "education will not be able to say, 'you people give us the dollars and don't bother us about the delivery systems for other kinds of services, for example welfare.' " It was his conviction that social needs, as represented in ecology, welfare, and education, needed "orchestration."

> Education needs to be seen as part of these other social needs. Some way must be found to bring about a blend of resources. Education should be considered a resource for meeting needs in welfare and ecology. You don't talk about formal educational needs versus welfare. There are just so many dollars available, and rather than having competition or conflict among the various human needs, we need to find a way to exploit the resources which one field can make available to the other.

Erosion of Support for Education

At the same time that there is increasing talk about "dollar accountability," there is apparent erosion of support for education. In fact, I was informed in one state that the only people defending higher education were those in higher education. The comment was only in part facetious. Disaffection with higher education, particularly on the part of legislators, has been referred to in previous chapters.

However, the problems are those of purpose as well as dollars. Even in states well known for their leadership in the community college field, people in state government claimed there was need for "a more adequate definition of institutional purposes." The reference in this case was to community colleges. Beyond this, they asserted the state needed to become much more proficient at setting educational goals and in seeing to it that those goals are reached. Displeasure was voiced at what appeared to be the competing priorities of community colleges, the senior institutions, and the vocational schools.

"These have not been brought together in a comprehensive plan which has some strength to it."

Chaotic Situation Exists

Legislators are coming to realize that close to a chaotic situation exists in postsecondary education. The dollar squeeze demands determination of priorities. But these are seldom stated. The buildup of institutions often is in response to local pressures. Some states have not spelled out the respective functions of their institutions. There may be unused capacity in some colleges and overcrowding in others. Community colleges have not come up with adequate occupational education plans in many states. And in some areas demographic, geographical, or financial problems prevent supplying services that are justified in light of educational needs. Obviously, there must be a state-level agency of some sort to address itself to statewide interests in the light of statewide resources. Two questions remain: Will the legislatures recognize this need? Will community college leadership develop the larger perspective, the statewide view?

Educators are deeply concerned lest their capacity to exercise initiative and maintain flexibility be removed by other agencies. The best way to inhibit that is for educational leadership itself to work actively for the reduction of the waste, the rivalries, and the institutional vested interests that make postsecondary education vulnerable to much of the present criticism.

However, the blame does not always lie at the doorstep of educators; often legislators, and citizens, too, respond more to vested interest than to public interest. Examples of prodigality and ineptness are not hard to find.

JOINT PLANNING

A public community college and a publicly supported state university were established in the same city. Actually they were built within a few blocks of each other. From a helicopter view they seem to be close together, and in public relations releases the same affinity appears. But actually they are far apart. Nine-tenths of the faculty from the university, according to the president, have never visited the community college. There is no provision for joint use of track and playfields, gymnasium, or library. Consider the possibilities, suggested the president, of a cooperative approach in developing a real community center. It might not have been a community college as defined by a two-year program, but it could have been a real community center for education. He deplored the rigid definitions that limit new approaches to such educational opportunities.

SHARED FACILITIES

In another large city a state university and a community college are only seven blocks apart. The university's facilities, according to spokesmen in the area, are closed "tighter than a drum" from 4:30 in the afternoon. At the same time the community college, with desperate need for facilities, was only a few blocks away. Representatives of the state higher education board said that "These facilities and services need to be shared, whether the people in those institutions want it or not."

THE VOCATIONAL-ACADEMIC SPLIT

In another state the personnel responsible for administering programs of vocational-technical education "don't come to this end of the building where higher education services are housed." And it has been made clear to the community college state-level official by "people at the other end of the building" that he is not to communicate with persons in the area vocational schools and technical institutes. The problem was eased when the community college director was designated chairman of a committee to study career education in the state. Personnel from the technical institutes were included on that committee. The committee's function was to help the state board of education determine where new technical institutes, vocational schools, and community colleges should be located to provide programs in career education. So, for the first time in that state community college and vocational-technical personnel were conferring.

But technical institutes are under one state board, community colleges are under another board. Vocational education funds are from one source, other community college funds are from different sources. Twenty-five area vocational schools have been "subcollegiate in the past but are being augmented" to make them quasi-collegiate. Tensions persist between vocational educators and community college representatives. At the national level, they acknowledge, there seems to be some accommodation of views, and communication takes place. But in the state, vocational educators charge that their national leaders have sold them out.

Separation Is a Wasteful and Unsound Influence

The obsolescent concept of separation of academic and vocational education works its wasteful and educationally unsound influence in yet another state. The state-level agency administering vocational funds may provide money for a community college building but will then require that the building and equipment be utilized solely for vocational-technical purposes. For example, typewriters are to be used only for such programs. The effect is to clearly divide the vocational from the academic facilities, students, and faculty. State-level officials report that with community college funds channeled through two separate agencies it is almost impossible to eliminate duplication of funds. The members of the legislature are becoming aware of obvious duplications, and it is feared that this will harm the institutions. The state commissioner of education called for an administrative structure which emphasizes unity and does not postulate a dichotomy of academic and vocational education. Changes in federal legislation may be necessary to put these pieces together. A sounder approach was voiced by a state superintendent of public instruction who pointed to a map of the state which hung on the wall.

There are forty-three technical schools in this state now and soon there will be fifty-four. I would like to see where these are located and where other programs are offered, for example in adult education, and then in effect pull down an overlay map which shows where community colleges are, to see what attempts could be made to bring these kinds of institutions together.

RESISTANCE TO CHANGE

In another state a system of two-year centers is in process of development. Those under the auspices of universities offer the first two years of the baccalaureate program. Separate occupational education centers prepare for employment. None of these centers had permanent campuses when the first community college was established in that state in 1962. A state-level official reported that his colleagues "got their ears pinned back" when they proposed that the university centers and some of the technical institutes combine to become, in effect, comprehensive community colleges. It was his view that it would take continuing persuasion to bring this about. Resistance to the proposal came from university branches where there was a strong desire expressed by people in the centers to retain identification with the university and from citizens who looked toward an eventual four-year college in the area. There was resistance from people representing the technical institutes because they feared that the institution would lose its "flavor" if the academic came in. The opposition was described as "very political."

The state at the present has an open-access law; that is, any high school graduate can go to a university. State-level planning officials in higher education are urging that the universities become more selective. This will require legislation. Alternative opportunities did not exist formerly, but now officials say that they do. The greatest concerns expressed by the state's planners in education with respect to these developments are "first, to find a way to rationalize all of these various institutions into a statewide system with both the academic and vocational-technical services made accessible throughout the state and second, a strong need to sell the people of the state on the system." They maintained that entry through two-year institutions should be desirable and popular. But, they added, "This is a tough one because there is a real hang-up about wanting admission initially to the university."

PUBLIC-PRIVATE CONTROVERSY

Tensions exist between colleges publicly funded and those privately supported. The public community college, with its comparatively low tuition, is perceived as "luring" potential clientele from the privately supported institutions. A representative of an association of private institutions said that his organization has no quarrel with vocational-technical education. "We need these people and these kinds of programs, but we are concerned with what we perceive to be the increasing emphasis of community colleges on college-parallel programs. The community college would be hard pressed to prove that this does not draw from the private colleges." He reported that a well-established four-year college suffered a severe loss in enrollment at the same time that a new community college was developing rapidly. The tuition differential was substantial—$350 to go to the community college for a year and $1,600 for the liberal arts college. "Rather than build little liberal arts colleges all over the state in the guise of community colleges," he said, "the space now available in private institutions needs to be utilized under a tuition-grant program."

In areas where private colleges had been in existence for many years before establishment of a community college, I asked two presidents what the effect of the community college had been upon their institutions. One of these had been a leading junior college but became a four-year college about the same time that the community college began operations. The president reported that the community college had not affected their pool of students adversely, in fact, quite the contrary. The institution has more day students than had been expected. Many students are transfers to the upper division from the five public community colleges within driving distance. There had been more transfers to the upper division than anticipated, and cooperative efforts are under way to dovetail programs. In his estimation a good working relationship has been established, including some sharing of faculty. Programs in teacher education, business, and medical technology are among those that appear to be most attractive to community college transfer students. If there had not been need for a four-year college in the area, however, he believes the story might have been different. "The private junior colleges," he observed, "are lost in the shuffle."

The president of a well-established church-related four-year college said that the public community college which began operations in his area in 1965 had little effect upon enrollments at his college other than on evening programs which were offered as a community service but discontinued after the community college began to offer them. He maintained that the community colleges are tapping a new clientele and that this is a significant factor often overlooked in estimates of future college enrollments. Continuing education and adult education as well as job preparation, he asserted, will attract large numbers of students who would not have been served by the programs offered by institutions of the type he represented. It was his impression that some students are going to community college because it is an easy next step. In effect they are buying time while they try to make up their minds what they want to do. Having the institution available means that they are not forced to make decisions they are reluctant to make. Many are confused and uncertain, and society is not providing good options for them other than the community college. As a result of wider observations, however, the president went on to say, in some areas, for reasons not clear, private institutions suffered a distinct slump in enrollments at the time community colleges were founded. They seemed to be drawing from the same clientele.

Whether direct causal relationships can be established or not, privately supported colleges, both two-year and four-year, *with unused capacity* look to the public institutions and to the most omnipresent of these, the community colleges, with some lack of enthusiasm.

A STATE SYSTEM

Changing characteristics of the students who make up the pool from which colleges draw and the much evident budget squeeze have heightened stress and tension among the educational institutions within the state. There is urgent need to define the scope and mission of the many institutions that represent resources for educational tasks. Comprehensive planning is critical, planning that promotes an increased "mingling" of elementary and secondary institutions, community colleges, and universities. After all, the funds come from the same source: the people of the state.

A master plan limited to higher education does not go far enough. All the educational resources need to be looked at so that resources are allocated on a rational, planned basis. And how does the community college fit into this concept? Some state leaders are nervous at overenthusiastic talk about the comprehensive community college. They wonder if community college leaders mean that they will try to do almost everything. I see growing emphasis on the importance of having a state system of education which does everything. Comprehensiveness is achieved through effective relationships among all the elements in the system. In effect, the state's many institutions are so interconnected in their services and reciprocal in their relationships that they provide a "university without walls."

COORDINATION AND CONSOLIDATION

At the same time that calls are heard for more specific designation of the role and scope of postsecondary institutions and coordination of effort is described as imperative, some state-level agencies with responsibilities for long-range planning and coordination are under attack. In fact, in a number of instances bills have been introduced to do away with coordinating boards.

How can we account for this apparent behavior? One explanation is that higher education planning commissions or coordinating bodies are not able to make decisions that will please all the vested interests. Furthermore, in the words of one informed individual, the state legislatures seem more and more to be "feeling their oats," and they often see the higher education commission as the creature of the governor. Therefore, they want little to do with it in accordance with their declaration of independence from the executive branch.

Another interpretation is that coordinating councils tend to be weak in terms of institutional control. This was a plus factor in the 1950s. Now, with what legislators perceive to be some lack of responsiveness by universities and colleges, plus a mounting distrust by legislators of these institutions and a strong desire to bring them into a more responsive position, there will be more control exerted than was so with "coordinating" councils. Very likely there will be a greater move toward consolidation. Coordinating councils helped to arrest expansionistic tendencies. In these days there are many students and not much money, and it will probably take a stronger type of organization.

And it is the latter that seems to be occurring. I heard many references to the need for a single board of education with responsibilities for education from preschool through adult education to "unify and strengthen educational efforts."

An Integrated System of Education Coming

Change appears to be in the direction of consolidation—a concept of an integrated system of education that relates more closely public and private institutions and higher education with the schools. The feasibility of states or cities contracting for educational services as well as utilization of plant capacity, which exists out on the job in employment settings, is viewed hopefully. Another factor to take into account in forecasting educational change is the development of post-high school programs in proprietary institutions.

In several states procedures have been established by which these institutions are formally recognized by state education agencies. In one state it was reported that two firms, Philco Ford and International Telephone and Telegraph, had purchased proprietary schools. Western Electric was reported to have a program in Princeton, New Jersey, and to be interested in the possibility of establishing graduate degrees. General Electric had a program in a space laboratory at Valley Forge in Pennsylvania. Other corporations with similar educational programs in that state included Westinghouse and Gulf Oil. A commissioner of education described such programs as effective, with the latest equipment, and he urged that they be "tied into community colleges."

"We need to take a look at these places. We cannot ignore them. They have implications for our organizations as we look ahead. There are over 300 of these proprietary programs in Pennsylvania, now enrolling over 100,000 students. We have tended to ignore the fact that they exist, but they are there, and they are growing rapidly and have implications for the work of our institutions."

STATE GOALS FOR EDUCATION

What changes are state plans and patterns of education calling for which would have implications for the future of community colleges? There are insistent pressures in the environment that require the states to specify educational goals. Some of these pressures have been referred to. An example of a recent statement is the New Jersey Master Plan for Higher Education. Its basis is found in *Goals for Higher Education in New Jersey.* These include:

1   To assure each individual the opportunity to be educated to the height of his potential
2   To eliminate financial barriers
3   To foster diversity and flexibility
4   To foster an integrated system of public and private institutions
5   To strive for excellence
6   To help meet the needs of society
7   To encourage research and advancement of knowledge
8   To sustain academic freedom
9   To contribute to the well-being of the community
10 To use all resources to full effect[1]

The report emphasizes that the establishment of goals is the crucial step in the planning process, and it is in the effort to reach the goals that all planning decisions are made. In New Jersey the higher education community and a special committee representing leadership in the state spent the better part of a year in discussion of possible goals and their final formulation. Each state will establish its own goals in terms of its historical precedents and current status.

DIVERSIFICATION OF EDUCATIONAL OPPORTUNITY

Diversification of educational opportunity is an aim in state plans. The Ohio Board of Regents takes issue with the law in that state which obligates the public universities to admit every graduate from high school who applies for enrollment. They see this legal provision.

. . . to imply that the taxpayers of Ohio have an obligation to provide every high school graduate with a four-year college education. A college degree is not just a job passport to which every child born in Ohio is entitled. An open-door

---

[1] New Jersey Master Plan for Higher Education, Number 1, *Goals for Higher Education in New Jersey,* New Jersey Board of Higher Education, Trenton, N.J., January 1970.

policy to Ohio's public universities can result only in the admission of innumerable youth destined to fail or else the reduction of a four-year college degree to a meaningless piece of paper.

The regents recommend that public universities be authorized by law to select the Ohio high school graduates to be admitted as first-year students in baccalaureate programs in accordance with the enrollment limitations, enrollment objectives, and special characteristics of each public university. Further, "Because of enrollment limitations placed upon certain state universities and because of the availability of a structure of two-year campuses throughout Ohio, ... the open-door admission policy for all Ohio high school graduates should be made applicable to two-year campuses."

Another educational option is made available through a recommendation of the regents for a program of contract services whereby a private college wishing to do so will agree to accept any graduate with an associate degree from a public two-year college who wishes to continue his or her educational program at the baccalaureate level. The private college or university "under the contract would agree to charge such student the equivalent amount of the instructional and general fees charged by the state universities and would receive from the State of Ohio the amount of the state subsidy provided for students enrolled in comparable instructional programs at the state universities." Regents' recommendations require implementation through the legislative process.

Another example of the growing emphasis upon a broader range of educational opportunities is found in the report of the governor's commission on education in Wisconsin.

There are other educational and occupational objectives that do not require four years of training, that have rigorous standards of performance based on differing types of talent and skill and that provide opportunities for satisfying transition from school to career. These goals deserve a higher priority than heretofore accorded them in state planning and administration of education.

Many state plans, such as Ohio's, suggest the advisability of limiting enrollments in the universities but of providing for open access into the educational system through other institutions—community colleges, technical colleges, and general colleges.

INCLUSION OF ALL INSTITUTIONS IN PLANNING

Reference has already been made to an arrangement proposed in Ohio whereby a private college may contract with the state to serve students transferring from two-year institutions. The state of New Jersey system permits this kind of arrangement among all institutions, public and private, at all levels of higher education. The notion of utilizing private as well as public resources to meet educational need is gaining greater acceptance. In some states, such as Iowa, a system of tuition grants is utilized. Phase III of the master plan in Illinois calls for a flow of students into all the institutions. Here the concept is of a total system of higher education for the state, public and private, and deliberate measures to make use of all available capacity. Even spokesmen for the public segment of education maintain that the continuance of strong privately supported institutions is advantageous to all of education and that such continuance can be encouraged by new programs of financial aid designed to achieve state goals. The private institutions will need to examine carefully the cost of services rendered along these lines. What is the state willing to pay for? Are the proposed educational services appropriate to the mission of this type of college? What constraints will develop out of exercise of the review-and-evaluation function by state-level agencies, including the legislature which appropriates funds? Can the distinctiveness which differentiates the public and private institutions be conserved or will there be encouragement under financial aid programs for the institutions to become much more alike?

Whether or not the private institutions receive public funds, it is likely that they will be involved in the projection which a state makes of its educational programs. The New Jersey plans hold that

... Each institution—public or private—has a unique role to play. Nevertheless, all colleges and universities, whatever their history and pattern of governance, must contribute to their maximum within the framework of the system if the state is to meet its educational needs in the years ahead. This integrated system must sustain the proper balance between cooperation and coordination on the one hand, and initiative and independence on the other.

COMPREHENSIVE AND CONTINUOUS EDUCATION

State plans look toward the concept of education as a continuum from preschool to graduate school and continuing education. I heard in my interviews many references to educational opportunity beyond the high school as a common experience, a right, and strong suggestions that the chasm between public school completion and postsecondary educational experiences be filled. A number of states are seeking to minimize this historic separation through organizational structures that bring all the educational elements together under one board of education, including the universities and the public schools. Also, although no one has proposed popular ways of doing so, it has been urged that the reward system in education be altered so that the social importance of the various parts of the educational structure take on more equal status. If postsecondary educational experience is to become ever more common, what happens to the pinnacle of prestige so long occupied by universities and their graduate schools? Is a peer relationship of functional responsibilities more realistic than a hierarchical structure of levels with declining numbers and higher esteem at each successive gradation? One report calls for the creation of a state education board which "would be a mechanism for unifying and strengthening educational efforts from preschool through adult education."

Questions are raised about whether present forms of planning and organization are truly suited to the optimum development of the various potentials of all the citizens of a state. Just as there is concern about whether the concept of a pyramidal structure of education (with public schools at the base and graduate schools at the apex) is outmoded, so there is uneasiness with what might be called a horizontal separation in education. The governor's committee in Wisconsin put it in a way which was seconded in other states:

> Our society must not retain outmoded status distinctions between technical and academic education. It must continue to develop high standards of performance and reward for differing types of aptitude and ability. Just as our educational system serves to enable some of our citizens to rise to high levels of scientific and professional development, it should enable others to prepare for satisfying careers and other kinds of occupations.

Both in Wisconsin and Ohio, where there have been institutional separations along the lines criticized in the report, mergers of institutions offering vocational-technical programs and those offering general and academic education are recommended as soon as is politically feasible. Although the complex demands of comprehensive institutions have been described in detail in this book, the advantages broad programs have in meeting the needs of a variety of students appear to state planners to outweigh the difficulties.

In order to achieve a successful merger of interests of state vocational and community college administrators, a new type of reward structure—one which positively reinforces close collaboration—is required. The recently debated comprehensive manpower bill recognized the need for a more coordinated approach to mobilizing available resources by authorizing state governors and the mayors of metropolitan areas to contract on a competitive basis for manpower training services. Any public or private agency would be eligible to respond. Mobilizing all resources within one location would presumably put that location into a better competitive position. Unfortunately, the bill was subsequently vetoed by the President.

A former superintendent of a unified school district (grades K to 14), now elevated to a national office, described how he succeeded in bringing about an articulation of high school and postsecondary vocational programs in his California district. A team of counselors had discovered that those students who were not planning to transfer to a four-year college following high school graduation—those who elected to enroll in the two-year postsecondary program at a nearby community college or those who were not yet certain what they wanted to do following graduation—were finding it virtually impossible to enroll in an articulated sequence of courses linking high school with the junior college. The responsible high school principals and junior college deans were requested by the superintendent to hammer out a well-articulated curriculum sequence following the recommendations of the investigative committee. As a result, high school students were permitted to enroll in one or two community college-based courses. High school counselors were encouraged to meet and jointly plan with their junior college counterparts. Thus, having communicated his interest and concern, this forceful superintendent was successful in forging new links between high school and the community college.

THE RELATION OF EDUCATION TO SOCIAL PROBLEMS

Our organized society engages in many tasks in order to meet the needs of its members. Education has frequently been looked to as a source of trained personnel for business and industry. When engineers have been in demand—or teachers, mathematicians, astronomers, or military personnel—the schools and colleges have prepared them. Now there is an underlying concern that in the future problems in unemployment, crime, welfare, health needs, environmental pollution, an aging population, and urban decay be examined to determine their relation to education. In each instance issues need to be identified, ideas discussed, values changed, skills developed, information communicated, research conducted, and organization effected. This is the work of education. State plans are taking note of elements in the social environment which will press upon educational institutions. An obligation is acknowledged to "participate in appropriate ways to assist these communities to solve their problems." But to date little has been said or done about the mechanisms by which education comes to grips with social needs. Organizationally, as far as state or local government is concerned, they seem to exist in separate boxes as does education. The proposed state plan in Oregon approaches recognition of the opportunities with encouragement to "each community college to serve whenever feasible as a regional coordinating agency for special educational or community service programs such as War on Poverty, Coordinated Childcare, or Manpower Training Projects."

DISTRIBUTION OF STUDENTS

How should students distribute themselves so that the broadest possible opportunities are provided? As I observed the growing attraction of community colleges and saw large numbers of students qualified academically and financially to enter directly the university or four-year college, I wondered what effect their presence would have on the opportunities of students who could take their work nowhere else—older people or those with family responsibilities, academic deficiencies, financial handicaps, or requiring a program not offered by the other institutions.

Will it be necessary to have selective admissions at community colleges? Here selective admissions must be defined not to demand a minimum level of academic achievement, but rather to assure that those students who could not be served well at other institutions would not be crowded out of community colleges.

How to administer such a policy is a question of sufficient force to discourage much rumination. The factors to consider are numerous and complicated and also resist identification and measurement. If the student merely lacked money, a grant-in-aid might make it possible for him to take his work at some other suitable institution. However, other matters of motivation—maturity, family respon-sibilities, age, employment commitments, and interests—would be difficult to deal with in establishing an order of priorities for students to be admitted to the college. And there is the old concern—if the college purports to serve those who could not be served elsewhere, would anybody want to go to it? The dumping-ground image has long been a bugaboo to community college personnel.

But the problem remains. In the final decision, who are the students to be given priority in community colleges? Answers will probably be found in better counseling in communities and high schools, moves toward a peer relationship among educational institutions, and the fact that it is the academic value rather than the socioeconomic characteristics of its students which seems to arouse more concern about the reputation of an institution.

Community colleges will continue to have a broad distribution of academic ability because of other factors—desire to stay in the community, family responsibilities, employment. But one fact remains: the community college cannot do everything. The community college within a state system of education will be required to have specific goals. Along with other institutions it will be put on notice to provide services clearly in line with the needs of the people.

SUMMARY

Each state needs to work out its own statement of educational goals. To achieve those goals, a pattern of educational services is required which takes into account the particular needs of its citizens, its resources, its history, and its culture. The organizational forms must be appropriate to the goals specified, with equal educational opportunity being the overriding consideration. An illustration of inappropriate and ineffective organization is the national and state structures for administering vocational-technical postsecondary programs in comprehensive institutions. The effect of current organizational forms is to divide rather than to meld.

An agency is needed at the state level to make tough decisions, to provide evaluation and review, and to address itself to statewide interests in the light of statewide resources to meet statewide needs. This "quality control" agency can take a dispassionate view of the capacity of institutions to fulfill their state goals with reasonable cost and effectiveness.

Emphasis needs to be upon the target student populations and the learning opportunities provided rather than upon the needs of the established structures. Critical points include questions of what is best for the potential consumer and how to provide access to needed and desired educational opportunities. Proprietary schools may be best for quick training and in this case a program of tuition aid may be suitable, along with the cooperation of industry. For those needing adult basic education, local satellite learning centers may be most suitable with supportive services provided, such as day-care centers. Alternative ways of providing services should be under continuous review. I am not so naïve as to suggest that a completely rational approach will be tolerated. Vested interests and political considerations will continue to have their impact. However, the size of financial resources in contrast with burgeoning social demands will necessitate more reliance upon reason and planning.

Many people (especially those in state legislatures) criticize education for "overlap and duplication." Unfavorable comments are heard about educational institutions "fighting each other and competing with each other before appropriations committees." The result has been "revulsion against institutional aspirations," said one key legislator. The search for order, economy, and consensus is justified, but there is the ever-present danger that uniformity and rigidity may replace initiative and creativity—along with their occasional associates: institutional jousting and commotion. What is needed is a pattern of organization which makes possible maximum cooperation, coordination, and sharing of resources among institutions and at the same time assists institutions in developing their own specialized strengths and unique identities.

Institutions will have to be clearer about what they are and what they intend to be. Something is wrong if a private, four-year residential college and a community college, publicly supported, are fighting for the same students. Community college programs ought not to be like those of traditional four-year, residential institutions. Or is the private institution changing its target populations in a struggle for survival? The institutions should be aimed toward different students and hence have different programs.

Chapter 10. Something Special– Independent Junior Colleges

No review of the so-called junior college movement can be complete without consideration of the independent junior college. It is a special kind of college with special resources and special problems. Its mission has been obscured, perhaps, by the onrush of the public community college; yet the independent junior college can take much of the credit for the development of the two-year college idea—it was there first.

The privately supported junior college has served as a defense against the possible "homogenization" of education. Its existence has provided a choice as well as a chance for many Americans. If there is any hope for diversity in higher education, then the private institution should be preserved and nourished.

As with all private education, however, the independent junior college stands at a critical point in its history. Support from the private sector is becoming much more difficult to obtain. Society's growing commitment to the democratization of higher education has worked against the independent college, which traditionally has been considered exclusive and expensive. The tradition common to many privately supported institutions of high tuition, selective admissions policies, and the consequent implied elitism has lost some of its charm. The whole question of "relevance" pertains to any consideration of the private institution, and students find this kind of cloistered education lacking in relevance to the larger social issues of the time.

My meetings and interviews with people of private junior colleges also point up another real problem; that is, the management, the administration of these institutions, reveals that they have by and large failed to plan ahead. They did not read the handwriting on the walls ten or fifteen years ago, the message that the fabric of American education would probably be rewoven in the decades to come. Little attention was given to spelling out purposes, to involvement of the community in planning and decision making, they say. Management and planning have generally been lodged in the hands and the offices of one man, the chief administrator, with some modest input from boards of trustees.

As I review the problems and the resources of these institutions, this central consideration should be kept in mind: the colleges themselves are going to have to move aggressively and quickly into fresh long-range planning, involving many people in the process. Only if this is done can there be positive gains both internally and externally. And I am talking here about the very survival of this important segment of higher education.

Admittedly, it is difficult to generalize about these privately supported colleges because they are so diverse. Some have developed out of New England finishing schools for women where the tradition is exclusive admissions and liberal arts curricula. Others had their beginnings in proprietary trade schools where the tradition was a special brand of open-door admissions and vocational studies. Add the church-related colleges, military schools, the YMCA colleges, and various other kinds of traditions and relationships, and you have the independent junior college mix.

But there is one thing which they share in common: they are not directly supported by taxes. Limited federal and state finances are now going to private colleges for facilities and certain specific programs. But for general operations, the independent colleges look to the student's tuition, gifts from alumni and friends, and other private sources of support. And this is proving to be a very difficult common bond to live with.

The rise of the public community college with its local tax support and its commitment to open-door admissions and low tuition has made life more difficult for the independent junior college. Many privately supported institutions have seen community colleges open nearby. And, as a business officer at one private junior college told me, "You cannot sell on one corner what someone else is giving away on another corner."

While community colleges have grown in number, the list of private colleges has declined. In 1960, for example, there were 273 independent institutions listed in the *Junior College Directory* published by the American Association of Junior Colleges. In 1970 there were 244 independent junior colleges listed. Some of the institutions that disappeared from the directory were closed, some became four-year colleges in the search for a different financial base, some were taken over by the states and became public colleges.

VALUE OF INDEPENDENT INSTITUTIONS

Many educators worry about the possible extinction of these institutions because of the distinctive values that private education brings to our system. Independent junior colleges have strengths which need to be preserved.

I found people on these campuses consistently articulate in enumerating these advantages: small enrollment, closer personal relationships between students and faculty, transferability of courses, good professional teachers with time and interest to help individual students. Mostly the students spoke of the value of this kind of institution in terms of size. They often referred to the "large university" as the only alternative, one which they did not relish. One young woman seemed to catch up the feeling of many students when she said with feeling, "Big schools are *yuk!*" I heard these same values referred to over and over again—and with conviction. I had the impression that the conviction came from personal experiences that had verified the virtues cited in the catalogs of small colleges.

Administrators of independent junior colleges also referred to the valuable freedom that private institutions enjoy: freedom to set their own objectives, choose their own programs, select their own students and faculty. The president of a church-related junior college in the Southeast speculated about how much freedom his institution would have to give up if state aid were to become available to his college. He recognized that state officials have to account for funds spent and that guidelines and regulations would go hand in hand with any aid that might be proffered.

Some administrators and faculty are concerned that their institutional freedom from state offices and legislatures tends to get boxed in by other institutions, namely the universities. Many independent junior colleges concentrate on traditional academic offerings with the goal of transferring their students into four-year colleges. Consequently they feel some real limitations on what they can do. Will it transfer? is a more important question on many independent junior college campuses than it is at community colleges. A large percentage of the community college students are in occupational programs and do not intend to transfer, and large enrollments give the institutions more "muscle" for transfer. But this problem may become less significant for independent junior colleges. The pressures that growing community college enrollments are putting on universities to work out articulation problems will probably work to the advantage of the independent colleges as well.

HOW TO USE INDEPENDENCE

A more important problem for independent junior colleges obviously is how to use the freedom they *do* have to create new educational roles. I found some excellent examples of institutions that have successfully pursued new approaches to the educational task.

An independent junior college in Maine has an interesting program called "II Plus You." Students finishing two years at Westbrook College can have their further college work monitored by the college, and when they have completed the equivalent of a four-year program, the college can grant them a baccalaureate degree. Westbrook is for women. The advantage of its innovative program is that the graduates can move about the country (or the world for that matter) with their husbands and families, collecting credits at a number of institutions as special students, taking as much time as needed, without the encumbrance of repeatedly taking entrance exams and meeting requirements of regular degree programs at each of the institutions. Yet, they can complete a bachelor's degree program. Their "home" institution, Westbrook, has been approved by the state to grant both the bachelor of arts and bachelor of science degrees.

Another independent junior college, this one in Iowa, has worked out a three-year option with several universities in the state so that their students can remain at the two-year college for an extra year, transferring only the last year in the bachelor's program. Students seeking a master's degree take three years at the junior college and two years at one of the universities, obviously an advantageous option for many. This institution is Grand View College in Des Moines. If, for example, a Des Moines student considers it advantageous to live at home and attend Grand View for one more year before transferring to Iowa City, Ames, or Cedar Falls where the state universities are, the way is clear for him. The flexibility is there. The president is proposing to public community colleges in his area that students graduating from those institutions may wish to transfer to his college for an additional year before moving into the university.

Mitchell College in North Carolina has announced that it will refund tuition to students if learning fails to take place. In other words, the institution is accepting responsibility for the learning process. It is saying that it will be accountable. The student must have spent a required amount of time in the learning labs. He must have tried. But if that requirement is met and if the student still does not succeed in his studies, he will receive a full refund. There is no publicly supported comprehensive community college in the locality. Mitchell College is serving as much as possible as an open-door institution for the community.

At Marymount College in Florida I found a block system of scheduling courses which was the kind of innovation that I had been looking for in my search for change. The freshman year is called a "Year of Reflection." Each student spends seven weeks in each of these four areas of reflection: Identity, Meaning, The World around Us, and Communication. For seven weeks the student reflects on the question Who am I? The major emphasis is Western civilization and psychology as the student seeks to know himself. Then for seven weeks the question Why am I? is considered. Philosophy and theology provide the framework and resources as they consider what man is. Where am I? represents a creative encounter by the student with the world around him as he works in zoology, botany, and mathematics. Finally, the basic nature of the ability to communicate is acknowledged. For seven weeks all students study literature, composition, and the related arts. With the modular approach students achieve greater depth in a subject than when the usual fifty-minute "shift-of-gears" type of schedule is observed. Other advantages are easy entry at several different periods during the year, the possibility of focus on one area of interest at a time, and flexibility in scheduling for the college. There seemed to be general approval by students, faculty, and administration with the way the block system was working.

Still another innovation is to be found at Mount Vernon College in Washington, D.C. The college is on a modular calendar, which permits students to devise their own calendars. They may take one course at a time, finishing each in three weeks; two courses at a time, finishing the two in six weeks; or four courses at a time for twelve weeks. Here again, the program is one that allows flexibility and departs from structures and artificial barriers to learning.

IT COMES FROM THE PRESIDENT

Ultimately these kinds of innovations in independent junior colleges seem to hinge a great deal on the initiative of the president or some other administrator. The institutions I visited left me with the strong impression that the faculty is seldom involved in thinking through the role of the college. Time after time I heard faculty say, "That sort of thing comes from the president." Seldom did I detect interest on the part of the faculty in being involved in discussions of purposes and goals and possible changes. It was not uncommon to hear this sentiment: "The college is okay as it is, if it can only continue to exist financially."

While the faculty members with whom I talked were competent, articulate people, they were not well informed on educational issues. They had not read widely in the current literature of higher education. They did not identify themselves with the effort to clarify the role of independent junior colleges in the changing pattern of American higher education. Yet they were there, on the scene, where such questions are going to be decided.

It was evident under such circumstances that the insights and personalities of the presidents were crucial in these institutions. Board members seemed to think so, too. One trustee told me, "The purpose of this board is to see to it that our president doesn't retire."

In discussions with students, faculty, administrators, and trustees at both public and private colleges I inquired about institutional purposes—what they were, how they were identified. In the case of publicly supported community colleges I found basic purposes that were relatively easy to identify and widely accepted in such discussions. For example, the primary purpose of making educational opportunity beyond the high school broadly and easily accessible to almost everyone is generally articulated quite clearly. In many of the independent junior colleges I found purposes difficult to identify. In fact, good clear-cut statements of purposes and goals were simply not often expressed.

A survey conducted as part of our project indicated that private college leaders were most concerned with fund-raising activities. Often this is an activity that begins with identification of purposes and goals so that these basics can be communicated to potential supporters. But, if purposes and goals have been identified, they evidently have not been sufficiently communicated to establish a wide acceptance or understanding within the institutions.

The same study showed independent junior college administrators perceived the purposes of the institutions in terms of intellectual, psychological, and moral values, while public community college administrators perceived their institutional goals more in terms of career education programs, adult education, and efforts to respond to needs in the communities. Obviously, the people from private colleges are thinking about concepts that are much more abstract and more difficult to articulate than their public counterparts. But that should not preclude effective communication.

One has the feeling that faculty, students, trustees, and others could give a good deal of help to administrators of independent junior colleges in working out statements of purpose and that, in the process, these groups would develop a commitment to the results. Many interesting possibilities exist. Might not an independent junior college use its freedom to be selective and choose for itself a specialized area of concentration? It might select students with special needs—perhaps those who have poor communications skills, for example—and seek to build an outstanding learning situation for persons with these needs. Such an exercise is going on at Bennett College in New York State. It is a strong institution. And it is probably going to be even stronger. A collegewide committee that includes trustees, administrators, faculty, and students is planning a new Bennett. It is seeking a sharp definition of purpose for the institution. Discussions with persons on that campus indicated that there is a real commitment to changing the institution in whatever ways necessary to fit the mission identified through the committee's efforts.

Another suggestion was made: in the case of private colleges that educate women from affluent families, women who usually are going to marry men who will have substantial incomes, would it not make sense to make a specialty of educating the students to be effective community workers in volunteer agencies such as the PTA, the League of Women Voters, and the United Fund? Is that a reasonable specialty for a college? The person who suggested it thought it might be, especially if some colleges took a close look at what their graduates do a few years after they leave the institution.

A PRIVATELY SUPPORTED COMMUNITY COLLEGE

A different kind of institution in the private sector was included in the study. Central YMCA Community College in Chicago is an independent junior college, but in many ways it has greater resemblance to a community college than to a private institution.

As the name indicates, the institution is supported by the YMCA. And as one might assume from that fact, the college is engaged in a wide-ranging program of services. The college has an enrollment of some 4,000 in credit courses and another 3,000 in noncredit courses. It is a comprehensive community college in its curriculum, serving the diverse groups usually found in a community college. But it has also sought to draw on the power structures of street gangs to bring students into the program. "Street workers" are used to encourage promising young people to enroll. The students enlisted this way often include former dope addicts and former prison inmates. In fact, the college has organized a program staffed by former convicts to help rehabilitate and find jobs for such persons.

Central YMCA Community College has a large number of new programs, some with government funding. It was exciting to hear from the persons involved in these programs. They all knew precisely the terms of the act under which their salaries were paid. One program sends young black students on to Ivy League colleges where they seem to do very well. In fact, one of these young men who had just finished his first year at Dartmouth said that his background in the ghetto gangs of Chicago seemed to be good preparation for campus leadership at Dartmouth where many of the students had no comparable similar experience in personal leadership.

The main reason for this reference to Central YMCA Community College is to illustrate the diversity that exists in the independent junior college field. And I should emphasize that it is a successful institution with clear-cut purposes with regard to the kinds of students it will serve and the programs it will offer. It is meeting needs, and it is being supported.

There are many persons who speak of the need to make the case for privately supported junior college education. There is no big case that can be written for the independent junior college in general; there is only the case that can be made for each college individually.

The diversity is too great for useful generalizations. And that is the way it should be.

EACH MUST FIND ITS OWN ROLE

There is no weakness inherent in the fact that one finds no well-defined general statement of purposes for independent junior colleges. But there is weakness when no such statement is found for an individual college. It is futile to lump these institutions together in a common prescription for success except to say that each must find its own prescription. It is possible to justify the existence of independent junior colleges in general only in that it is good to have institutions with such freedom to become something special. But each institution has to find for itself its own special something and justify its existence in that context.

Following that line of thought, one can see the difficulty in developing programs of common endeavor. The American Association of Junior Colleges has in its membership 200 member institutions which are independent junior colleges. Within the Association is a National Council of Independent Junior Colleges embracing 70 institutions that hold memberships for which they pay additional dues. What kinds of programs can be successfully launched in the face of such diversity? What efforts can be made to advance these institutions in general when their real value becomes apparent only in looking at their individual programs or potentials?

Independent junior colleges have special problems. Some special efforts are going to have to be made to help them develop their full potential. As the executive officer of a national association, I believe that some things can be done nationally to benefit all such institutions. The advancement of the idea of the two-year college is bound to help both public and private institutions. A project to improve instruction in two-year colleges is bound to help both kinds of institutions as will a project to improve facilities planning or one to improve the preparation of counselors. Efforts to make government and foundations more aware of the capabilities and needs of these kinds of institutions are bound to help all two-year institutions, both public and private.

MANY KINDS OF COMMUNITY

Community can be defined many ways. When we talk about the public community college, we are most often talking about a geographic locality. But there are other kinds. The Fashion Institute of Technology, a publicly supported community college, has as its community the garment district in New York City. But its community can also be defined as the New York fashion industry. The same sort of community can be identified for the Academy of Aeronautics in New York. These are communities of interest bound together by elements other than geographical proximity.

What gives the community college strength is its identification with a constituency that is willing to support it—its community.

But, in the case of the independent junior colleges, most of the work to identify the potential—to find its own community *and* to fulfill it—will have to be done by each college itself. That may sound like a tough assignment; it is. In fact, it is one of the most challenging tasks in America higher education today. But, I am impressed with the resources available to our private institutions. I referred earlier to the untapped help from the faculty in thinking through and working out institutional purposes.

In a sense, the independent junior college has an advantage over the public institution. It does not have a locked-in community. It is free to find its own community of interest, and to identify with it and to be strong too.

One possibility immediately apparent is the community of interest represented by the independent junior college's board of trustees and its alumni. What interests do they *really* represent? The man who suggested that this question be researched by means of follow-up studies had an idea that needs to be examined by many colleges searching for a new statement of purpose. A similar idea was being offered by the administrator of one of the private colleges I visited. He said he felt his institution had to be increasingly aware of what its students were actually doing when they left the institution and to work to prepare them for those roles.

ALUMNI AND TRUSTEES CAN HELP

The trustees and alumni of independent junior colleges are in a good position to help their colleges identify a sense of educational purpose. And most privately supported junior colleges try to stay in close touch with their alumni. They know who they are and where they are. They should be able to draw on them for help. But they will have to do more in the way of follow-up than gather information that is used in the typical news-and-notes pages of the alumni magazines. And they will need to talk to their former students on a level different from the expected chatter at an annual chapter meeting. An effort to go into this kind of "community," to really probe its educational needs, and then to structure appropriate educational programs could result in the same strength as in an "aware" public community college seeking to identify the needs of its locality and to serve them. This kind of pursuit could result in the discovery of unique services such as those at Westbrook in the "II Plus You" program.

As I talked with persons in the independent junior colleges, I was particularly impressed with the resources represented by trustees. One college I visited gave an interesting example of how a board can be meaningfully involved in planning. The president said that the college's purpose was to give young people, many with a rural background, a basic liberal education. The college is virtually open door; in fact with respect to two counties, it *is* open door. Students, faculty, and trustees had been involved in a study of whether to become a four-year college. The decision had been made to remain two-year. Their present size of 1,600 was seen as near optimum. The board has been planning five years ahead and is now moving into a ten-year financial plan.

Many private two-year colleges have people on their boards who are seasoned planners and executives accustomed to providing leadership for organizations every bit as complex and expensive as junior colleges. Many of these persons have been very successful. Their basic skills are the ability to analyze problems and formulate solutions.

One observer said that enlisting this kind of resource person should be the first priority of most independent junior college presidents. He said he would work hard to identify and secure the help of several such persons for his board and then involve them as deeply as possible in working out a viable role for the institution. He was speaking about a continuing role, not just several meetings. And he was talking about a major investment of time on the part of the college's leadership. But he felt it would be worth it.

THE COMMUNITY AS A RESOURCE

Another resource which independent junior colleges must not overlook is the local community, the same one with which the public community colleges identify. Obviously a private institution like Central YMCA Community College does this. But I saw some other interesting illustrations too. For example, one independent junior college in a large city found that many of its students were attending because of geographical proximity. According to the director of admissions, ten years ago most of the students, perhaps 85 percent, were members of the church to which the college is related. They came from a large geographical area. But, today the denominational population at the college is down to approximately 25 percent. And now he estimates that as many as 85 percent of the students come from homes within a 10-mile radius of the campus. The institution has a rather traditional liberal arts curriculum with an admission policy for the day program that is somewhat selective. But the evening program is open door, and students can come into the college via that route, later qualifying for the day program. The president of the college and the trustees, some of whom are ministers, were not at all uneasy about seeing the college become less and less "an extension of the parish," as they put it. They were looking for ways to identify more closely with the world of business in the community as well.

This same college had found another interesting way to clarify its identity: by working with the other higher education institutions in the city. I was impressed with the division of labor that had been worked out. The independent junior college was specializing in a good-quality two-year liberal arts program. The publicly supported community college in the city was growing rapidly as an institution with a reputation for serving "remedial" needs, students with interests in occupational education programs, and students with limited funds. The university in the same city was doing a good job of working with both institutions in a consortium arrangement. The three colleges together will work through their consortium to help direct students to the appropriate institutions. It was interesting to note that the three colleges in this consortium had more black students than the three public universities in that state. The U.S. Department of Health, Education, and Welfare made a grant of $106,000 for the academic year to support a special program by the consortium to provide services to economically disadvantaged and physically handicapped students.

Some of the faculty at the independent junior college felt a little uneasy about trying to reach out to disadvantaged ghetto popula-tions in the city. Their uneasiness stemmed from a question about their own abilities to do this kind of work. But the board did not seem to have this same reservation. They felt they had just begun to tap their resources for offering services to educationally dis-advantaged students.

I could not help but compare the fine working relationship this college seemed to have with the other institutions in its city to the situation I found in another private junior college in another state. The second college was located virtually across the street from a university with which it might have related very well, and very profitably too. The university was a strong institution. But, as far as I could determine during my visit, there was no real communication between the two institutions. It was not long after that I found out that the two-year college was going to close its doors and cease to exist.

SUMMARY

Independent junior colleges represent a special resource in our society and in the American scheme of higher education. They enjoy an enviable freedom which is also their special challenge: they have the ability to identify their own assignment.

In the public sector, to a large extent, the community college receives its mandate when it is established and supported by the local community it serves. This is not so for the independent institution. It can offer a quality two-year program to any specialized community it finds to serve. That "community" may be local, regional, or national. In a complex society, there are many communities of interest that need postsecondary educational services. The challenge of the independent junior college is to make this identification for itself.

The value of this kind of education in the perceptions of the persons involved is often related to size. To them a small college means better instruction, better relationships. The main problem is usually seen as a lack of finances. But the institutions visited seemed to bear witness that when an appropriate role is found for the institution, the funding will follow. There was an observable tendency to rely on the president to define the purposes and goals of the institution and to plan its program.

These colleges will be stronger in the long run, it seems to me, if they will make a genuine effort to involve more persons in the dialogue necessary to define their individual roles and promote understanding and acceptance of them. They have some impressive resources available to them for this task. If they use them well, the results may be equally impressive.

Part 5.
Trends in Community Relations

It's not the location, but what you do. You could sit right in the middle of the ghetto and not serve it.

A Board Member

Chapter 11.
The College
Should Be There

There is a meeting place for America's diversity, a common ground, a means for communication. Every day in Miami, Florida, and Kansas City, Missouri, in Cleveland, Ohio, and Booneville, Mississippi, in a thousand locations across this land people as different as the communities in which they live are coming together. They are interacting. They are talking. They have not left their communities nor surrendered their identities. Their aims are varied. Common needs bring them together, and common interests are discovered. Their meeting place is America's community colleges.

As I moved around the country, I listened to people talk about "their" college. What I heard was not the old cliché about "town and gown."

"It has pulled the people together," said someone in North Carolina. "Bankers and welders, black and white, Democrats and Republicans, all support the college, even the chronic critics."

"Everybody has a little piece of the academic pie in this community," was the way somebody described the college in a Midwestern city. And as a student saw it, "This college serves the street corner guy, the man sitting in the office. This college has a fit for all of them."

And that is close to the impression I had. Community and college were moving beyond mere speaking terms; they were getting to know each other and were ready to call theirs a close relationship.

However, nobody could attribute the multiplying of community colleges throughout this last decade to a deliberate move by civic leaders to provide a mechanism for bringing community segments together. The reasons for establishment were usually much more conventional than that. They dealt with community pride that said, "This city needs a college." Or they were considered part of a state plan for dispersing educational opportunities, making college possible for people living at home. Or their function was to ease the load of the university, especially of students who were not ready for university entry. Motivations in the sixties were pragmatic and conventional.

In the late sixties society was beset by divisions and struggles for identity as part of a cultural nationalism; it was concerned about the youth culture and generation gaps, the haves and have-nots, the hard hats and the longhairs. It was the cracks in the culture and changes demanded of education that thrust into the foreground of community college values an element that had been perceived as incidental, a happy by-product. And this community institution, in the process of doing its job of providing educational opportunity on an open-access basis, emerged as a means to cut across the conflicting forces. The effect was cohesive. How did this occur?

PLANNERS LOOK AT THE COMMUNITY

One explanation for the move toward a merger of community and college is the simple fact that some educational planners are taking an honest look at the potential service area of the college and from there drawing clues for the college services and programs. This is a dramatic shift from starting with traditional ideas of what a college is and does. It is a turnabout from referring to "higher" education as a body of knowledge and processes to referring to the sociology, the economics, and the psychology of the people to be served. Who are these people? What are *their* characteristics? How are their needs to be identified? What educational services are unmet? This basic, most essential shift in orientation is beginning to take place. An obvious reason for this, of course, is the insistent pressure of the social environment.

In the past, community colleges had not made much of an effort to find out about the communities they served. The dean of the evening division of a large college told me that until she was given responsibility for the direction of long-term planning for the college she had no idea that in her county there were more Indians than in any other urban area of the country save one—20,000 in the metropolitan area and another 8,000 to 10,000 on reservations.

In Miami with its large Cuban population, now about 300,000, there are an estimated 100,000 who speak no English. If help were needed, for example, from the police department or fire department and if those agencies had no one who could speak Spanish, there could be serious consequences. Using Spanish, college personnel telephoned some 70 downtown companies or agencies and found that, indeed, they did not comprehend the language. As a result the college is training people to respond to calls bilingually.

Community Needs Differ

The nature of the needs may differ as widely as the communities. In North Carolina a dean told me his perception of the area's educational needs. He didn't have to refer to notes or papers. He knew the figures:

20,000 adults over age twenty-five who are functional illiterates

40 percent of the school population who drop out of high school

Underemployed individuals

Those needing preparation for job entry

Students preparing to transfer to a four-year college

Older persons having interest in utilization of leisure time

I was impressed. It is not often that the needs are so precisely articulated. But then I felt a chilly draft of realism as he went on to tell me that while the needs were as he described them, the college program then corresponded almost negatively. The priorities were:

Students preparing to transfer to a four-year college

Those needing preparation for job entry

Older persons having interests in utilization of leisure time

Underemployed individuals

20,000 adults over age twenty-five who are functional illiterates

40 percent of the school population who drop out of high school.

Accounting for the discrepancy between the two lists, in his view, was the difficulty in getting acceptance of the first three educational needs he listed as worthy of college response. He attributed this generally to the thinking of faculty coming out of graduate schools.

Three community leaders on the West Side of Chicago talked with me about the issues in their area that were central to the mission of a college. There was nothing casual about these conversations. They were describing life-and-death issues. They had been there through the burnings and the riots. Now the college had given them hope. Businesses were beginning to emerge. There was a significant change from emphasis on protest to emphasis on production. In that part of Chicago 65 percent of the youth drop out of high school.

"How else do you sit at the planning table rather than being programmed by somebody else?" asked these men. Community control and economic development are the keys to realization of hopes, and education the backup. They call the college their "city hall." For the first time community leaders had the information necessary to ascertain needs and to proceed with community planning and development. They had the capacity for analysis, expertise to deal with other agencies at the planning levels, and brainpower to plan.

A state commissioner of education saw the community colleges as a tool to achieve social objectives, to break the poverty cycle, to meet the needs of racial minorities. He believed that the major portion of continuing education would be done by community colleges, and he emphasized their potential in serving rural areas in the role of centers of community activity. He saw this role as important enough to be recognized by state planners.

A Need to Refocus Efforts

If community colleges want to be in the forefront in the 1970s, they need to refocus their efforts to respond to the needs of older people rather than recent high school graduates who will probably go on to college anyway. This position was forcibly expressed by a state superintendent of public instruction concerned about the need for educational services, to people eighteen to sixty-four and older. A way must be found, he felt, to bring together the community schools, the adult basic education services, high school equivalency programs, adult vocational skills centers, the off-campus collegiate offerings, and the community service programs so that no adult is ever denied the opportunity of these kinds of services. A regional approach is needed to bring these various services together into a coordinated pattern. He saw the community college as the most effective regional unit for the work of coordination.

One of the basic needs, in fact, the implied prerequisite of the community college, the sine qua non, is knowledge of the area where the college is located and which it services. Not enough is known now by most community colleges about their target populations, nor is there assurance that the interpretation of what is known is correct. Both are required—the disposition to look into the community for data and the capacity to probe its meaning for college programs.

THE COLLEGE CANNOT GO IT ALONE

No institution can go it alone, least of all the community college. The name itself connotes a sense of relationship, a community of interest. And there are evident pressures to enforce relationships if they do not flourish voluntarily. Rapidly mounting social needs suggest the wisdom of exploring every possible way for various community services to minimize the need to compete for available resources.

It is clear that the public schools and community colleges have overlapping interests and that each has a stake in the productivity of the other. Much more needs to be done in recognizing this common ground. In fact, self-interest warrants such recognition. If only for our own defense, said a president, we must tie into earlier school experiences. The load of reclaiming people coming out of public schools ineffectively prepared was impossible, he felt. Some educators have proposed that the responsibility for inadequately prepared students should be borne by the elementary and secondary schools. Obviously it would be better if students learned to read and write before they sought entrance to the community college. This is where the solution should be sought over the long haul. But now the college assumes the role of meeting the student where he is and at the same time linking up with the schools in supportive and helpful ways.

Deans and presidents give the impression of having more rapport with college and university personnel than with the professionals in public schools. A state commissioner of education was blunt about this. In his state he thought the presidents and deans tended to turn up their noses at the high schools. He called for better relationships between these institutions and suggested that the deans and presidents ought to meet with high school principals and teachers to build a stronger and more understanding relationship. Faculty members in a community college took up that same theme. They urged administrators of both kinds of institutions to work together and faculty to tackle problems of counseling, curriculum planning, and other matters of mutual interest.

An Example of Ineffectiveness

One of the most blatant examples of ineffective relationships is that between community colleges and area vocational schools. Fortunately, some improvement is now taking place. For example, in New Jersey there are several counties with coordinating councils for occupational education. These are made up of the community college president, the superintendent of comprehensive high schools, the county superintendent of schools, appointees from labor, and the director of the area vocational school. A county coordinator of occupational education represents the state and the local area in convening the group. This device compels joint examination of who can best deliver the services. Some funding assistance is provided by foundations.

Questions are being raised more frequently about what is often called the "luxury of duplication." Two prominent civic leaders in a Midwestern city wanted some answers. There were seventeen school districts and numerous universities, colleges, and community colleges in their city. They wondered whether these institutions were not to a great extent doing the same things. Was there not some way they could relate to each other? They insisted that duplication and overlapping existed and that the costs were too great. As they put it, the taxpayers will demand some kind of unification. They saw an area council on higher education to perform a planning and coordinating function as only a partial answer.

But quite justifiably their criticism and concerns were not limited to the educational scene. The need for regional government was stressed, a government that could transcend county and state lines. Their attitudes were fully representative of those expressed in many other places. Is it the responsibility of the community college to serve as a catalyst toward area planning and as a mechanism for agency and organizational relationships? What should the community college do in this situation? In acquiring a site for a new community college and preparing that site for construction, $6 million is spent. Of that money 20 percent is being expended for parking space. At the same time, in that area there is a large medical complex under development as well as large business buildings. Parking needs exist for the whole area. Should the community college, the hospitals, and the businesses get together and take a look at their common needs—including parking? Seldom are people sitting down together to look at these common needs and the most economical ways to meet them. Somebody should exercise this kind of initiative. In the long run, an institution that relies upon substantial public support will find that its interest will have been advanced by taking such leadership.

The College Is One Influence among Many

The concern for economy, persuasive though it is today, is not the only important reason why the college cannot go it alone. The college is one influence among many which touch the lives of those who look to educational opportunities as a means of liberation from the poverty cycle, but who may find themselves enmeshed in a whole system of interrelated and often competing forces. If the college is to be successful in its work with the student, it must be aware of those elements in his environment that counter his efforts to become self-determined. What is the responsibility of the college in a case like the following?

Just out of military service, a young man enters the New Careers Program at a community college. He is employed in juvenile court work and preparing to be a paraprofessional. He hopes to go on for a degree in social work. The New Careers Program is funded by the Department of Labor, and its purpose is to make the employee more effective in his job in human services. He works 24 hours a week and studies at the college. Joe reported that when he went into this program, his income went up slightly. So his rent was raised. The man at the housing authority said that he admired what Joe was trying to do, but when Joe was unable to pay, he turned off the lights. And there was the problem of trying to change the date of payment of rent from the first to the fourteenth so that it would match up with the time that he got his check. The new student was discouraged. He told me:

> I could have drawn the $800 I had coming to me after the service, and I could have just sat there and used it up. So often it looks like the props are knocked out from under you while you are trying to climb. The program seems designed to keep you alive, but not to advance you. You really have to have zap to go ahead with it.

Many welfare and social agencies—housing, food stamps, unemployment, vocational rehabilitation—impinge upon the lives of low-income people. Often there is little or no communication among agencies. Perhaps one role of the community college ought to be that of providing interagency communication so that the individual's interest in self-improvement could be advanced rather than defeated. But the college needs to maintain its unbiased position even as it helps to break this institutional cycle. To take sides is a questionable measure, but the college can be a public forum. It can and should provide opportunity for expression of points of view. Although it should maintain its independence, it can work to reduce the existing barriers among such agencies and organizations so that educational objectives will be so fully achieved that one day there would be no need of them.

SELF-IMPROVEMENT OPPORTUNITIES PROMISED NEAR TO HOME

A commitment was made by the state of North Carolina and many other states during the sixties. It was a noble commitment, one with far-reaching implications for the citizens, and their children, of those states. It was a democratic plan.

Every adult citizen would be afforded at reasonable cost an opportunity near his home to learn a trade or technical occupation, to continue to upgrade his economic capacity, to further his general education or even to learn to read and write if for some reason he failed to acquire those basic skills earlier in life.

The intent was to put the services of community colleges within reach of most citizens. Sometimes geographic accessibility was referred to as commuting distance, perhaps 30 miles or an hour's travel time. College campuses were built in most of the states. Frequently they were planned in connection with the new interstate highway system. Access was generally good for persons with automobiles. Parking lots were usually ample. But for those who relied upon public transportation or whose time was limited because of employment or other responsibilities, access was not as easy. And for prospective students to whom the ways of the majority culture were either alien or suspect, the college campuses were not inviting. In many parts of the country people affirmed that the process of dispersion of educational services throughout the state needed to continue beyond those units designated as campuses. These were needed as administrative and resource centers, but the rapidly increasing population of students over thirty years of age and others who were more at home in their neighborhoods needed to be served there.

People who work all day find it difficult to drive 30, 40, or 50 miles to get to the college campus. Why not transport college faculty to locations closer to the homes of these people—in the schools or churches or neighborhood centers? Or why not offer the programs in the place of employment, the hospitals, nursing homes, newspaper offices, and factories? There seems to be less hesitancy to take courses in familiar and convenient surroundings. Registrations could be held in the plant, paper work reduced to the minimum, textbooks and other materials provided there, and full credit given for work taken without the necessity of going to the college campus. The accessibility principle is a logical extension of state policy, but its application is limited because of the conventional notion that a college is something to go to and that all people are equally equipped to make that journey.

Struggle for Recognition

In the struggle to be recognized as a respectable institution of higher education the community college sought to move out of the high school buildings and the "temporary" facilities in which many started. If the institution looked like a college, the chances seemed better that recognition and acceptance would come.

This was a necessary stage in the evolution of the community college. Many would agree with those administrators who say that some central facilities are needed. But now services also need to be housed either in existing facilities or in smaller and more widely dispersed units. It seems a little disrespectful to refer to a new campus as that "damn brick pile," but the administrator who was talking was frustrated. He believed that the institution would have to "de-institutionalize" itself and that learning opportunities in that city needed to be taken out into the churches and the livingrooms of people. He knew that some of the young people he was trying to reach were not going to embarrass themselves by coming to the college. On the other hand, the faculty member who moved out into the neighborhood would have to be good or he wouldn't be able to stay there. So the community college outpost gets the people ready; it develops the kind of confidence needed to sit in a room with a professor, the professor who, they said, initially scared the hell out of them. The phrase *near to home* may have a psychological significance as important as its meaning in miles.

WHERE THE DRAMA IS REAL

Community and college interfused. To accept that view means a different way of judging many things the college does or does not do. For example, students commonly call their community college "Apathy U." Why? Out of several thousand students only a few hundred vote in a student government election. For three weeks an appeal was posted on the bulletin board for people to volunteer to be cheerleaders. There were no takers. One community college had a championship football team, but most of the spectators were not students. Student leaders said there was no school spirit, and then they searched for explanations. Some were pretty standard. Most of the people who attend work part time. They live in the area, and as soon as classes are over, they leave. They still have their roots in the community. Perhaps if there were residence halls, more would be done.

Probe this kind of thoughtful searching awhile. You begin to realize that your definition of college spirit is in terms of the classic stereotype of the residential campus where students live for a few years apart from the world in their own cloistered community, with its folkways and mores, its own language, its own life. After a period in this setting the student "goes out into the world." An institution of this kind has its value. It has its own place. The community college is a different kind of institution. Morale, college spirit, cannot be measured with the same yardstick. *Apathy* may be a misnomer for the degree of participation of community college students. They have a different set of challenges, a different setting for participation.

The setting is a real-life situation. The macrocosm rather than the college microcosm is the center of activity. There is the widow who has to work, the veteran who has come back to college, people who have limited time to spend with their families.

The day is just so long, and you have only so much energy. Residence halls might be good, but we have other people enrolled in apprentice training and secretarial programs, mothers taking children's literature courses. There are general education development programs and apprentice programs and programs for mothers on welfare.

At the same time that it is difficult to find people to work on the college newspaper, there are many students who are paid employees of the city newspapers.

Apathy May Mean Something Else

What appears to be apathy toward college activities could well be a result of involvement in employment, family responsibilities, or other commitments where the students live. These social facts about community college students can be looked upon as handicaps and deterrents toward learning with a consequent hand-wringing about student apathy, or they can be seen as a reality which cannot be escaped and which ought to be utilized to strengthen motivation and to facilitate learning. For example, with the eighteen-year-old vote, shouldn't the college program and outlook encourage enlightened, informed participation by college students in the political and governmental life of those areas in which they live? Shouldn't students with interest in journalism be encouraged to seek opportunity for work with community publications? And for those in theater, music, and the arts, wouldn't this encouragement enhance identification with civic organizations representing these interests?

There has been some movement in this direction in the occupational fields through cooperative programs and work-study experiences, but even here a vast expansion is in order. The underlying philosophy for this approach is to accept the characteristics of the community college student as living in the community, usually employed, often with family and neighborhood responsibilities and developing educational programs based upon that experience, as contrasted with simulation.

A director of student activities might spend time in negotiating these links with the community rather than stirring up enthusiasm for a scheduled student activity on campus. Not all students would have interest in moving in this direction, nor are all communities ready to absorb the shock of having students in their presence rather than having them confined to the campus. But the institution should be encouraged in that direction. The idea of "acting out" where the drama is real would not only enliven the college experience but would also provide a context in which students who are already residents of the community interact with their fellow citizens in cultural, political, and occupational situations. In this way an experimental base exists for communication. Often suspicion and sometimes hostility exist toward the college. There is apprehension and lack of understanding. An approach that minimizes separatism and maximizes common participation wherever possible would change such attitudes. What goes on then would be "where the people are."

THE COMMUNITY COLLEGE AS A FOCAL POINT

The factors of impermanence and transiency so well documented by
observers of contemporary America are nowhere more evident than
in the service areas of community colleges. People move from farms
to cities and within cities from place to place as economic and social
factors push and pull.

In an area served by a California community college the
population increased from 10,000 to 110,000 in ten years. So much
movement into the area had made it difficult to establish any sense
of identity for the district as a whole, any concept of a single
community. Many people who lived there drove to other places for
employment, and people who lived in other areas worked in the
college district. A college administrator in another situation
wondered how you could keep your fingers on the pulse of a district
of 600,000 people made up of a large number of communities and
community interests. To what community does the college relate? Is
it possible to establish a sense of community out of the variety and
disparity of a changing, widely dispersed population? I heard the
question raised frequently and the difficulties described. Finally,
though, the conclusion was reached that somehow such a sense of
community must be sought. And there is no other institution that
offers as much potential because it covers broad interests and needs.

Pulling the People Together

There is urgent need for the college to serve as a focal point, said the
president of a community college in the South. On the east side of
his city there was no focal point other than the churches. He saw
the feeling of community at a low level. The east side was cut off
from the cultural activities serving other areas in the metropolis.
People felt little or no relationship to those other centers. Nobody
had hit upon anything to pull the community together. He felt that
it was up to the college to identify the needs of the people and to get
programs set up.

The trend toward larger districts in the name of efficiency and
economy heightens the probability that the population will be even
more varied in income, culture, race, and interests. To imagine this
conglomerate as uniform in its expectations of the college program
and services verges on the ridiculous. There are many components to
the area served, many communities to acknowledge. What the college
does is provide a focal point, a center, places and reasons for coming

together. The many communities and the varied constituents meet in the context of the college. In this process more conversations take place, some differences are accommodated, and some overarching common interests may emerge.

PARTICIPATION IN COMMUNITY CHANGE

Should the community college be viewed as an agent for social change? There are mixed answers to that question. Some define the college's role as transmitting society's professed values with little or no examination of the discrepancy of actual social performance. However, a growing chorus is heard of statements like these:

It needs to become an advocate for the community. It should be socially oriented, a community storehouse for immediate knowledge. It should take over community action programs, have human relations activities and programs for the aged.

The community college should be on the forefront of ethnic and cultural integration, whether this is stated or not.

Fifteen years of chronic unemployment. The community college ought to be doing something about it.

In our city the college through its community services program is providing some political education. It is assisting in the registration of voters, encouraging the people to vote.

As a change agent? Not as a revolutionary force but as the cutting edge to help foment constructive change.

The college participates with the community as a change agent. Perhaps it has changed more than it has brought about change. The community college is different from a university working on a study of the community. The college has a long-term investment in the community, and it is not a matter of trying to improve on the community. But it is a matter of working with the community, for example to help the police department raise the level of competence of law enforcement officers through community college programs.

The College as an Agent, Not Advocate, of Change

Those who question the definition of the college as an agent of change are often concerned that this means advocacy of a political or partisan position. Advocacy of one position, by definition, can mean elimination of other considerations. It can also mean continuous struggles for power to control the college. With power to control as the prize sought, power can become an end rather than a means to strengthen the institution. A community college, by virtue of its place in the community, may find its work threatened by the very element that can give it success—its primacy of relationship with the components it serves.

On the other hand, by its very nature the community college is an advocate of a position on values. It declares that educational opportunity should be available to all. Implied is recognition of each individual's value to himself and to society. In an extension of this position about people the admissions policies of most community colleges acknowledge differences among people in motivation, interests, achievement, age, and objectives. In a society which has established educational institutions as a means of mobility, the very existence of the publicly supported community college with its open-door stance clearly demonstrates a viewpoint about the desirable directions of social change.

The variety of programs offered by the college also reveals the orientation of its values. Some are now under question and examination. Do these values show a preoccupation with the world of work? Do they reveal enough concern for other aspects of human life such as self-knowledge, family relationships, civic participation and obligations, lifelong learning, and creative expression? The leadership role of the college is to encourage such questions, their discussion, and thus clarification of issues through the experiences of people. It should also offer assistance in projecting the probable results of actions and values. The college programs will appropriately change to relate to social needs.

Housing Patterns Transcended

In another important way the college serves as an agent of change: the first genuine interaction among the various racial and cultural groups takes place in some cities when the student reaches community college. This is due to the ethnic geography of the district. The community college can transcend the housing patterns that have limited elementary and secondary education. Much the same thing could be said about age distribution as about racial and cultural differences. The colleges are responding to both ends of the age spectrum, day-care centers on one hand and services to the elderly on the other. Interaction of age groups may have much more social significance than is commonly recognized at this time.

It was more than coincidental that the number of public junior colleges doubled and enrollments tripled during the decade of the interstate highway, Appalachia, urban explosion, racial tension, violent dissent and protest, and men on the moon. An educational instrument, the public junior college which had been forged in another time to meet other needs, showed promise of possessing an adaptive and responsive quality to new needs. These needs related to the concept of the word *community* which was more often modifying "college" in the name of these institutions. Historically, it could be said that first came the change in name, then came the conditions that pressed the college to become what the name stood for.

Equal opportunity, human rights, quality of life, the value of cultural differences—so many elements considered implicit in America's social fabric are challenged and questioned. Consequences of social and economic policies become painfully apparent in unlivable cities, smoggy skies, and dirty water. It is clearly a time for new emphasis on the value of the person, his place in the group, and the importance of interrelationships of people. These conditions call for the educational institution which has been on the scene since the turn of the century as a junior member of the higher education establishment to reshape its priorities and its purposes. Now the community college is called to significant work in its own right and in its own name.

SUMMARY

The community college is a meeting place for ideas and people. It's a place for communication and interaction. Academics are the concern of the people. They can be critical, they can raise questions, they can have something to do with what happens.

There are good explanations for the coming together of people and the college. Social pressures have made educational planners recognize the need for it. Rather than view higher education as some isolated part of the community, planners have begun to see it, particularly with regard to the community college, as a central part. Community control and economic development are the keys to realization of hopes, and education the backup.

To realize the full potential of being where the action is, the community college will want to refocus its efforts in the 1970s. It will need to consider older people as well as youth in its programming efforts. A wide range of services will be needed. Present arrangements for meeting needs of all the people will need to be

228 TRENDS IN COMMUNITY RELATIONS

altered. What works for the young students may not be appropriate for the older students.

The community college cannot go it alone. It must link up with earlier school experiences. There are overlapping interests between public schools and colleges, with each having a stake in the productivity of the other. College administrators and faculty must seek better rapport with public schools in order to bring about necessary interaction.

Just as it should work closely with public schools, the community college should help bring about better articulation among other agencies. Many welfare and social agencies impinge upon the lives of the people. The community college can encourage cooperation and communication among these agencies so that the lot of the people can be improved.

Accessibility is the key to community college promise. But is accessibility to be measured only in geographic distance, in mileage? Colleges can make education more accessible by taking programs where the people work and live. Put programs in churches and the living rooms of the community.

The community college, whether it wants to or not, is going to be an agent of change. It is in and of the community. Thus, it should wear the mantle of change proudly and ensure that in its philosophy and program it seeks to bring about change that will provide for the individual self-fulfillment that is so important in the lives of Americans.

Conclusion To Achieve the Goals

CHANGES IN THE STUDENT POPULATION TO BE SERVED

In forecasting what the community college will be like five to ten years from now, the basic question is, What kinds of students should this college serve? Resolution of virtually all other issues—learning strategies, locus of decision making, and patterns of financial support—depend on the answer to that question.

It was on this matter that interviewees showed substantial agreement. This institution, they said, should provide educational opportunity to those who have not had it before—the financially handicapped, minority groups, those who wish to prepare for early employment, those who need to be retrained, older persons wishing to use their time constructively and creatively. These were some of the target groups.

Others will come in large numbers for a multitude of reasons. State policies may "divert" entering freshmen from state colleges and universities to the community colleges. The financial crunch may encourage students to conserve their financial resources by attending the low-cost community college close to home for the first two years and then transferring to another institution. More students say they are seeking a learning environment that seems to highlight the individual's interests and needs, and they perceive the community college as offering that promise.

Whatever the reasons, prospects are for more students and greater diversity among them. Although the spiraling enrollment increases of the last ten years will probably not continue, steady growth and changing proportions of constituent groups are expected. For example, enrollment of veterans is expected to increase. There will be many more students beyond the conventional "college age." There will be large numbers who have not completed high school, and in several states adults will be offered basic education programs. More students will attend the college on a part-time basis, and more may move from college to work (or to other experiences) and back to college as interests and personal needs change. The enrollment of minority group students has risen sharply over the last few years and is expected to represent a major sector in the community college population.

Many students seek more than academic experiences. They will be looking for a sense of personal worth, acceptance and encouragement, and their place and role in society. Such broad outreach has many implications. An open-admissions policy, with its broadening variety of students, will bring differences in motivations, ages, life-styles, and levels of academic achievement that pose extremely difficult teaching tasks.

CHANGES IN HOW THEY ARE SERVED

What changes are anticipated in learning strategies, teaching styles, educational programs, and supportive services? What do the data show? Many hours of discussion ensued about this part of the community college forecast. Most of the discussion dealt with problems, searching questions, and deep concerns. Not much time was devoted to solutions, although some creative efforts were reported in a few institutions.

A deficiency immediately apparent is the limited knowledge most institutions have of their students and their community settings. Either the information is not secured, or if it is, it seldom gets to the professionals who have firsthand contact with students. Further, there is a tendency to use traditional labels that don't fit community college students and institutional purposes. It is inaccurate and misleading to evaluate community college services in terms of data on "dropouts," "degree-credit students," "college grade," "college age," and other well-known terms that may be suitable to colleges with different tasks.

To be at all useful measures of evaluation must relate to the tasks performed. Current data collection efforts in the community college field do not satisfy this criterion. To correct this shortcoming, federal and state government offices, the national associations involved, and the individual institutions must take a new look at their data collection methods as well as at their interpretations of information. Evaluative information based on institutional goals will enable the community college to adjust its course according to experience.

CHANGE LAGS

Although a new consciousness of educational mission seems to be emerging, changes in organization, administrative concepts, teaching styles, and learning strategies lag. Community college planners appear to be saying that they cannot initiate change but must wait and respond to change initiated by other institutions and agencies. They seem hemmed in by educational codes, traditions of higher education, the number and diversity of students, and minimal collegiality among faculty.

Faculty members say that the goals of the institution are ambiguous. They are often very frustrated. The frustration may stem from uncertainties or differences of opinion about who the college is to serve. Or, if student diversity is accepted as appropriate to the college role, then the question is, How do we do it? Those who hold teaching responsibilities are spending little time examining basic educational issues affecting the institution and their work. Many felt their skills did not match this changing, complex educational assignment. They were critical of their graduate schools and of their own institutions for not providing the opportunity to rectify their deficiencies.

In the basic matter of how the student is served, is there hope that the community college can be the flexible, dynamic, creative, and self-determined institution it is commonly envisioned to be?

PRESIDENTIAL LEADERSHIP CRUCIAL

The element crucial at this stage of community college evolution is the quality of presidential leadership. Constraints on creativeness and initiative in problem solving spring from uncertainties about the educational task coupled with the tepid spirit of noninvolvement. The greatest desire I heard expressed was for leadership which involved the participants so that common goals could be identified. Then there would be a common understanding of what it was they were to do together. It has been reported earlier: the role of the president is changing. The "bricks and mortar man" is being replaced by presidents with the training and personal qualities such as those specified by one of the nation's largest community college districts:

We seek a superior leader in education with demonstrated competence. Although we prefer a person with community college administration experience in urban settings, this does not foreclose consideration of candidates from other areas of educational experience. However, he must be committed to community college goals.

Among personal qualities considered important are the following: capacity to inspire trust among associates and to respect diverse viewpoints; forceful but not demanding; decisive but not defensive; capable of purposive listening; emotionally secure.

We seek a strong administrator:

a   To provide leadership for those involved in the work of the district so that common goals are identified and accepted.

b   Capable of nurturing an atmosphere of openness, trust, and cooperation among college personnel and the community toward accomplishment of college goals.

c   Capable of attracting and developing competent staff to whom responsibility is delegated.

d   Able to secure participation of people affected by decision making.

e   With capacity to organize for procurement and interpretation of data to be used by appropriate personnel in program and policy evaluation and review.

f   Aware of the finite nature of resources available for the educational tasks.

g   An independent thinker capable of interacting effectively with the board with recognition and respect for the particular and different responsibilities of the administrative and policy-making bodies.

The chief executive officer for the district will have the facility to become acquainted with the dynamics of this urban environment and will in turn have leadership responsibilities in interpreting the district goals and programs to the district community. Age: 35-55 preferred. However, a high level of vitality, physical energy, and enthusiasm are essential regardless of age. Special needs: Experience with a split board, a critical press, with teacher unions, militant faculty groups, and complex administrative organization.

GOALS OF THE ENTERPRISE

The criteria developed by this board reflect their perceptions of urgent present needs. A similar document prepared ten years ago might emphasize substantially different qualities. The community college president's leadership role is extraordinarily important now. He must make clear the institution's goals. Once the mission has been specified, many questions can be resolved.

Financial pressures are demanding an ordering of priorities. What sectors of the population represent the most urgent educational needs? How will the resources of the college be deployed? Choices must be made.

The growing press for institutional accountability necessitates measures of output. What yardsticks are appropriate?

Faculty members reveal more than moderate frustration with respect to their teaching assignment. And it seems to them to be exactly that, an assignment about which they had little to say.

National and state-level developments require better coordination and common planning among the various kinds of educational institutions within a state. Respective roles and missions will need to be determined.

Legislatures need to establish new patterns of funding for community colleges in the light of court suits over the constitutionality of using property taxes in support of education. How will the legislature determine what financial measures will facilitate effectiveness in the institutions?

In each instance (and each represents a significant contemporary issue) the only way toward resolution is through the development of a clear understanding of the institutional mission—the goals of the enterprise. Without this, judgments cannot be made of college priorities, selection and appropriate training of faculty, how well the institution is doing, its part in the total educational program of the state, an effective financial reward system, or finally, what kind of person is best qualified to serve as president. The president cannot escape responsibility for this task. Only one other responsibility parallels it in importance—establishment of a process to evaluate the effectiveness of resources and programs in achieving the agreed-upon goals.

THE NEED FOR TRAINING

There is no need confronting the community college more critical than for administrators with sophisticated conceptual ability as well as a working understanding of the fundamentals of human relations. But there is no large-scale, systematic effort to identify and train administrators or to retrain present leaders in terms of the changing requirements of their positions. The military forces have their staff colleges. The Department of State has its specialized training institutions. Corporations continuously search for talent among their personnel and establish management training programs.

Apparently it is assumed in the community college field that success will come from a generalized background and a fortuitous sliding into an often poorly defined role. A mechanism is needed to make possible a massive commitment to self-improvement. Institutions must provide time and the financial means for its leaders to utilize resources for professional improvement when they become available. Moreover, the task of the president requires clarification. A continuous process to identify potential and a program for development and evaluation are needed. Community college boards could benefit by assistance in identifying persons with the specified personal attributes and training to meet the requirements of their institutions.

Occasional efforts have been made in the past to prepare community college presidents. Most noted are the junior college leadership programs supported by the W. K. Kellogg Foundation which were initiated in 1960 at the beginning of the dramatic increase in the number of public community colleges. Those programs were primarily preservice, and graduates now hold leadership posts in scores of institutions. But the needs are even more critical today. Society's expectations have changed. The student population has not only skyrocketed; it has grown infinitely more complex. The pressures of state control, collective bargaining, inflation, various social needs, the requirements of minority students are all current problems beyond the comprehension of the planners of 1960. Now there are students in these institutions, and the leadership now required is in the area of learning processes. That's even more difficult than getting institutions under way. Where can presidents look for help to achieve the necessary qualifications for this task?

Much of what I have said about presidents can be said about faculty. A special kind of person with special skills and attitudes is needed for community college work. Faculty come with good academic credentials but not necessarily good preparation for the actual work they will do. Faculty are deeply concerned that their skills do not match this changing, complex educational assignment. The assignment is complex partly because the reference point has changed from academic disciplines to the students in the community. Therefore, alternatives are needed to formal graduate programs, alternatives that relate to the nature of the community college teaching task. More and better in-service training is essential. Strong support from the administration is needed to encourage faculty to learn new and improved practices. This support must include time and financial resources. Other states could well follow Florida's leadership in setting aside a percentage of state-level financial assistance (e.g., 5 percent) for staff development.

CHANGES IN ORGANIZATION AND GOVERNANCE

More decisions which affect the goals and priorities of community colleges will be made in the state capitols. The move toward state-level power comes at the same time as a rising demand from the local level for the college to respond quickly to community needs as well as offer to the faculty, students, and community representatives participation in goal setting and program development. Among parties on the local scene and between those on local and state levels the result is tension and struggle for decision-making authority. Dominant among the state-level forces will be the state legislature, which shows not only increased interest in educational matters but also a new consciousness of its own role and responsibilities. In some states, people at the local level are apprehensive that power will be centralized in a state-level agency.

There is more active exercise of local board authority than in the past. Mounting competition for tax funds and public concern about student behavior require board members to have an up-to-date knowledge about college programs and policies. Board members called for more board time on institutional purposes, goals, and policy evaluation. Large numbers of board members are relatively new to their tasks. Either their community college districts have been established only in recent years, or they have been appointed or elected recently.

Faculty members are seeking more power in the governance of community colleges, and there is general agreement among board members, administrators, and faculty that this is widespread enough to constitute a trend. In a number of institutions power is organized and expressed through collective bargaining.

Student participation in governance appears related to the political characteristics of the college location. In general there does not seem to be a groundswell toward more student power—student apathy was frequently cited.

The movement of decision-making power toward the state level raises the question of how the locally oriented, community-responsive nature of the community college will be affected. The community college will have greater difficulty carrying out its mission as it is further removed from local control. To conserve the value of localism three things are needed: (1) a clear statement of institutional goals, as a reference for legislative personnel considering new enactments which might affect governance, (2) highly qualified education personnel in the state-level agencies which deal with the local institutions, and (3) strong, able presidents supported by informed and influential boards.

Faculty involvement in institutional governance has already been mentioned. There is some indication that when faculty members are responsibly involved in policy and program development, they are not inclined to push for contract levels that could jeopardize other essential services of the institution.

For the large number of new board members as well as for those with more experience who are confronted with new responsibilities, an organized program of in-service training may be welcomed. Although the president has a role in counseling and advising the board, it may be difficult, even presumptuous, of him to serve as mentor. A national approach to assist board members in carrying their responsibilities wisely could best be organized by board members themselves. Although two national organizations are at work in this field, their efforts have not begun to match the need.

Illustrative of the rudiments to be mastered in boardmanship is the agreement entered into by one board of trustees.

AGREEMENT

1 Dialogue and discussion of matters under consideration by the Board shall be carried on in a constructive, forthright manner devoid of hostile personal references to Board colleagues who may hold opposing views.
2 During Board deliberations, major efforts shall be exerted to focus on the merits and/or demerits of issues rather than presumed motives of proponents or opponents of such issues.
3 Board members shall at all times give and expect to receive the undivided attention of colleagues when they have been properly recognized by the presiding officer. Interruptions shall be avoided since they are in violation of both parliamentary law and common courtesy. With this right goes the responsibility of keeping oral contributions succinct and pertinent to the issue before the group.
4 News releases and/or comments shall be funneled through channels established by the Board for the dissemination of information on district matters.

5   Proposals conceived by Board members for official action by the Board shall
    be submitted to the Chief Administrator of the District for study and
    analysis prior to submission by motion for Board action.
6   While exemplary performance of duties as a member of a college Board of
    Trustees may result in an opportunity for service in a more exalted public
    office, extreme care should be exercised that actions and behavioral patterns
    are not calculated to promote self-aggrandizement at the expense of honest,
    efficient Boardsmanship.

In carrying out the responsibilities enumerated in this code of conduct, attention
shall be given to the spirit and intent of the commitments as well as the more
narrow literal aspect of such code.

SHIFTS IN FINANCIAL SUPPORT

Interviewees say that a financial crisis exists. Not only is property tax
overloaded, but also its constitutionality as a major source of funds
for public education is challenged. There are pressures to increase the
student's bill. Fears are expressed that he is being priced out.
Institutions are pushed in the direction of conventional programs for
conventional students—generally these cost less. There is a trend
toward more state-level support, raising the big question about how
this will affect local control. Does the agency that pays the bill call
the shots? The states say they are broke, and they look to
Washington. There are many indications that the present financial
support patterns do not facilitate the achievement of community
college goals.

What is to be done? Certainly improved management practices are
in order to assure the most efficient possible use of resources
available. And the community college cannot do everything. Its role
needs definition and delimitation in relation to the services of other
agencies and institutions. Given its role definition, the college must
of necessity operate in concert with such organizations. It cannot go
it alone. Educational leadership needs to take initiative in reducing
waste, rivalries, and vested interests that make postsecondary
education vulnerable to much of the criticism it now experiences.

The theme is repeated again and again: society needs to
understand better what community colleges are capable of doing, to
determine more precisely what community colleges are to do, and
then to make a commitment to support the colleges in that work.
This is an appropriate time to encourage legislators to consider how
new financial measures can relate to community college goals. If
comprehensiveness, low cost to the student, local responsiveness,

continuing education, community services, and developmental education are desired characteristics of community college programs, what kind of financial "reward" system should be developed? Not many support patterns at either state or federal levels are now deliberately designed to encourage institutions to move toward generally approved goals.

TRENDS IN COMMUNITY RELATIONS

One of the notable changes in American education is the movement toward state-level planning and coordination of public and private institutions, the colleges, universities, and in some states the public schools. For example, the state of Illinois has a concept of a total system of higher education for the state, public and private. Deliberate measures will be adopted to assure use of all available capacity. The community college will be affected by these developments. It will be required to have specific goals within that state system. Statewide planning can minimize unnecessary duplication of effort and assure that all the citizens are served. At the same time, special care must be taken to help institutions develop their own specialized strengths and unique identities.

The community college particularly will take its clues for service from knowledge of the area in which the college is located. Insistent social pressures are forcing educational planners to take an honest look at their potential service area, and they express surprise at what they are finding. Differences among communities are recognized. The overlapping interests of public schools and the community colleges are acknowledged and in some cases (still not enough) the community of interest is being exploited with distinct advantages to the student in terms of an educational continuum.

There still exists a stereotype of "college" which leaves the community college looking ill-formed and deficient by comparison. But that stereotype does not fit, and there is need to see the community college for what it is—a community institution serving its people. That is the pattern against which the institution needs to be measured, and then the results are quite different.

In the decade of the sixties, hundreds of these institutions were built, and the students came. It was a decade of bricks and mortar, of staff recruitment and program development, of advisory committees and master plans. This decade is one to fulfill the promise, to achieve the goals; its dominant theme is the learning process. Signals in the environment register no diminution in social importance of the community college. Its essential place in a changing society is widely recognized. Community colleges are doing more than respond to change—they influence the direction of change in our society by the priorities they establish. In my visits to community colleges and in my conversations with people in state capitals nothing impressed me more than the call for the college "to be there," a kind of people's college, an educational resource center for the community, a liberating means for people in a society where opportunity of education means opportunity to live as a person.